Rome and Attila

Rome's Greatest Enemy

The Fall of the Roman Empire
Book Three

Nick Holmes

Published by Puttenham Press Ltd

ISBN 978-1-7397865-4-0

British Library Cataloguing in Publication Data.
A catalogue record for this book is available from the British Library.

Typeset in the United Kingdom by Indie-Go
https://www.indie-go.co.uk

History is merely a list of surprises

– Kurt Vonnegut,
Author of *Slaughterhouse Five*

Beneath his great ferocity he [Attila] was a subtle man, and fought with craft before he made war

– Jordanes,
Sixth-century Gothic chronicler

Contents

Part III: The Scourge of God

Part IV: The Last Days of an Empire

Illustrations

Photographs are from the Author's Collection unless stated otherwise.

Maps

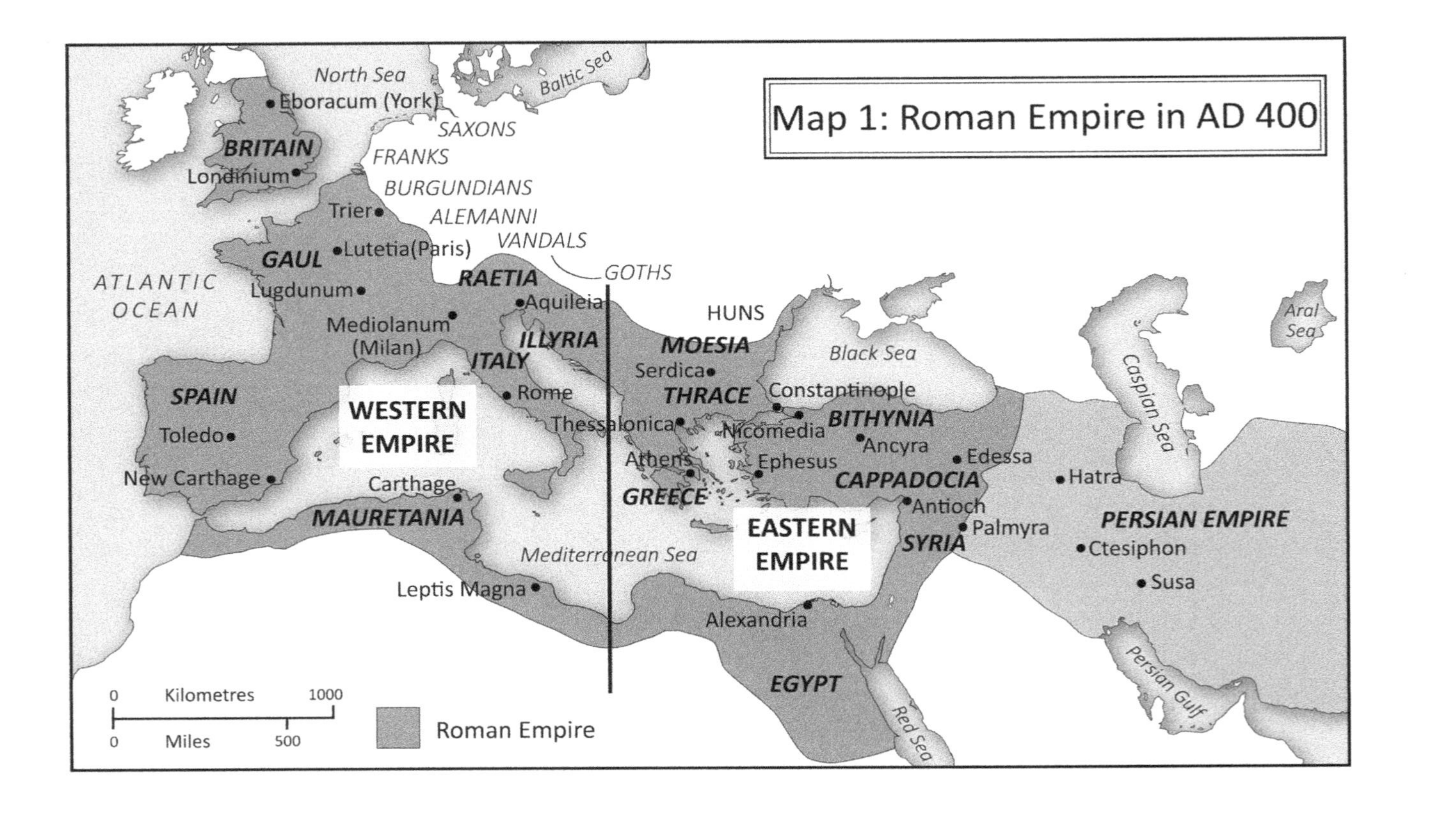
Map 1: Roman Empire in AD 400
North Sea
Baltic Sea
Eboracum (York)
SAXONS
BRITAIN
FRANKS
Londinium
BURGUNDIANS
Trier
ALEMANNI
VANDALS
GAUL
Lutetia(Paris)
GOTHS
ATLANTIC OCEAN
Lugdunum
RAETIA
Aquileia
HUNS
Aral Sea
Mediolanum (Milan)
ILLYRIA
MOESIA
Black Sea
Caspian Sea
ITALY
Serdica
SPAIN
Rome
THRACE
Constantinople
WESTERN EMPIRE
Thessalonica
BITHYNIA
Toledo
Nicomedia
Ancyra
Athens
Ephesus
Edessa
New Carthage
Carthage
CAPPADOCIA
Hatra
GREECE
Antioch
MAURETANIA
EASTERN EMPIRE
Palmyra
PERSIAN EMPIRE
SYRIA
Mediterranean Sea
Ctesiphon
Leptis Magna
Susa
Alexandria
EGYPT
Persian Gulf
Red Sea
0 Kilometres 1000
0 Miles 500
Roman Empire

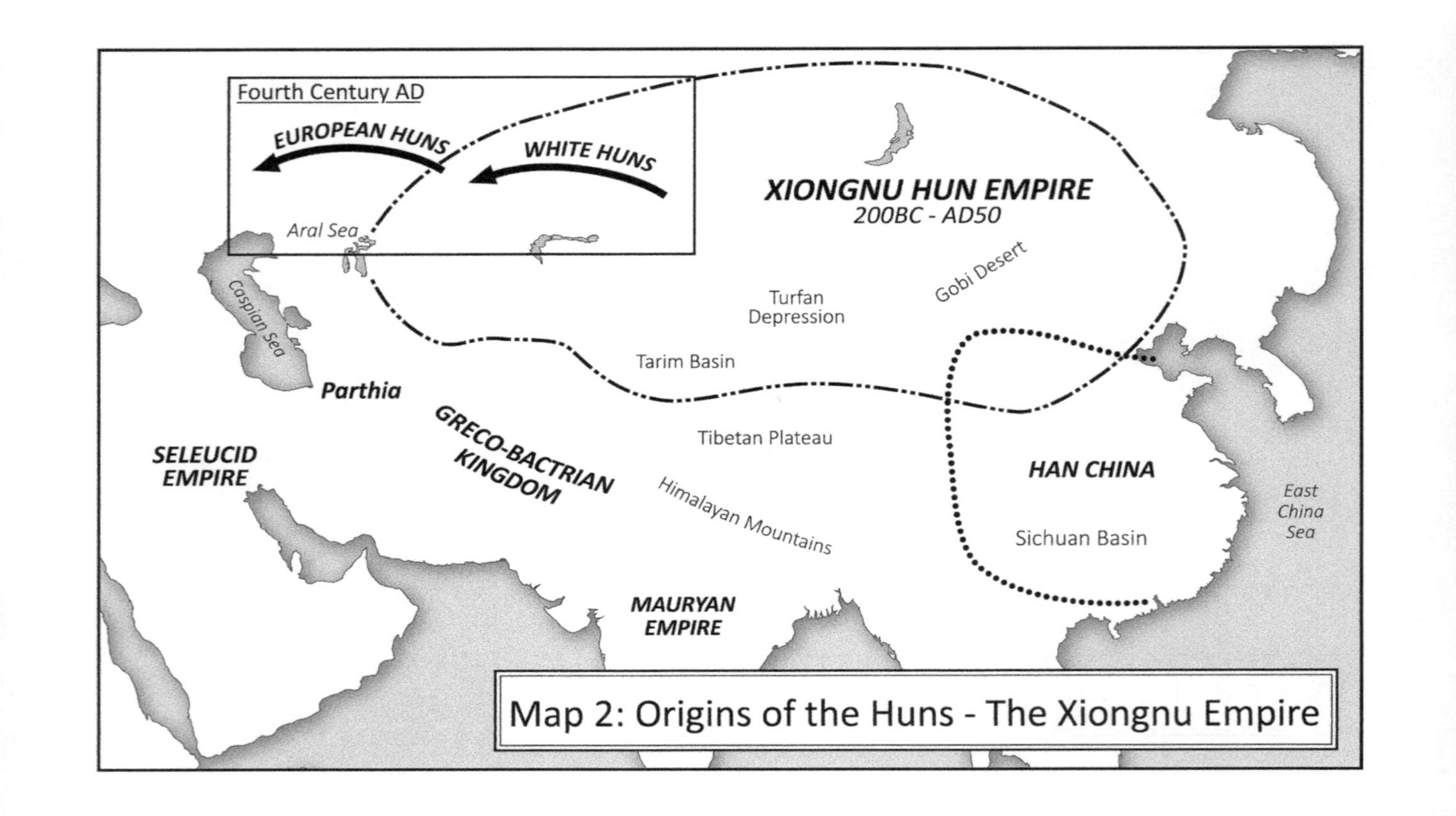

Map 2: Origins of the Huns - The Xiongnu Empire

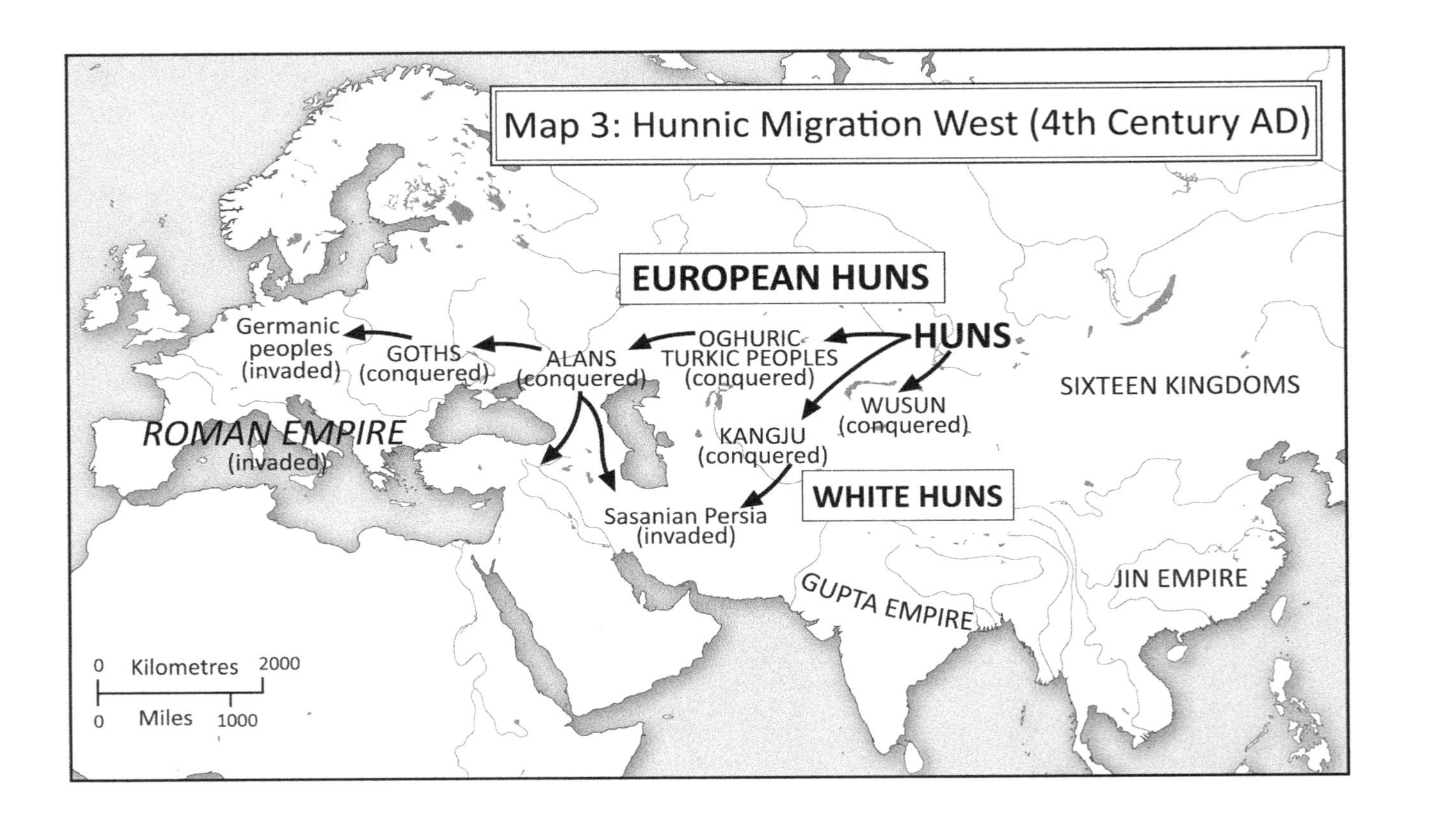
Map 3: Hunnic Migration West (4th Century AD)
EUROPEAN HUNS
HUNS
Germanic peoples (invaded)
GOTHS (conquered)
ALANS (conquered)
OGHURIC TURKIC PEOPLES (conquered)
WUSUN (conquered)
SIXTEEN KINGDOMS
ROMAN EMPIRE (invaded)
KANGJU (conquered)
WHITE HUNS
Sasanian Persia (invaded)
GUPTA EMPIRE
JIN EMPIRE
0 Kilometres 2000
0 Miles 1000

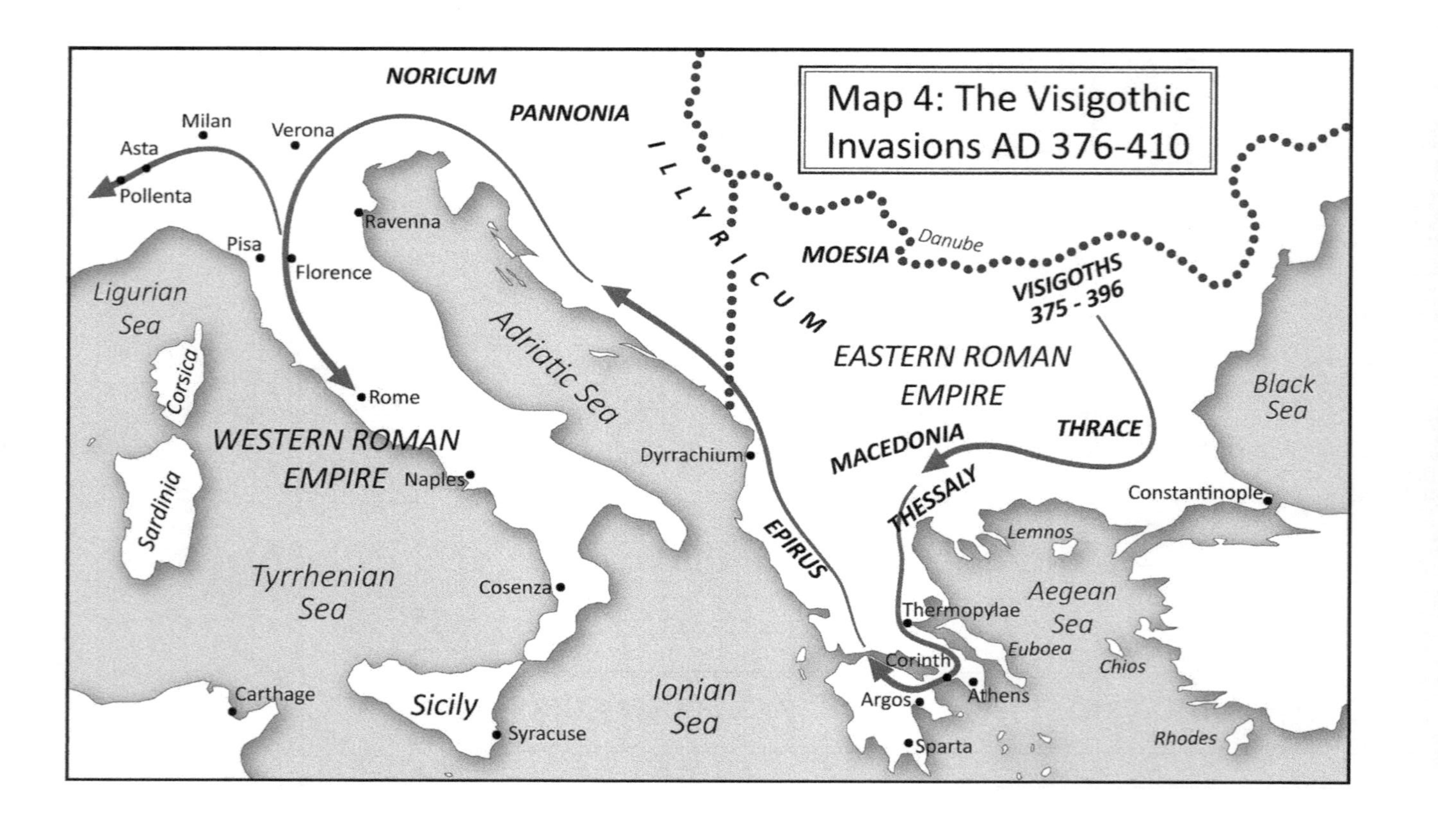
Map 4: The Visigothic Invasions AD 376-410
NORICUM
PANNONIA
ILLYRICUM
MOESIA
Danube
VISIGOTHS 375 - 396
EASTERN ROMAN EMPIRE
THRACE
MACEDONIA
THESSALY
EPIRUS
Black Sea
Constantinople
Lemnos
Aegean Sea
Euboea
Chios
Rhodes
Thermopylae
Corinth
Athens
Argos
Sparta
Milan
Verona
Asta
Pollenta
Ravenna
Pisa
Florence
Ligurian Sea
Corsica
Sardinia
Rome
Adriatic Sea
Dyrrachium
WESTERN ROMAN EMPIRE
Naples
Tyrrhenian Sea
Cosenza
Carthage
Sicily
Syracuse
Ionian Sea

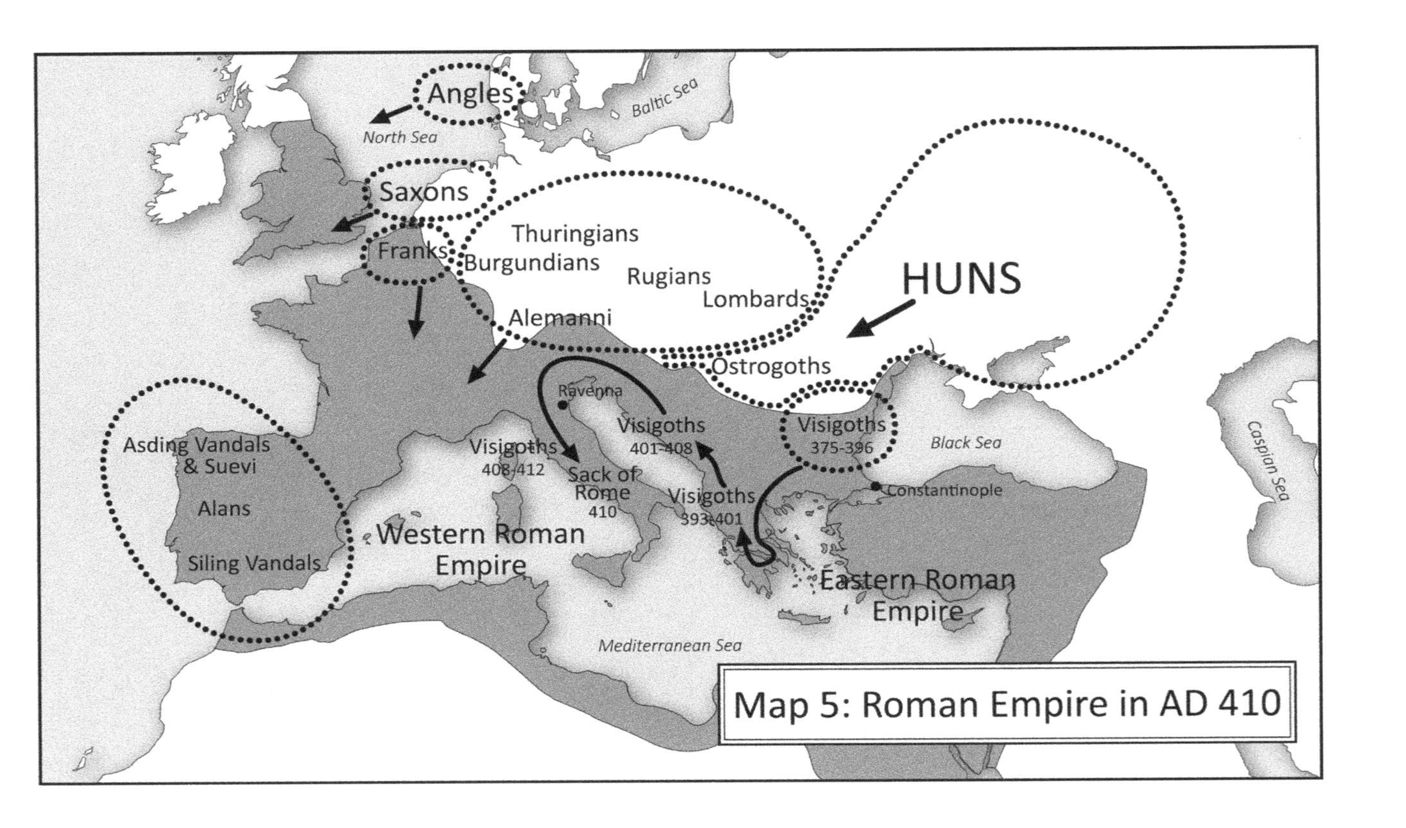

Map 5: Roman Empire in AD 410

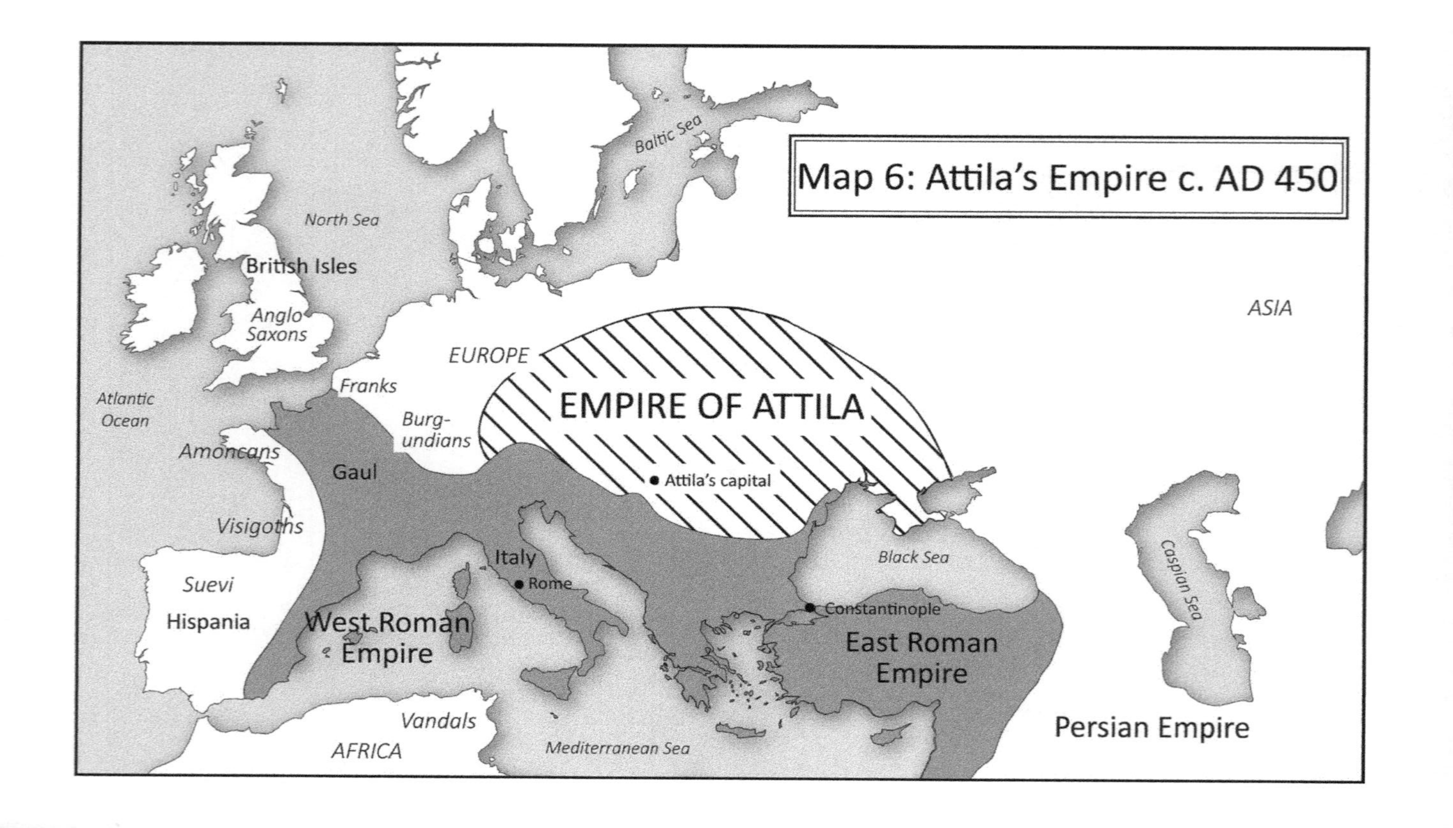
Map 6: Attila's Empire c. AD 450
Baltic Sea
North Sea
British Isles
Anglo Saxons
ASIA
EUROPE
Franks
Atlantic Ocean
Burg- undians
EMPIRE OF ATTILA
Amoncans
Gaul
Attila's capital
Visigoths
Italy
Black Sea
Caspian Sea
Suevi
Rome
Hispania
West Roman Empire
Constantinople
East Roman Empire
Vandals
Persian Empire
AFRICA
Mediterranean Sea

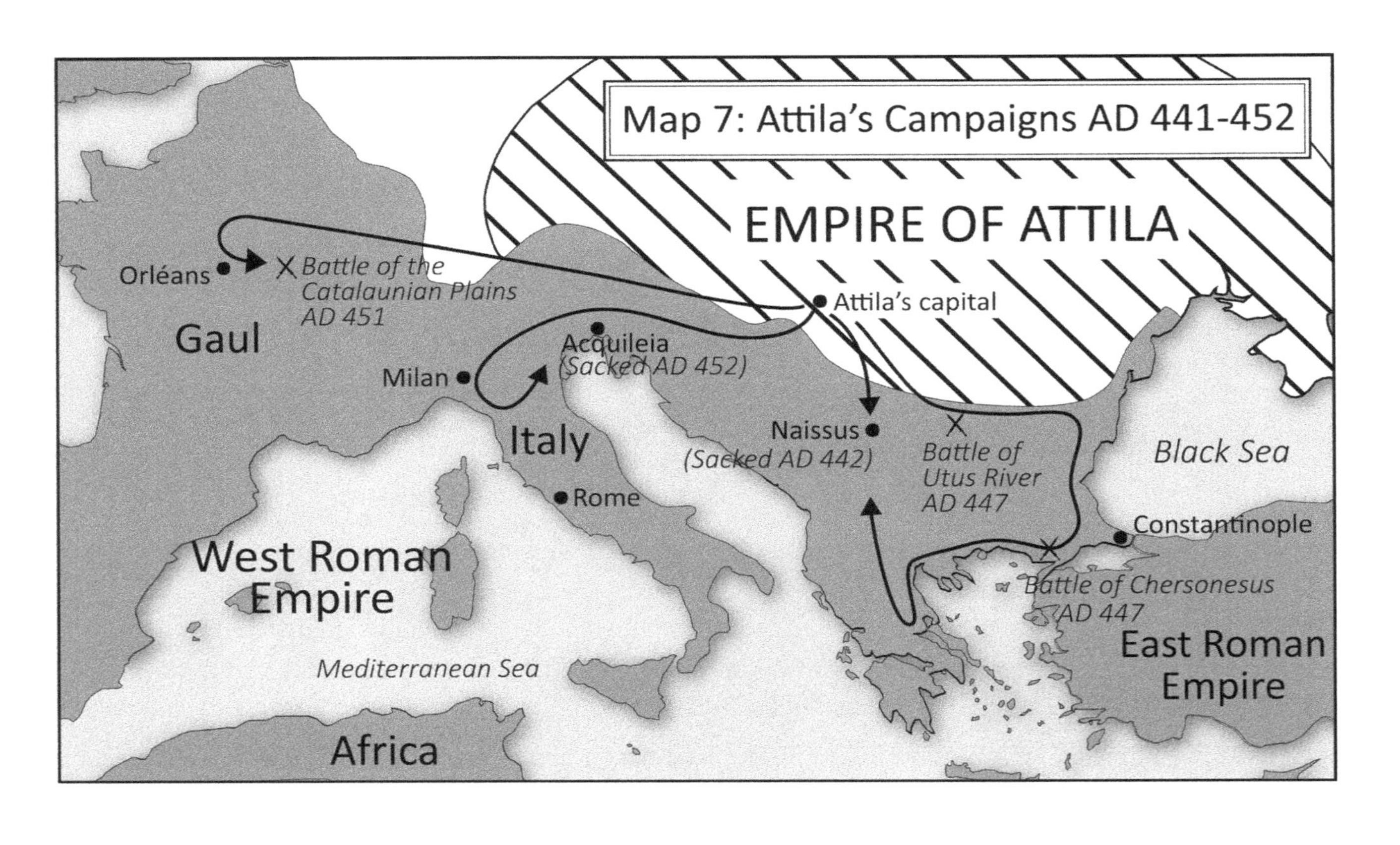
Map 7: Attila's Campaigns AD 441-452
EMPIRE OF ATTILA
Orléans
Battle of the Catalaunian Plains AD 451
Gaul
Attila's capital
Acquileia
(Sacked AD 452)
Milan
Italy
Naissus
(Sacked AD 442)
Battle of Utus River AD 447
Black Sea
Rome
Constantinople
West Roman Empire
Battle of Chersonesus AD 447
East Roman Empire
Mediterranean Sea
Africa

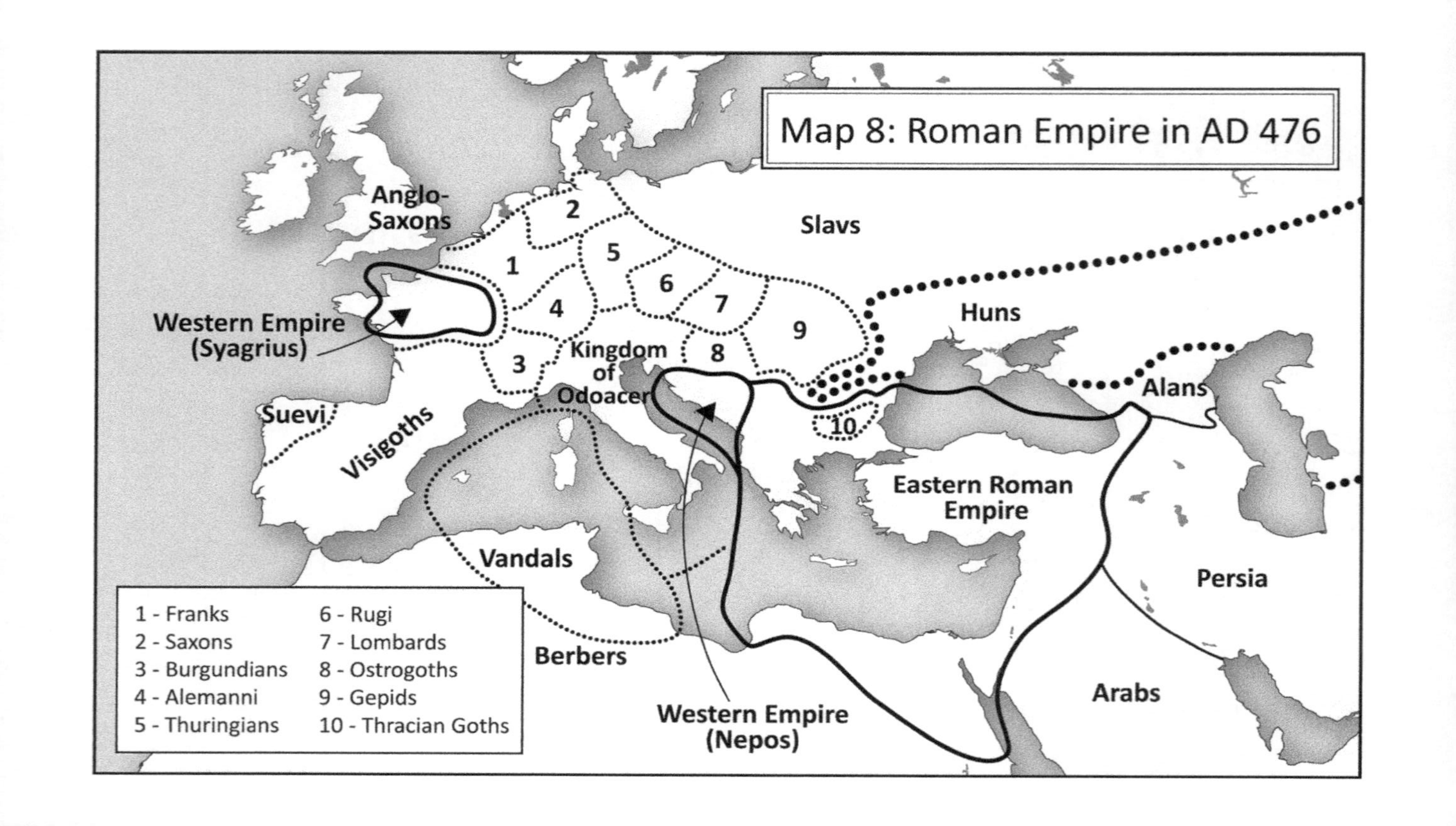
Map 8: Roman Empire in AD 476
Anglo-Saxons
Slavs
Huns
Alans
Western Empire (Syagrius)
Kingdom of Odoacer
Suevi
Visigoths
Eastern Roman Empire
Vandals
Persia
Berbers
Arabs
Western Empire (Nepos)
1 2 3 4 5 6 7 8 9 10
1 - Franks
2 - Saxons
3 - Burgundians
4 - Alemanni
5 - Thuringians
6 - Rugi
7 - Lombards
8 - Ostrogoths
9 - Gepids
10 - Thracian Goths

Map 9: Ancient Rome

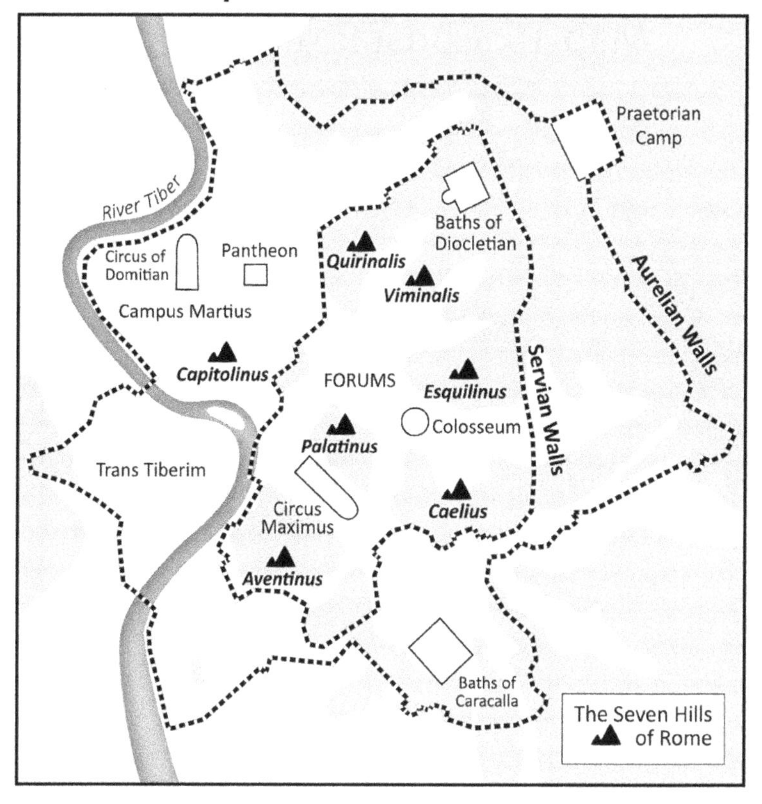

Map 10: Constantinople

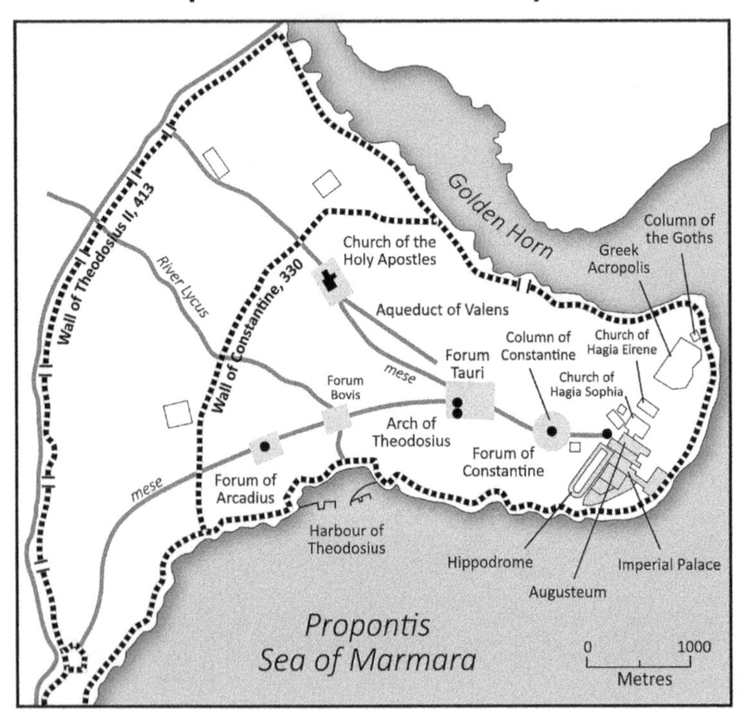

Introduction

Like a kestrel circling in the air for its prey, Thorismund, son of king Theodoric, waits to strike.

The high ridge of Montgueux conceals him and over 2,000 heavily armoured Visigothic horsemen. Below them on the plains, they can hear the screams of the wounded and horses neighing in agony. Attila's army is winning. As it always does. The deadly Hunnic cavalry is in the centre, furiously pushing all before them. On their flanks follow hordes of their German subjects. Against them, the coalition of Romans, Visigoths, and Franks is losing ground.

In the distance, Thorismund can see his father's royal standards. He doesn't yet know he lies dead on the battlefield. He raises his spear and calls to the horn-blowers to sound the advance. Eager for battle, the Visigoths crowd forward, horses rearing.

Their charge is majestic. Brightly coloured shields. Long dragon pennants streaming in the wind. The sun glittering off their chain-mail. Sharp spears bristling. An unstoppable phalanx of horsemen rides down the hillside.

They catch the Huns in the flank. The steppe nomads have no time to use their famous bows. The ferocity of the Visigothic attack scatters them. Attila's army caves in. For once, the Huns are beaten. They retreat. Back to their camp. There, Attila orders a vast funeral pyre to be constructed from the wooden saddles of the dead. The flames leap into the fading evening light. He watches, unable to draw his gaze away from the burning of his dreams. He wants to throw himself into the fire. To burn the ignominy of defeat.

*

On 20 June AD 451, Attila the Hun was defeated at the Battle of the Catalaunian Plains in Gaul. The battle marked a turning point in history. The westward expansion of the Huns was halted. Never again would Asiatic steppe nomads reach so far into Europe and threaten to overrun it.

To the Romans, Attila was the 'scourge of God'. Just his name was sufficient to strike terror into the hearts of not just the Romans but all the peoples of Europe. Remarkably, his legend has endured from late antiquity to this day. But was this deserved? And what was his true place in history?

This book searches for the answers to these questions. What emerges is a very different man from the legend. For example, our only eyewitness account describes him as someone who despised ostentation, was respectful towards those he admired, and devoted to his sons.

As for his place in history, there is no doubt he dominated the history of western Eurasia in the fifth century. He engulfed Europe in war. His campaigns stretched from Constantinople to Gaul. Cities burned. Kings and generals died in battle. Pitched battles were fought on a scale not seen since the days of Julius Caesar and Trajan.

But against this well-known backdrop, it may surprise you to hear that historians have long held widely differing views of Attila. Was he a genius or a bungler? Was he a side-show or someone who changed world history? The debate continues. This book offers a new perspective by reconstructing his campaigns against the eastern Roman Empire. In particular, historians have underestimated the strength of the new Roman army that emerged out of the ashes of defeat to challenge Attila. It was strong enough to enable Constantinople to defy him by refusing to pay tribute. Attila turned west not, as most historians think, because he was victorious in the east but because he had met his match there. This rewrites the story of both Attila and Rome.

While Attila is central to this book, its larger focus is on the story of the fall of the Roman Empire, and so it continues the narrative begun in the first two volumes in this series. We meet an extraordinary cast of characters, from Flavius Aetius, the resourceful general nicknamed 'the last of the Romans', to his nemesis, the feeble Valentinian III, who jealously stabbed him to death. From Gaiseric, the wise and cunning king of the Vandals, who conquered North Africa, to Galla Placidia, the imperial princess, and one of several powerful women in this era, who ruled the western empire when her half-witted brother, the emperor Honorius, was incapable of ruling anything other than his pet chickens.

Finally, we consider one of the great conundrums of ancient history: why did the western Roman Empire fall while its eastern half survived and prospered? For example, as Roman Britain slid into a prehistoric level of barbarism, Egypt, Syria and Anatolia were enjoying unprecedented economic growth and cultural sophistication. I hope this book provides new insights into how this happened.

But before we embark on the above, let us start with a fundamental question.

Who were the Huns?

PART I

The Origin of Our Destruction

1

The Huns

The men are small by European standards and have long black hair and brightly coloured shields strapped onto their backs. Quivers of arrows are at their sides. In the carts are women and children. This is an entire people on the march. A people fleeing not a human enemy but a natural one. Drought has brought them here, in search of pasture for their flocks. They are the Huns.

Suddenly, a shout goes up from Hunnic horsemen at the front of the long column of travellers. Ahead of them is a band of warriors. Unlike the Huns, they are tall men with long blond hair. They wield iron swords and carry round wooden shields. But they wear no body armour. Their blue eyes are arrogant. They prize courage in battle more than anything else. The Huns are trespassing on their lands.

Behind them lies their land of green valleys and well-watered springs. Their settlements are full of women and playing children. The women boast they would rather see their husbands dead than cowards. Today, it will be victory or death.

The Gothic horsemen gallop forward. Behind them, a mass of infantry advances. Dust swirls in the air. They have no tactics or tricks to play on their enemy. They ride to punish them.

But they never get there. The Huns are too quick for them. Massed together in a crescent shape, they ride small steppe ponies, more obedient to their riders than a dog to its master. Dry dust billows from the Gothic horses' hooves into the air so they cannot see the enemy ahead until it is too late. Arrows fill the air. Thousands of razor-sharp, flint-headed arrows pour out of the sky into the Goths. They tear through their shields. They pierce heads, arms and shoulders in a deadly storm. The Huns encircle them, taunting them and drawing them forward. When the Goths charge at them, they throw lassos around the horsemen and bring them floundering to the ground. The Goths have never seen fighting like this before.

Restringing their bows as effortlessly as if they were threading a wicker basket, the Huns loose arrow after arrow. The Goths drown in a storm of arrows. Soon, the Huns close in on their kill. Drawing sabres and maces, they butcher those who have survived the dreadful aerial onslaught. Bodies cover the ground. The screams of the wounded fill the air. The Huns cut the heads off their leaders and fix them to spears in triumph.

Only now have the Gothic infantry caught up with the dreadful fate that has befallen their horsemen. They have one thought: to save their women and children from this terrible enemy. With shields raised, they hold their ground. Gothic foot archers answer the Huns' barrage of arrows. For a time, there is a stand-off. But the Goths must swallow their pride and retreat. Retreat. Retreat.

Although we have no specific records of conflicts like this, there must have been many like them for our most trusted chronicler of the fourth century, Ammianus Marcellinus, narrates:

> *Terrifying rumours got about of a new and unusually violent commotion among the peoples of the North. Men heard that over the whole area extending from the Marcomanni and Quadi to the Black Sea a savage horde of remote tribes, driven from their homes by unexpected pressure, were roaming with their families in the Danube region.*[1]

The 'savage horde of remote tribes' was the Goths. The 'unexpected pressure' mentioned by Ammianus was the Huns. So, who were the Huns? And why were they so successful at displacing the German tribes?

Ammianus provides us with a vivid description, the best outside Chinese sources: 'The people of the Huns, who are mentioned only cursorily by ancient writers, and who dwell beyond the Palus Maeotis (Sea of Azov) near the frozen ocean, are quite abnormally savage.'[2]

The frozen ocean appears to refer to the Arctic Circle, which is a bit too far north, but ancient geography was not perfect. He describes them as barely human:

> *They have squat bodies, strong limbs, and thick necks, and are so prodigiously ugly and bent that they might be two-legged animals, or the figures crudely carved from stumps which are seen on the parapets of bridges. Still,*

their shape, however disagreeable, is human; but their way of life is so rough that they have no use for fire or seasoned food, but live on the roots of wild plants and the half-raw flesh of any sort of animal.[3]

You may be forgiven for thinking that Ammianus is describing Orcs out of JRR Tolkien's *The Lord of the Rings*. Indeed, it would not surprise me if Tolkien's inspiration was derived from Ammianus. But, aside from the ferocity of their alleged physical appearance, which was surely exaggerated for effect, why were they so terrifying?

The answer is they were good at fighting. This was really because they were excellent horse archers. As usual, Ammianus gives us an insightful description:

The Huns enter battle drawn up in wedge-shaped masses … And as they are lightly equipped for swift motion, and unexpected in action, they purposefully divide suddenly into scattered bands and attack, rushing about in disorder here and there, dealing terrific slaughter … They fight from a distance with missiles having sharp bone, instead of their usual points, joined to the shafts with wonderful skill; then they gallop over the intervening spaces and fight hand to hand with swords.[4]

The Huns' superiority in battle lay with their superb equestrian and archery skills. As Zosimus, another chronicler, wrote: 'The Huns were totally incapable and ignorant of conducting a battle on foot, but by wheeling, charging, retreating in good time and shooting from their horses, they wrought immense slaughter.'[5]

Like most steppe nomads, the Huns used a composite recurve bow comprising separate sections of wood and bone, glued together to create strength, making the shape of the bow into a sort of 'W'. These differed greatly from the bows typically made in Europe from a single stave of wood. European bows were effective for infantrymen who could stand up and use a relatively long bow. But a horseman needs a shorter bow that can pack more punch. This was what the Huns excelled at.

And Hunnic bows were exceptionally powerful, even by steppe nomad standards. Whereas most nomad bows were about 30 inches long, the Huns' bows were even longer, between 50 and 60 inches. So, how did they fire a bow that was so long from the saddle? The Huns' answer was to make the bow asymmetric, with the upper half of the bow longer. Why did their opponents not do this? The reason was skill and comfort. Considerably more skill was required to shoot an asymmetric bow. It was also larger and less easy to carry. But the Huns considered the power and distance of the shot outweighed those disadvantages. For example, the Huns' asymmetric bows gave them the ability to shoot arrows through chain mail and all but the most robust armour. Thus when they came up against the Goths, who rarely wore metal armour at all, the ferocity of their archery was overwhelming.

It is also worth clarifying that, contrary to popular belief, the Huns were not helped by stirrups. They used heavy wooden saddles which allowed them to grip the horse with their legs and create a firm firing platform. Stirrups were unknown in Europe until the Avars introduced them in the sixth century, about 200 years after the Huns first appeared on the edge of Europe.

The Huns are one of the most under-researched peoples in global history. Yet their impact on the ancient world was nothing short of phenomenal. At one time or another, they conquered and dominated all the major civilisations in Eurasia from China to India, Persia and the Roman Empire. Their story began in Mongolia with a tribe called the Xiongnu (see Map 2). They first came into conflict with the powerful Han Chinese Empire in the third century BC. Indeed, the Great Wall of China was originally built to keep them out. But under the rule of a remarkable leader called Modu, they broke through the wall, slaughtered the Chinese armies and then subjected Han China to vassalage. Modu turned the skulls of his enemies into drinking cups and took the Chinese emperor's daughter as one of his many concubines. He created an empire that stretched from Manchuria to Kazakhstan and was larger even than that of Alexander the Great. On his death in 174 BC, the Xiongnu Empire was probably the most powerful state in the whole of Eurasia.

After that, the balance of power see-sawed between the Xiongnu and China for the next five centuries. While Han China momentarily rid itself of the Xiongnu in the first century AD, they returned with a vengeance in the fourth century, conquering Jin China (the Jin dynasty replaced the Han) and burning its capital Luoyang to the ground. Thereafter, the Xiongnu and Chinese continued to fight while also becoming increasingly integrated. One historian[6] has argued that China's entire military, political and administrative development was effectively taken over by the Xiongnu who established a 'barbarian' military aristocracy ruling over the Chinese people with the help of native bureaucrats. Interestingly, this has close parallels with what happened in the western Roman Empire in the fifth century, when barbarian German tribes ruled over Latin-speaking Roman populations.

In the mid-fourth century AD, a group of Huns – the European Huns – arrived on the edge of Europe in modern-day Ukraine. We will discuss how and why they came to be there in a later chapter. But whatever their origin, the Roman chronicler, Ammianus Marcellinus, was clear of one thing – Rome's decline was due to them.

> *The seed-bed and origin of all this destruction and of the various calamities inflicted by the wrath of Mars, which raged everywhere with unusual fury, I find to be this. The people of the Huns.*[7]

Let us find out why.

2

Refugees

The immediate threat the Huns presented in the fourth century was *not* an invasion of Europe. This would come later in the mid-fifth century, led by Attila. Instead, it was the domino-toppling effect they created by pushing the Germanic tribes west into the Roman Empire. Bishop Ambrose of Milan summed this up with impressive clarity: 'The Huns fell upon the Alans, the Alans upon the Goths, the Goths upon the Romans, and this is not yet the end.'[8] In short, what precipitated the fall of the Roman Empire was not the Huns themselves but a massive inflow of refugees, fleeing from the Huns.

The Huns arrived beside the mighty rivers Don and Volga sometime around AD 360–70. There they met and subjugated the Alans, a steppe people with strong links to the Germanic world, and, according to Ammianus, skilled metal workers capable of fielding armoured cavalry. Despite this, the Huns' deadly arrows made short work of them, and the Alans joined the Hunnic armies. Then the Huns advanced south over the Dnieper River and into the Gothic lands in modern-day Romania. The Goths tried to stop them and, although the details are limited, Ammianus says many battles were fought, but the Goths were always defeated. He recounts that one Gothic leader, Ermanaric, even offered himself to be sacrificed to appease the gods.

By the 370s, the Goths were in full retreat. In the summer of 376, hundreds of thousands of Goths arrived on the Danube to ask the Romans for asylum from this terrifying enemy. Ammianus Marcellinus wrote: 'Our people paid little attention to this [the news of the Goths' defeat by the Huns] at first, because news of wars in those parts generally reached distant hearers only when they were already over or at least quiescent. Gradually, however, the story gained credence, and it was confirmed by the arrival of the foreign agents begging and praying that the host of refugees might be allowed to cross to our side of the river.'[9]

Ammianus says that the number of these barbarians was so vast that, 'To try to find their number is as vain as numbering the wind-swept Libyan sands.'[10] Another source is more precise, saying they numbered over 200,000.

What happened was a huge migration of Goths. And the word here is migration. Two entire Gothic tribes, the Greuthungi and Thervingi, had fled to the Danube, including men, women and children. They wanted asylum. They were refugees.

Normally the Romans followed a strict code when allowing barbarians to enter Roman territory. This allowed them into the empire only once they had been defeated, disarmed and integrated as farmers. But when the eastern emperor Valens heard of the Gothic request, he broke this rule, and allowed some of the Goths to cross the Danube still fully armed and remaining an independent political unit. This would prove to be a disaster.

So why did he do it? There were several reasons. One is that he knew the leader of the Thervingi tribe personally and trusted him. He was called Fritigern and had helped Valens in the First Gothic War in 367–9, when Valens successfully beat off the Goths who supported a Roman rebel Procopius. These Goths were led by a Thervingi chief called Athanaric. Fritigern was a rival of Athanaric's and more than willing to help Valens fight him. Fritigern had also converted to Christianity. In brief, Valens trusted Fritigern.

Second, Valens did not give the Goths carte blanche to cross en masse. He only allowed Fritigern's Thervingi to enter Roman territory. He forbade the other Gothic tribe with them, the Greuthungi, from crossing. These were at least half of the 200,000 Goths in total. He also insisted that Fritigern's senior followers convert to Christianity as Fritigern had done.

Hostages from the Thervingi were taken to guarantee honourable conduct, and the Goths agreed to supply soldiers for the Roman army. This latter point was important to Valens because he was building an army to fight the Persians, and he did not mind having a few additional regiments of Gothic auxiliaries. Fritigern's men had been helpful fighting against Athanaric, so why not against Persia?

All of these reasons influenced Valens' decision to allow the Thervingi to cross the Danube. He thought he had the situation under control. But one thing he underestimated was the sheer number of Goths. The Thervingi numbered around 100,000 people – men, women and children – and having an additional 100,000 mouths to feed in the Thracian countryside put pressure on food supplies. Suspecting there might be trouble, the Romans wisely moved the harvest of 376 to fortified strongpoints that could resist the Goths. This seemed a good idea, but it also made some unscrupulous Romans think they could exploit the situation.

According to Ammianus, it was Roman greed that lit the Gothic bonfire. For the Roman governor of Thrace, Lupicinus, and a general called Maximus, decided that the hungry Goths offered a tempting opportunity to get rich quick by selling them overpriced food. Allegedly, they gathered up stray dogs for the Goths to eat, offering one dog for a child to be sold into slavery. Whether or not that was true, not surprisingly tensions between the Romans and Goths started to rise.

Exasperated with Roman corruption, the Goths protested outside the legionary fortress at Marcianople, in eastern Thrace, close to the Black Sea. Lupicinus, who should go down in history as one of the most incompetent governors of all time, responded by gathering his troops stationed along the Danube to intimidate them. This only meant that the other main Gothic tribe, the Greuthungi, who had been barred from crossing the Danube, took advantage of the absence of Roman river sentries and crossed over to join their cousins the Thervingi. So, double trouble.

Faced with an ever-increasing number of Goths, and sensing that things were about to get out of hand, Lupicinus resorted to an old Roman tactic. He invited the Gothic leaders to a grand banquet intending to kidnap or kill them. This was a favourite Roman fourth-century trick. Unfortunately for them it seldom succeeded.

Lupicinus spectacularly mismanaged the entire event. Ammianus suggests that this was because he enjoyed the banquet too much himself: 'After a long sitting at an extravagantly luxurious meal followed by a noisy floor-show, (Lupicinus) was muzzy and dropping with sleep.'[11] What followed is not entirely clear from the Roman sources, but it seems Lupicinus failed to spring his trap on Fritigern immediately. Perhaps the two of them were actually becoming friends as they enjoyed the floor-show. But what spoilt the party, literally, was that, during this banquet, fighting broke out between the Goths and Roman soldiers outside the town, as the Goths demanded food and the Romans refused them. When Lupicinus heard this, he panicked and seized Fritigern, killing his bodyguard. Fritigern cleverly saved his own life by persuading Lupicinus that if he killed him, the Goths would storm the town. Instead, he persuaded the incompetent Roman that if he released him, he would pacify his followers and everything would be fine.

Why Lupicinus fell for this is anyone's guess. Perhaps he had drunk too much, as Ammianus says. But whatever the reason, he released Fritigern, who immediately went back on his promise to Lupicinus by telling his men the Romans had betrayed him and it was now war.

Lupicinus had achieved the exact opposite of what Valens wanted. He had started a war. The very next day, he asked his soldiers to sort out the mess he had caused. Gathering his men, he marched to meet Fritigern. But his performance on the battlefield was no better than at the banquet. We do not have any details about the battle but the Goths trounced the Romans, who, according to Ammianus, suffered considerable casualties, losing their standards with several tribunes killed. Lupicinus managed to escape; as Ammianus says, 'While others were fighting, his one aim was to get away.'[12]

Part of the explanation for the miserable performance of the Roman troops lies with their being second-rate garrison troops, the *limitanei*, as the Romans called them, and not the field army, or *comitatenses*, which comprised better soldiers. This, together with Lupicinus' incompetence, now ignited a Roman Gothic war that would last from late 376 until 382 and would prove to be a turning point in Rome's history.

By defeating Lupicinus' regiments, the Goths gained control of the countryside of Thrace, since the only other substantial Roman forces were some distance away in Illyria under the western emperor's command (Gratian, Valens' nephew). As mentioned, Valens' main army was also far away in the east, massing to fight the Sasanian Persians.

The Goths controlled the countryside but not the towns. All the major towns were heavily fortified, and the Goths had little skill in siege warfare. The credit for these strong defences must go to the emperor Diocletian, whose idea it had been in the third century to construct extensive fortifications in all the frontier provinces, especially in the major towns and cities. What archaeological evidence we have suggests these walled towns were extremely well fortified, with tall walls and often huge U-shaped bastions designed to carry the brutally effective Roman wall artillery. Against this, the Goths stood little chance.

So instead, they resorted to pillaging the Roman villas that dotted the countryside. They put these affluent centres to the torch, and killed, raped and enslaved their inhabitants, if they had not fled. In addition, considerable numbers of slaves and poorer peasants chose this moment to rise against their masters and take revenge for their mistreatment.

Completely oblivious of this chaos in Thrace, Valens was still in Antioch, putting the finishing touches to his projected offensive in Armenia against the Sasanians. When he heard there was a full-scale war in Thrace, his initial shock turned into a determination to avoid a war on two fronts. First, and with great reluctance, he cancelled his whole Persian expedition. He sent his general, Count Victor, to sue for peace with Persia. The Persian king Shapur demanded that the Romans give up their attempts to control Armenia and recognise his own king in the kingdom of Georgia in the Caucasus, known as Iberia, which was Christian and pro-Roman. These demands were reluctantly accepted and the Persians strengthened their position in the east. Second, he had already asked his nephew, the western emperor Gratian, for help to fight the Persians, and he now sent messengers urgently asking for help to fight the Goths instead.

With the Persian frontier secure, Valens began the laborious process of moving the eastern army hundreds of miles west to Thrace. By the summer of 377, two generals from the eastern front, Traianus and Profuturus, arrived with the first batch of troops from the east. Gratian sent a small force under his general, Richomer, through the Succi Pass, in what is now western Bulgaria, to join them. The Goths retreated north towards the Danube. The two Roman forces joined up and offered battle to the Goths. At a place called Ad Salices, in the narrow piece of land between the Danube and the Black Sea, the two armies met. There is no detailed account of what happened, but it seems to have been a bloody slogging match resulting in a draw. Ammianus describes the battlefield littered with corpses. The Goths withdrew into the safety of their wagon circle for a week, suggesting they sustained heavy casualties, and the Romans withdrew to Marcianople.

It was now a stalemate until the Goths were reinforced by a large number of Huns and Alans, who, having heard of the enormous booty to be stolen from the Romans, were eager to take part in the raiding and plunder. This encouraged them to venture towards Constantinople once again, but they were put off, according to Ammianus, when some Goths near the city were attacked by a group of Arab auxiliaries working for the Romans, who took them prisoner, slit their throats and drank their blood. Appalled by this behaviour, the Goths never ventured near the city again.

Meanwhile, the Romans were also getting stronger. By early 378, the bulk of Valens' eastern army arrived at Constantinople. However, Valens did not want to commit to a fight unless he had Gratian's support from the west. This meant that the Goths, with their Hun and Alan allies, devastated Thrace yet again. 'The barbarians poured over the wide extent of Thrace like wild animals escaping from their cage,'[13] as Ammianus put it. This time it was even more brutal than the last time. 'Everything was involved in a foul orgy of rape and slaughter, bloodshed and fire and frightful atrocities.'[14]

The delay in confronting the Goths hurt Valens' popularity. The mob in the hippodrome at Constantinople taunted him by calling 'Burn Valens alive.'[15] They mocked him for taking no action against the Goths who had ravaged Thrace. They called for Gratian to rule both halves of the empire. Valens felt vulnerable. He had to act fast. But the western army was slow in moving east, and in early 378, a major assault on the Rhine frontier by a tribe of Alemanni called the Lentienses held it up. This happened in February 378 and the ensuing conflict lasted until May, when Gratian won a resounding victory. Ironically, this only put more pressure on Valens to defeat the Goths.

By August 378, Gratian was still some distance away in Illyria (see Map 1). Other news reached Valens. One of his generals, Sebastian, won a resounding victory over a minor Gothic war-band near Adrianople. Fritigern withdrew to the north of the city. This emboldened Valens to wonder if he could defeat the rest of the Goths by himself and boost his battered image.

Valens advanced the eastern army towards Adrianople. Scouts informed him that only the Thervingi Goths were in the area. They said their allies, the Greuthungi Goths and some Huns and Alans, were dispersed, foraging around Thrace. The scouts reported the Thervingi warriors to number about 10,000. Against this, Valens had around 30,000 troops, including the elite regiments of the eastern army. Surely he could win a prestigious victory? He decided to strike.

3

The Battle of Adrianople

On the morning of 9 August 378, the roads and fields north of Adrianople were choked with Roman legionaries and cavalry. Dust circled in the air, kicked up by horses' hooves and nailed sandals on the hard summer earth. Coughing and spluttering, the soldiers marched forward in long, seemingly endless columns.

The eastern Roman emperor, Valens, rode with his senior officers. He was convinced he would defeat the barbarian Goths. Although Gratian's legions were only a few days' march away, this only made him more impetuous. He would defeat the Goths by himself without any help from Gratian. He wanted to prove the mob wrong.

As the sun rose and the heat became more intense, the Roman cavalry found the enemy. At the top of a steep slope, an immense circle of barbarian wagons, a couple of miles long, came into sight. Trying to buy time, the Gothic king Fritigern sent a last-minute deputation to discuss peace. The emperor Valens accepted and discussions began.

Meanwhile, the Roman army deployed into its battle formation. A mixture of cavalry and infantry mustered on each wing, with the bulk of the heavy infantry in the centre. The August sun was burning. The Roman legionaries felt they were being cooked in their heavy armour. They were already tired and sweating from the eight-mile march to reach the Goths. Then the Goths set fire to the dry grass in front of them and the air became even hotter and more oppressive.

Both sides waited while Fritigern played for time by making offers of peace. His deputies even promised that he would come to meet Valens himself if high-ranking hostages were exchanged. The western general, Richomer, courageously offered himself as a hostage, and was actually on his way towards the Gothic lines when something completely unexpected happened.

On the Roman right wing, a couple of regiments began an unauthorised attack on the wagon circle. But no sooner did they advance than they retreated. Richomer wisely decided not to offer himself as a hostage. Negotiations ended, and the battle began.

The Roman chronicler, Ammianus Marcellinus, has left us with the best account of the battle even if it is a little disjointed. What seems to have happened was that, although the first fighting was on the Roman right wing, Ammianus says that it was the Roman left wing which made the most progress, advancing right up to the Gothic wagon circle. But then disaster struck for the Romans. The Gothic cavalry arrived. These were the Greuthungi and Alans who Fritigern had been waiting for. They transformed the battle. Ammianus says, 'They shot forward like a thunderbolt and routed with great slaughter all they could come to grips with…'.[16] Their onslaught seems to have destroyed the Roman left wing, and because of this the Roman legionaries in the centre found themselves outflanked by the Gothic cavalry, while also facing a horde of Gothic infantry in front of them.

Although these soldiers were the elite regiments of the eastern army, they were too penned in on all sides to use their weapons effectively. Ammianus says they were:

> *...so closely huddled together that a man could hardly wield his sword or draw back his arm once he had stretched it out. Dust rose in such clouds as to hide the sky ... In consequence, it was impossible to see the enemy's missiles in flight and dodge them; all found their mark and dealt death on every side.*[17]

They were using the densely packed *testudo* formations (meaning 'tortoise' in reference to the shields forming a protective shell), normally what gave the Romans an advantage, but this time they did not work against the Goths. 'The barbarians poured on in huge columns, trampling down horse and man, and crushing our ranks so as to make orderly retreat impossible.'[18] Despite this, for quite a while the legionaries held their ground. Ammianus describes a bloody battle with both sides taking heavy casualties: '...you might see the barbarian towering in his fierceness, hissing or shouting, fall with his legs pierced through, or his right hand cut off...'.[19]

Finally, Valens' legionaries '...weak from hunger, parched with thirst, and weighed down by their armour...'[20] broke under the pressure of the Gothic attack. Only the most elite Roman regiments, like the Lancearii and Mattiarii, kept fighting while the others fled. The result was slaughter. 'The barbarians spared neither those who yielded nor those who resisted.'[21]

It was one of Rome's most disastrous defeats. Contemporaries were unanimous in acknowledging its significance. Ammianus said it was the worst defeat since the disastrous Battle of Cannae in 216 BC, when Hannibal had destroyed most of the Roman army in Italy and left the Republic on the brink of collapse. Two-thirds of the eastern Roman army were killed by the Goths in the space of a few hours, maybe 20,000 legionaries and cavalry.

The roll call of Roman dead was truly astonishing. It included the eastern emperor Valens himself, and almost all his senior military officers – 35 tribunes (commanders of legions and so equivalent to generals), as well as the *magister peditum* and *magister equitum* (Traianus and Valerianus respectively, the two most senior commanders in the eastern army and equivalent to field marshals). No one knows exactly what happened to Valens. He was either killed randomly on the battlefield or, as one story recounts, he fled to a farmhouse which was burned down and he died in the flames.

The Battle of Adrianople need not have marked the beginning of the fall of the Roman Empire. But it did for two reasons. The first was that most of the eastern army's elite regiments were destroyed and not replaced. This meant that the eastern army was unable to eliminate the Goths who remained in Roman territory. Second, it resulted, quite fortuitously, in the elevation of an eastern emperor, Theodosius I, or 'the Great', who, contrary to his glowing epithet, sowed the seeds for the destruction of the western empire, as we will now discover.

4

Theodosius the Not So Great

The day after their victory, the Goths attacked Adrianople. But the city's tall walls, equipped with the brutally effective Roman artillery, and manned by soldiers and every able-bodied citizen, were waiting for them. Like waves crashing against rocks, they threw themselves against the Roman defences, only to suffer horrendous losses as missiles and artillery poured down on them. Eventually, they retreated, cursing they had ever entertained the idea of taking the city.

What the Goths encountered at Adrianople set a standard for the rest of the Gothic war. They simply did not have sufficient knowledge about siege warfare to take any walled city. After Adrianople, they marched to Constantinople. But one look at its walls, even though these were not yet the mighty Theodosian walls we can still see in modern Istanbul, built over 30 years later, convinced them it would be impossible to take the city.

The result was a stalemate. The Goths could not take any of the Roman cities but the Romans did not have an army left to face them in the field. Or at least not in the east. In the west, there was still a formidable Roman army, and this prevented the Goths from advancing west to the Adriatic. To the east, they were confined by the Bosphorus, which prevented their crossing into Anatolia. This meant the Goths stayed in Thrace, plundering at will whatever it was they had missed in the previous two years.

Meanwhile, the Romans prepared to take their revenge. The western emperor, Gratian, appointed Theodosius in January 379 to replace Valens. Theodosius was a soldier with no dynastic claim to the purple, but he was the son of Gratian's father's (Valentinian I) main general, also called Theodosius, and he was appointed to shake up the eastern army and secure a victory over the Goths.

Gratian respected and trusted Theodosius and gave him the task of rebuilding the eastern army and leading it to victory over the Goths. The problem was that the defeat at Adrianople had eliminated nearly all the elite regiments of the eastern Roman army. Rebuilding an army to anything like the same level of experience and ability would take years, if not decades. And Theodosius had just over a year to do it. He recruited from three sources – veterans recalled to the ranks, new recruits needing training, and barbarian mercenaries. It should have been clear to anyone this new army would not be anything like as good as the one destroyed at Adrianople.

Strangely, Theodosius did not realise this and, in the summer of 380, only 18 months after he became emperor, he tested his rooky army against the Goths in battle. He should have waited longer to train it. There are no detailed records of the battle, but it was a clear Roman defeat. Theodosius had failed.

Despite this, Theodosius survived the political backlash against and found a diplomatic solution to the problem of the Goths. This was possible because, after six years of war, the Goths were as exhausted and keen to make peace as the Romans. Although they had now defeated two Roman armies – one at Adrianople in 378, and Theodosius' new model army in 380 – they were incapable of taking any of the Roman towns and cities. The western army successfully pinned them into the Balkans and prevented their migration westward towards Italy. Running out of food, they were ready to negotiate.

In October 382, Theodosius agreed on a landmark settlement with the Goths. Hailed by his courtiers as a Roman victory, the treaty of 382 was, in fact, the opposite. It was the first agreement the empire had made in its history to hand over a portion of territory for occupation by a foreign invader. Theodosius agreed the Goths could settle in an area south of the Danube, and although we do not know precisely where it was, it seems to have been mainly in Moesia and Macedonia. This meant that the Goths evacuated Thrace, and the devastated region returned to Roman rule.

Our knowledge of the details of the peace treaty is poor. We only know three things for certain. First, the Goths were still fully armed and autonomous, and they were not Roman citizens. This was a Roman admission of defeat, for never had a group of barbarians settled in Roman territory while fully armed. Second, there was a regime change demanded by the Romans. Fritigern disappears from the history books, presumably on Theodosius' insistence. This makes sense since he had become the symbol of Gothic defiance. It may also suggest that his own political standing had fallen. The Goths wanted peace and they were willing to oust Fritigern. Third, the Goths promised to supply troops, albeit under their own commanders and not Roman ones, should they be called on. The Goths took this commitment seriously, suggesting they now saw themselves as Roman allies.

But what was hailed at the time as a Roman victory spelled the death of the Roman army. This was because Theodosius compensated for his failure to restore the eastern legions after Adrianople by using the Goths as mercenary troops. He fought two vicious civil wars against rivals in the western empire using the Goths as his front-line troops to defeat the western legions. In 394, he won an enormous battle at the Frigidus River against the western legions led by the usurpers Arbogast and Eugenius. His Goths destroyed the heart of the western legions.

The Battle of the Frigidus River was an overlooked turning point for Rome. Had Theodosius' rivals, Arbogast and Eugenius won, as they nearly did, the Goths would have been defeated and Theodosius overthrown. This would have been a far better outcome for Rome since Theodosius' victory made the Goths into the empire's premier fighting force. With the professional core of the legions destroyed, in the east at Adrianople, and in the west at the Frigidus River, the Roman military was effectively outsourced to barbarians. Historians have referred to this as the 'barbarisation' of the Roman army, but this term is misleading because it was not the legions that were barbarised. It would be more accurate to say that they were de-emphasised and replaced by mercenary barbarian units, led by barbarians, starting with the Goths, but in the early fifth century this came to include other German tribes, Huns and Alans. Inevitably, as the Roman army became dominated by barbarian mercenaries, so its command structure was also increasingly dominated by barbarians. 'Roman' generals were increasingly Germanic, as we will see in the next chapter with Stilicho.

But before we turn to Stilicho, we need to say a last word about Theodosius. His epithet of 'the Great' suggests he achieved something spectacularly good for the Roman Empire. However, the evidence suggests the exact opposite. So, where does his inappropriate epithet come from? History, as they say, is written by the victors, and our sources for Theodosius are a good example of this. The only victor from Theodosius' reign was the Catholic Church, and it is no surprise the Catholic bishops named him 'the Great' since he was a firm believer in the Nicene Creed, and opposed their greatest enemy: the Arians. The difference between the two sects may seem obscure to us today but for fourth-century Romans it was as important as the difference between Christians and Muslims is today. Arians regarded Christ as subordinate to God; Catholics (as followers of the Nicene Creed became known) regarded him as equal.

This theological division tore the Roman Empire apart in the fourth century. Theodosius helped the Catholic Church to triumph by enacting pro-Catholic legislation early in his reign, such as the 'Edict of Thessalonika' in 380, which stopped Arians from attending churches in Constantinople (although not elsewhere in the empire). He was also passionately anti-pagan. An edict issued in 392 clearly stated that Christianity was the empire's favoured religion and all but banned paganism. Therefore, it is little wonder that today's Catholic Church regards him as one of its most important founders.

But for the Roman Empire there was nothing great about Theodosius or his reign. Indeed, just the opposite. Only 15 years after his death, the city of Rome itself was sacked by the Goths.

5

A Tale of Two Barbarians

If Theodosius' reign sowed the seeds for Rome's decline, it was his sons who reaped that grim harvest.

In 395, Theodosius died from heart failure, aged 48. His death was unexpected and he left the empire in the hands of his two young sons, Arcadius in the east, and Honorius in the west. Arcadius was 17 and Honorius 11, both too young to rule. On his deathbed, Theodosius appointed regents to govern for them: in the west, Stilicho, the barbarian *magister militum*[22] (commander-in-chief of the army), and in the east, the praetorian prefect, Rufinus.

Not only were the two boy-emperors too young to rule, but even when they came of age they proved to be incapable. It was an ironic twist of fate that in Rome's greatest hour of need, its nominal rulers were the most weak-willed ever to wear the imperial diadems. In another age, they would probably have been quickly overthrown, but Constantine the Great had established a deep-rooted respect for hereditary succession that now cost the Romans dear.

Into the breach came generals and ministers intent on wielding the real power behind the throne. Two men in particular rose to the fore in the years leading to the sack of

Rome in 410: Stilicho and Alaric. Both of barbarian descent, their rivalry would determine the fate of Rome.

Stilicho was a fascinating example of a new breed in the fifth century – half barbarian, half Roman. His father was a Vandal, serving in the Roman army, and his mother a Roman. All we know about his early life is that he joined Theodosius' imperial guard and his career breakthrough came when he married Theodosius' niece, Serena. For an ordinary guardsman to marry into the imperial family would normally have been out of the question. But Serena was no ordinary woman. Theodosius I had always had a soft spot for her, preferring her to his own children. She knew her own mind and when she fell in love with Stilicho, who was presumably a handsome guardsman around the palace, she did everything to persuade the emperor to permit the marriage and then to promote her new husband.

Stilicho was also no slouch. A cynic would say he married Serena to further his career, and this was no doubt partly true, but he was also a devoted husband up until his death when, as we shall discover, he submitted to the sword to try to save his wife. But what took him to the very top of Theodosius' government was the relationship he forged with the emperor. Theodosius took a liking to him. He became his right-hand man, entrusted with a series of crucially important jobs from negotiating peace with Persia to being commander-in-chief of the eastern army. On his deathbed, the person Theodosius most wanted to discuss the future government of the empire with was Stilicho.

In contrast to Stilicho, Alaric was an outsider. Born beyond the Roman frontiers, he was a migrant, one of the many Goths who had crossed into the Roman Empire and was settled by Theodosius in Pannonia. Little is known of his early life except he rose to command a Gothic unit at the Battle of the Frigidus River in 394, and by 395 he was king of most of the Goths who had entered Roman territory and were nominally serving the Romans as *foederati*.

Alaric was ambitious. His sole aim was to secure power for himself. But the interesting point is that he did not care whether he secured this as a Roman general, a Gothic king or a combination of the two. He and Stilicho immediately came into conflict after Theodosius' death. Returning home from the Battle of the Frigidus River, where they had defeated the western legions, the Goths felt they had not been properly paid for their vital role in securing Theodosius' victory. Alaric took the lead by raising a rebellion in the Balkans. Some historians think part of his motivation was to unite the disparate Gothic tribes under his control since, although he was referred to as king of the Goths by most chroniclers, he was in fact probably only king of the Thervingi. To frighten the eastern Romans, Alaric led his Gothic army to Constantinople itself.

There was panic in the city. No eastern army existed to face the Goths since most of it was in the west with Stilicho, having just fought the Frigidus battle, and the rest of it had been sent east to Armenia to face a Hunnic invasion through the Caucasus. Although the Goths were no masters of siege craft, and it was extremely unlikely they could have taken Constantinople, the eastern minister Rufinus was sufficiently scared, according to Zosimus, to agree to meet Alaric and offer him Greece to ravage if he left Constantinople alone. Gold almost certainly also passed hands.

Meanwhile, in the west, Stilicho, who was in command of the remains of both the western and eastern Roman armies that had fought at Frigidus, watched Alaric's antics with a mix of outrage and envy. Outrage at the news of Alaric's rebellion and the fact a former Roman ally had betrayed his oath to Rome. Envy at the way Alaric had intimidated Rufinus, for the latter was the main obstacle to his own claim on power in the east.

What followed was an extraordinary game of cat and mouse between the two barbarian generals as they vied for power. Alaric skilfully exploited the tension between the eastern and western halves of the empire. The cause of this lay with Stilicho's assertion that on his deathbed Theodosius I had whispered to him he should be guardian to both his sons, in east and west. But Arcadius and his court rejected this. They had no wish to be subservient to Stilicho. When Stilicho marched into Thessaly and seemed to have Alaric at his mercy, the eastern minister Rufinus feared he would try to seize Constantinople. The divided Roman Empire was its own worst enemy for Rufinus intervened to save Alaric and his Goths and thereafter used them to shield the eastern empire from Stilicho. The only winner was Alaric.

In 397, Stilicho mounted a second expedition against Alaric who was still at liberty in Greece, albeit on friendly terms with Rufinus' successor, Eutropius. When Stilicho transported his army across the Adriatic and pushed the Goths back, Eutropius feared he was again aiming to seize Constantinople. For a second time, Eutropius helped the Goths escape and even made an alliance with Alaric giving him the title of *magister militum* of Illyria. Again, Alaric was the winner.

But Alaric's love affair with the eastern empire ended when Eutropius was replaced by Aurelian, and the eastern court severed their ties with him. Being the duplicitous chameleon he was, Alaric first offered his services to Stilicho, and when he was refused, he invaded Italy. Stilicho defeated him at the Battle of Pollentia in April 402. Alaric's own wife was captured and the Goths fled east. Stilicho pursued them and won another battle outside Verona. But unexpectedly, Stilicho did not capture Alaric and put his head on a spear. He spared him and allowed him to return to Illyria, this time as his vassal.

Yet again, the damaging division between the two halves of the empire saved Alaric. Stilicho's clemency to him was simply because he wanted his help against Constantinople. In late 406, he instructed him to join in a march on Constantinople. Civil war now threatened the empire – the worst of all possible situations.

It was Stilicho's obsession with controlling the eastern empire that destroyed him. Although in 406 he was at the height of his power, having defeated not just Alaric but another formidable Gothic invasion of Italy that year, led by another Gothic king, Radagaisus, he failed to spot a major crisis building on Rome's western frontiers. This would prove to be the most disastrous event in Roman history since the Battle of Adrianople.

6

Disaster in Gaul

According to Edward Gibbon, the fall of the Roman Empire began on the night of 31 December 406, when vast numbers of Germans crossed the frozen Rhine into Gaul. Although, in fact, no Roman, or any other source, mentions the Rhine freezing that night, Gibbon can be forgiven his poetic licence, since this proved one of the greatest events in Roman history. What probably happened was that a huge horde of Germanic tribes crossed the Rhine over several days in December 406, using various Roman bridges.

The invaders were a diverse collection of tribes, including two groups of Vandals, the Asding and Siling, a large group of Alans, who were an Indo-European nomadic tribe by now fairly well integrated into Germanic culture, and a large group mysteriously called the Suevi by the Romans, which probably comprised a collection of Alemanni and Burgundians, although the majority of those tribes seem to have remained east of the Rhine.

Similar to the migration of Fritigern's Goths in 376, which led to the Battle of Adrianople, this Germanic onslaught was not a raid but a proper migration of men, women and children. The intention was to settle in Roman territory, in a repeat of what Alaric's Goths had achieved in Illyria.

Why did this invasion happen and why then? Yet again, most historians believe the Huns were the culprits, exerting the same domino-toppling effect on the Germans by pushing them into the Roman Empire as they had done with the Goths. Why was the invasion so successful? The answer was that the Roman army was losing its grip on the west. The debilitating civil wars fought in Theodosius' reign had reduced it to a shadow of its former self. On top of that, Stilicho had withdrawn detachments to fight Alaric in 401/2, and then Radagaisus in 405/6. So, in 406 there was almost no Roman army in Gaul to oppose the Germans.

The result was a blitzkrieg-like invasion by the Germans as they streamed through Gaul. There is no surviving record of exactly what happened. The best we have are fragments from the writings of some Christian Gallic poets who bewailed the unfolding disaster as marking the end of civilisation. Most famous of these is the often-quoted one-liner from Orientus, who said that, 'All Gaul was filled with the smoke of a single funeral pyre.'[23] Another poet believed that the end of civilisation was nigh and described the invasion as the collapse of 'the frame of the fragile world'.[24]

The most detail we have is a long list of sacked Roman towns compiled by Saint Jerome. This includes almost all the main Gallic towns and cities except for those in the south in Roman Provence. Mainz on the Rhine frontier was the first to go, followed by Rheims. The former Gallic capital of Trier might have held out, helped by its enormous walls. The invaders moved into central Gaul, sacking Tournai, Arras,

Amiens and Paris (I am using the modern French names since they are easier to identify). Then they moved both west and south, sacking Orléans, Tours and Toulouse. By 409, after spending over two years devastating Gaul, this group of Vandals, Alans and Suevi reached the Pyrenees. Then they crossed into Hispania.

Exhausted by their long journey of destruction, they settled in Hispania. Again, there were few Roman defenders to oppose them. They carried on through Hispania to the Strait of Gibraltar, where they stopped. If they had found boats to ferry them across to Africa, no doubt they would have done that, as the Vandals were to do two decades later. But instead, they partitioned Hispania between them, with the Alans taking the centre, while the Asding Vandals and the Suevi occupied the north and the Siling Vandals the south.

As if the devastation and loss of Gaul and Hispania were not bad enough, there was also a rebellion in Britain. The British legions proclaimed two emperors in quick succession – Marcus followed by Gratian, both of whom were quickly rejected and executed – before choosing Flavius Claudius Constantinus and naming him Constantine III. He quickly proved himself a capable leader although little is known about his early life other than he was an experienced soldier. His name Constantine was said to have been part of his attraction, since it reminded the legionaries of Constantine the Great, whom the British legions had proclaimed emperor in York 101 years before in 306.

He crossed over to Gaul, where the battered remains of the Gallic legions immediately rallied to his standard. The few Roman soldiers in Hispania also declared for him. This was very similar to what had happened in the third century AD when Britain, Gaul and Hispania had broken away from Rome under the Roman general Postumus to create an independent Gallic Empire. Constantine III created another breakaway Roman state comprising the demoralised troops and landowners abandoned by Ravenna.

For Stilicho, these developments struck him like a bolt from the blue. Why he was unconcerned about the fragile condition of the Rhine frontier remains a mystery. After all, he was the commander-in-chief of the western army and should have known the situation better than anyone. As mentioned, the answer seems to lie with his ambitions to rule Constantinople which blinded him to the realities in Gaul. He would now pay a full price for his blunder. The fall of the west had begun.

7

A Noble Death

Things went from bad to worse for Stilicho in 408.

First, he failed to stamp out Constantine III's rebellion in Gaul. Indeed, as the majority of the German invaders passed through Gaul into Hispania, Constantine III was able to establish a Roman base around Soissons in northern France that would, ironically, outlast the western empire.[25] In one fell swoop, Stilicho had lost the tax revenues from Britain, Gaul and Hispania. This crippled what was left of the western Roman army. But a more immediate threat was developing in the east, and this time it came from his old enemy Alaric.

By the spring of 408, Alaric was getting impatient. It was over a year since he had dutifully followed Stilicho's orders to await the western Roman army for their intended march on Constantinople. During that time, his followers had received no pay or provisions from Stilicho and were almost certainly complaining. Because of this, he now demanded 4,000 pounds of gold as compensation and threatened war if this was not forthcoming.

Yet again, Stilicho was caught out. Alaric marched north from Epirus to the Roman province of Noricum (modern

Austria) ready to invade Italy. With Constantine III in Gaul, and Alaric in Noricum, Stilicho was surrounded. In desperation, he appealed to the senate in Rome to pay the Goths. Initially, they resisted. Resentment was growing against Stilicho. Rumours circulated he was actually in league with Alaric. The senate was also dissatisfied with the growing use of German mercenaries in the army instead of Roman legionaries, although this was partly their fault since many of the wealthy senators were reluctant to allow able-bodied, young men working on their estates to be recruited into the army. One senator criticised Stilicho by declaring in a speech that paying the Goths 'did not bring peace, but a pact of servitude'.[26] Nevertheless, the senate paid and Alaric was appeased.

Stilicho's growing unpopularity offered an opportunity for his rivals at court. In particular, a man called Olympius, who was *magister scrinii*, master of the imperial secretaries, and ironically Stilicho's own appointee, realised he could use it to his advantage. His job meant he was almost always at the emperor Honorius' side, and he used this to foment conspiracy theories against Stilicho in the weak-willed, young (24 years old in 408) emperor's mind.

Stilicho's relationship with Honorius was further damaged when news arrived from Constantinople of the death of Honorius' brother, the eastern emperor Arcadius, in May 408, leaving his seven-year-old son, Theodosius II, heir to the eastern throne. Honorius showed a rare moment of ambition when he declared he wanted to go to Constantinople to arrange the governorship of the eastern empire since Theodosius II was too young to rule. Stilicho objected, saying that if anyone went, it should be him. Stilicho had of course always hankered after power in the east. He also no doubt rightly feared that should Honorius go alone, he would fall under the influence of the ministers in Constantinople, not least the highly capable Anthemius, who was no friend of his.

Stilicho got his way. In the end, no one went to Constantinople and Honorius felt insulted. Stilicho attracted further criticism when he proposed to send Alaric to Gaul to confront Constantine III. Superficially, this made sense in view of the huge amount of money the Romans were paying Alaric. But it did not go down well with either the senate or the Italian legions. Both remembered the fear in Italy when Alaric had invaded in 401/2 and neither wanted him back on Italian soil. In particular, the legionaries and their officers had long disliked the use of Gothic and other German mercenaries in the army and particularly resented the payment of gold to Alaric's men. On hearing that Alaric's army could be transferred to the Gallic front, they feared they would be told to report to Alaric. This was too much for them. Rumours spread like wildfire that Stilicho was actually in league with Alaric against Rome.

It was the scheming Olympius who did his best to work the rumour mill against Stilicho. According to the Roman chronicler Zosimus, he said that Stilicho 'was planning the journey to the east in order to plot the overthrow of the young Theodosius and the transfer of the east to his own son, Eucherius'.[27] This view went viral. Not only did it shock Honorius, but it was also the last straw for the Roman army in Italy, headquartered at Ticinum (modern Pavia), ready to defend the Alpine passes from Constantine III.

A mutiny erupted there in August 408. Officers who supported Stilicho were rounded up in a military *coup d'état* and executed. The emperor Honorius happened to be present at the time and was shocked by the insurrection. Indeed, one story said that when a pro-Stilicho officer, the *quaestor* Salvinus, fell at the emperor's feet begging for his life, the soldiers simply dragged him away from the speechless Honorius and butchered him. Honorius, who normally enjoyed a quiet life tending to his chickens, ran away scared for his own safety.

When Stilicho heard the news, he was in the town of Bononia, midway between Pavia and Ravenna. At first, he did not know what to do. Did the emperor want to punish the mutinous soldiers or forgive them? If the latter, it meant he was finished. As usual, Honorius himself was undecided. The real architect of the revolt was Olympius. He now told the emperor the army answered to him, not Stilicho. Honorius accepted this. Stilicho's death sentence had in effect been signed.

However, despite Olympius' betrayal, Stilicho was still in a powerful position, since with him in Bononia he had most of the barbarian mercenaries who were the real muscle in the Roman army. His supporters, including his trusted Gothic general, Sarus, told him to advance on Ticinum and punish the mutinous Roman regiments. But Stilicho refused to do this, knowing it would mean a costly civil war with Honorius. Instead, he earned himself a place in the pantheon of Rome's most noble leaders by refusing to plunge the west into even worse chaos. He retired to Ravenna hoping he could argue his case with Honorius. His reasonable behaviour only infuriated his barbarian supporters. Sarus deserted him in disgust.

Shortly after Stilicho arrived in Ravenna, messengers from Honorius reached the city with orders to arrest him. Stilicho sought sanctuary in a nearby church. At daybreak on 22 August 408, soldiers led by an officer called Heraclian entered the church. They pushed aside the bishop who was protecting Stilicho, saying they wanted to arrest him not execute him. Yet the moment Stilicho agreed to leave the church, Heraclian produced a second letter, condemning him to death for 'crimes against the state'. Stilicho's servants and bodyguards raised their weapons, ready to save their leader, but Stilicho told them to put away their weapons and submitted his neck to the sword.

Why did Stilicho not put up a fight? Many have praised his selflessness in wanting to avoid a damaging civil war. Others have seen him as foolishly loyal to the incompetent Honorius. I suggest another answer: he wanted to save his family. In that he succeeded, at least initially. His son, Eucherius, who was with him in Ravenna, was allowed to leave for Rome to join his mother, Serena, Stilicho's devoted wife. They were both allowed to live. But not for long. Both would die within the next two years as catastrophe enveloped the western empire.

Opinion is divided about Stilicho. Some see him as the barbarian who nearly saved Rome; others as the man who failed it in its hour of need. But all are agreed on one point: he died a noble death.

8

The Sack of Rome

When Stilicho's head was severed from his body, government passed into the hands of Honorius' minister, Olympius, who proved as incompetent as he was treacherous.

Almost the moment he took office, a tragic error of judgement sealed the fate of the western empire. This occurred when the Roman army based in Ticinum turned against the German mercenaries that were now so prominent in the western army. The objects of the Romans' anger were the Gothic families who had been quartered in various Italian cities while their menfolk served in the Roman army. This arrangement had been Stilicho's idea following his defeat of Radagaisus' invasion in 404 and had worked well. Now, these innocent women and children were rounded up and massacred. This horrific act backfired on the Romans spectacularly, for it achieved nothing from a military standpoint other than to send the husbands of the slaughtered families – some 12,000 Gothic soldiers recruited by Stilicho from Radagaisus' defeated army – rushing to join Alaric, who in the meantime had advanced into northern Italy.

The fact these Goths were not integrated into the Roman regiments meant they could easily move en masse to form a Gothic supergroup in Italy far more powerful than any of the regular Roman forces. For Alaric now commanded the largest Gothic army Rome had ever faced, probably around 40,000 strong, including his own army of over 20,000 and Stilicho's 12,000 Goths. In contrast, the regular Roman army at Ticinum was a shadow of its former self. It probably numbered only some 10–15,000 men. Italy was now effectively in the hands of Alaric and his Goths. The city of Rome now stood like an abandoned lamb waiting to be slaughtered.

Despite this Alaric was in no rush.

In complete contrast to Hannibal, who never felt he had the resources to take Rome, Alaric knew he had the city at his mercy and could occupy it whenever he wanted. But Alaric was not Hannibal. Whereas Hannibal had wanted to destroy Rome, Alaric wanted to be accepted by Rome. In the fourth century AD, Rome was still a legendary city, similar to how the Vikings would later regard Constantinople. It was a city of undreamed-of wealth and prestige. And Alaric wanted all of this. He wanted Roman wealth, titles and recognition. So, he tried to use his military power as a bargaining tool to secure Roman accolades.

Over the next two years, he conducted three sieges of the city. The first resulted from his request to Honorius for another payment of gold, similar to the one he had secured from Stilicho earlier that year. Olympius, the power behind the throne, refused. It is very doubtful whether Ravenna had the money to pay Alaric. Alaric led his troops south. When they reached Rome, he took Ostia, Rome's port and its supply base for the North African grain that fed its population. There was panic in the city. Serena, Stilicho's unfortunate widow, was arrested and strangled to death for fear that remorse for her husband might induce her to betray the city to the Goths. Honorius' sister, Galla Placidia, also resident in the city, raised no objection, although in her youth she had been brought up by Serena and Stilicho. Placidia's hard-heartedness was the first sign of the ruthless determination that would help her survive and prosper over the next few decades.

Alaric held the city in a tight grip. Aqueducts were cut and the Tiber River was blockaded. No supplies could reach it. Food quickly ran out. The population, estimated at around 800,000, began to starve. Unburied bodies filled the streets. Famine led to plague. 'The stench arising from the putrid corpses was sufficient to infect them with disease,'[28] according to Zosimus, our best source on the sack of Rome. The Romans were holding out, hoping a relief force would arrive from Ravenna or the army based at Ticinum would move south. But no help came. Honorius and Olympius were too worried about their own precarious position to save Rome. In desperation, a group of senators sought an audience with Alaric. When they told him the people of Rome would fight just like their ancestors, Alaric laughed. When they asked him what he wanted, he said all their gold and possessions, as well as the freedom of the slaves. When they asked him what he would give them, he said, 'Your lives'.

The senate resorted to invoking help from the ancient Roman gods. Even Pope Innocent I agreed to this. But when there was no divine intervention and there was no food left, the senate returned to Alaric to beg for terms. He demanded

5,000 pounds of gold, 30,000 of silver, 4,000 silk robes, 3,000 scarlet fleeces and 3,000 pounds of pepper. The terms were accepted, and the senate levied the ransom from the city's inhabitants according to a means test. Zosimus recounts that the miserly senators, although many possessed enormous wealth, did their best to avoid contributing. All the gold and silver in the churches, and what remained in the pagan temples, was stripped to pay the Goths. Zosimus says that ancient statues made of gold and silver were melted down, including one of Virtus, the Roman god of Valour. 'With this being destroyed, all that remained of Roman valour was totally extinguished.'[29]

Alaric was as good as his word and, once he had been paid, in December 408, he withdrew north to Tuscany. Food supplies flooded into the city to the relief of its starving inhabitants. Rome had been saved. But for how long? In January 409, the senate sent an embassy to Honorius in Ravenna begging for a peace treaty with Alaric to prevent him from attacking Rome again.

However, Honorius, under Olympius' thumb, refused. A palace coup ousted Olympius and the praetorian prefect for Italy, Jovius, took over. But there was still no agreement made with Alaric.

Frustrated, Alaric returned to Rome for a second time and put it under siege in the autumn of 409. But this time the senate had no faith in being rescued by Honorius. Nor did Alaric expect to extract a senior appointment from him. So, they joined forces. They agreed to circumvent Honorius and appointed their own emperor, a senator called Priscus Attalus.

Honorius realised his mistake in alienating both the senate and Alaric. He panicked and decided the best course of action was to flee to Constantinople. But there was yet another twist. As he was waiting to board ship to join his young nephew, Theodosius II, a fleet from Constantinople itself appeared, containing 4,000 elite troops from the eastern empire. The eastern empire had come to his rescue in the nick of time. He immediately rethought his plans and stayed in Ravenna.

Alaric's frustration was now reaching boiling point. Honorius would not recognise him. His puppet emperor, Priscus Attalus, was in fact only a puppet. And his vast army had not been paid since December 408, when the senate ransomed the city. When a final meeting with Honorius' delegates ended in failure, he marched on Rome for a third and final time.

On 24 August 410, someone, perhaps a vengeful slave, opened the Salarian Gate,[30] one of the main gates in the Aurelian walls to the north of the city. The Goths flooded into the city. Nevertheless, Alaric did his best to ensure moderation. He ordered the Goths to plunder but not to kill. In particular, the two main Christian churches, the basilicas of St Peter and St Paul, were nominated as places of sanctuary where Roman citizens would be safe, if they could get to them. The Goths were Arian Christians and, although most Romans were Nicene Christians, there was at least some sort of religious kindred spirit between the invaders and the invaded. Certainly, the sack was mild compared with the utterly brutal sacking of northern Italian Roman cities 40 years later by Attila the Hun and his pagan hordes.

In particular, two stories illustrative of Gothic clemency have become well known. One, recounted by Saint Jerome, is of Marcella, a nun who protested to the Goths ransacking her house that she had no wealth, for she had no need for material possessions, which so impressed them they took her to the safety of St Peter's.

Another, recorded by the Christian writer Sozomen, says that a fierce Gothic soldier fell in love with a pretty young Roman woman, 'conquered by her loveliness', and escorted her to the safety of St Peter's, where he paid the guards to protect her until the danger was over.[31]

Nevertheless, the pillage of the city would *not* have been a pretty sight. It is almost certain the Goths seized a huge amount of gold and silver and other precious possessions from the city's inhabitants. Although they seem to have respected most of the churches, they could not resist taking a 2,000-pound silver ciborium (a canopy covering an altar) which had been a gift from Constantine the Great. They burned several large Roman administrative buildings, including the senate house itself and the basilicas of Aemilia and Julia.

No one came to Rome's rescue. The Italian legions at Ticinum did nothing. Still guarding the frontier against Constantine III, they did not move south to confront the Goths. In Ravenna, the story goes, according to the sixth-century Roman writer, Procopius, that the feeble-minded emperor Honorius was feeding his chickens when a eunuch rushed in to tell him that Rome had perished. The emperor looked up in horror and said, 'And yet it has just eaten from my hands!' The eunuch had to explain he was referring to the city of Rome and not the chicken which Honorius had nicknamed *Roma*. Apparently, Honorius breathed a sigh of relief and said, 'But I thought my chicken had perished.'

While Honorius might have been relieved his chicken had survived, most of the inhabitants of the empire regarded the sack of Rome as a turning point. Not for 800 years had Rome fallen to a foreign invader. The last time was in 390 BC, when the Gauls sacked it, and even then the Capitol still held out, according to Livy, with the help of its geese, who warned the defenders of Gallic attacks. In Constantinople, the first minister Anthemius told the nine-year-old Theodosius II to proclaim three days of mourning. Saint Jerome, one of our principal sources for this period, wrote, 'If Rome can perish, what can be safe?'[32] Christians blamed the pagans in the empire, and the pagans blamed the Christians. Orosius, a leading Christian theologian, blamed the impious pagans for the sack of Rome. But the pagan chronicler Zosimus blamed the Christians for causing the pagan gods to be rejected. Everywhere, divine vengeance was cited as the reason for the worst disaster to afflict the empire in 800 years.

Amidst this confused and vengeful anger surrounding Rome's demise, there rose to prominence one of the Catholic Church's most influential thinkers – Saint Augustine. He was the bishop of Hippo in North Africa in 410 when Rome was sacked, and he wrote *The City of God*, a treatise that became foundational for the Catholic Church. This great work would run to 22 volumes and was not completed until 425, but by 413 he had written the first three books, which put forward the view that the sack of Rome was not a defeat for Christianity, since the Roman Empire was not the same as the Christian Church. This was a revolutionary idea when most early Christians argued it was no coincidence that Augustus, the first Roman emperor, and Christ had lived at the same time. Augustine suggested that this was *truly* just a coincidence, and that the city of Rome and the heavenly city of God existed independently of each other, with the latter far more important, as he described: 'The Heavenly City outshines Rome beyond comparison. There, instead of victory, is truth; instead of high rank, holiness; instead of peace, felicity; instead of life, eternity.'[33]

But for most people, the sack of Rome was a shattering blow. It certainly marked the beginning of the city's rapid decline to little more than a village in the Middle Ages. Refugees fled the city and flooded into Africa, Egypt and Constantinople. One historian[34] has estimated that Rome's population fell from around 800,000 in 410 to some 500,000 by 419. The city's decline proved irreversible. By the year 600, there were fewer than 20,000 people left, barely enough to fill a corner of the Colosseum.

PART II

The False Dawn

9

Heads on Spears

In AD 410, it looked as if the western Roman Empire was finished.

Rome had been sacked. The Goths were wandering freely around Italy. Hispania was mostly in the hands of the Vandals and Alans, and much of the periphery of Gaul was in the hands of the Franks, Burgundians and Alans.

To make matters worse, the empire was more divided than ever. In 410, it had no fewer than six emperors. In addition to the two legitimate members of the Theodosian dynasty – Honorius in the west and Theodosius II in the east – there were Constantine III and his co-emperor son, Constans, in Gaul; Priscus Attalus with the Goths and even a sixth usurper, Maximus, was proclaimed in Hispania in late 410.

But one of the lessons of history is always to expect the unexpected. And just when it looked as if the west would implode, so it staged a partial recovery. Of course, this was nothing like a return to the glorious days of the empire under Diocletian and Constantine, but nevertheless it allowed the west to limp on for another few decades before it finally faced extinction.

First, let's turn to Alaric, the man who sacked Rome. After three days of looting, he called a halt, and the Goths left the city. Together with their plunder, they took Galla Placidia, Honorius' sister, whom they treated with great respect as befitted an imperial princess. So, where could the Goths go now? Alaric had destroyed any chance of a peaceful settlement with Honorius. There was apparently dissatisfaction within the Gothic ranks. Although Alaric had delivered the riches of Rome to his followers, they were frustrated with their itinerant lifestyle and wanted to settle down. So, he promised them a land of plenty, a land where corn grew in abundance, a land of sunny warmth beside the Mediterranean Sea, a land with civilised Roman cities that they could occupy. He promised them North Africa.

The Goths marched into southern Italy, which was still untouched by war. Our records are meagre, but they may well have sacked the cities of Nola and Capua. However, their plans came to nothing. When they reached the Strait of Messina, the ships they gathered for the crossing to Sicily were wrecked by a storm. The Visigoths were not sailors, and they turned back, unable even to reach Sicily, let alone North Africa. Then, another misfortune hit them. Alaric died in the winter of 410/11 of unknown causes. According to the Romano-Gothic historian, Jordanes, his death was 'untimely'. Historians have speculated malaria might have been the cause. Whatever the truth, his death just months after the sack of Rome was a blow to the Goths, who lacked a powerful leader to replace him. His brother-in-law, Ataulf, was crowned king. Lacking Alaric's vision, Ataulf led the Goths back north to find new lands.

Alaric was buried with a hoard of treasure in the bed of a river which had been diverted temporarily. Once placed in his grave, the river was redirected to flow back over it. To prevent any discovery of his resting place and the treasure, the Goths killed all the slaves who had dug it. Thus, in a rather grisly fashion, ended Alaric's remarkable story.

Ataulf led the Goths north towards Gaul. We know next to nothing of Gothic thinking behind this decision. Indeed, Roman sources have left almost no record of their actions in Italy from 410 to early 412, when they crossed the Alps close to modern Geneva, and descended into Gaul. One source suggests Italy was ravaged by them but, whatever the truth, they did not try to sack Rome a second time, or Ravenna or any major Roman cities that we know of. In tow was Galla Placidia, although again we have no record of her time with the barbarians.

Meanwhile, back in Ravenna, Honorius' blinkered vision focused on eliminating his rival, Constantine III. Before the sack of Rome, he had asked Constantine for help by sending him a purple cloak, recognising his imperial aspirations. But now that the Goths were leaving Italy, Honorius felt safe enough to plot his death.

Since Honorius left government to his ministers, the man he commanded to do this was a general named Constantius who assumed the post of *magister militum* of the western army in 411, effectively becoming the new Stilicho. For the next few years, Constantius will be an important figure in our story. Unfortunately, we know little of his background other than he was an Illyrian born in Naissus, and seems to have inherited the stern military outlook of the Illyrian soldier-emperors of the third century, many of whom came from that city, lightened by his liking for a party, as recounted by Olympiodorus:

> *In public processions Constantius was downcast and sullen, a man with bulging eyes, a long neck and a broad head, who always slumped over the neck of the horse he was riding, darting glances here and there out of the corners of his eyes, so that all saw in him a 'mien worthy of a tyrant', as the saying goes. But at banquets and parties he was so cheerful and affable that he even competed with the clowns who often played at his table.* [35]

His job was made easier since Constantine's empire started to fall apart when what remained of the Spanish legions, which had supported him initially, turned against him and defeated and killed his son, Constans. These Spanish Romans were led by a general named Gerontius who declared someone named Maximus emperor, about whom we know nothing, with some historians suggesting he might have been his son.

As Gerontius advanced from Hispania into Gaul, Constantius led a small force across the Alps. Were they in league? In fact, there's no evidence they were, but it was convenient for Constantius that Constantine's army was fighting on two fronts. He besieged Constantine III in Arles and forced him to surrender. In vain, Constantine tried to save himself by entering a church in the city where he was ordained as a priest. But he and his son, Julian, were taken prisoner and beheaded. Their heads were then sent to Ravenna where they were put on spears and displayed amid a growing collection of such trophies, including the head of the unfortunate Stilicho.

With Constantine III and his son, Constans, eliminated, the imperial roll call reduced to four emperors, with the remaining usurpers Maximus in Hispania and Priscus Attalus with Ataulf's Goths. But almost immediately there was yet another rebellion in Gaul, this time led by a Gallo-Roman called Jovinus. In these dark years, usurpers appeared and disappeared a bit like moles in a game of whack-a-mole. Jovinus was a Roman officer stationed at Mainz. But, in a clear sign the times were changing, his support base came less from the remains of the Roman army on the Rhine than from the armies of the Burgundian king, Gundahar, and the Alan king, Goar.

Constantius was smart, and he saw an opportunity to pit the two barbarian sides against each other and watch them fight it out. With that in mind, he retreated into Italy while Jovinus advanced south with the Burgundians and Alans. Meanwhile, Ataulf's Goths marched north over the Alps on a collision course with Jovinus. The two sets of barbarians met at Arles in southern Gaul. Constantius' hopes for a punch-up were dashed when Priscus Attalus persuaded the barbarians to get along with each other. But this didn't last long.

Fortunately for Constantius, they fell out when the Gothic general, Sarus, was killed by Ataulf on his way to join Jovinus. Sarus had been a rival of Ataulf's, and previously Stilicho's second-in-command. Jovinus disliked the fact Ataulf had not consulted him before killing Sarus and, in a fit of pique, he made his brother, Sebastianus, co-emperor against Ataulf's wishes. This annoyed Ataulf sufficiently for him to promise to Constantius he would send the heads of Jovinus and Sebastianus to Ravenna. In 413, he did just that when the Goths fought and defeated the Burgundians and Alans, capturing and beheading Jovinus and Sebastianus, and sending their heads to join the ever-expanding collection in front of Ravenna's walls.

But Constantius had little time to celebrate this victory before yet another pretender raised rebellion. This time it was more worrying because the rebel was in North Africa, still the breadbasket of Rome and Italy. His name was Heraclian, and the root of his rebellion lay in a personal feud with Constantius. This went back to the days of Stilicho when Constantius had been one of his most trusted officers and was deeply upset when he was beheaded. Heraclian, as mentioned in Chapter 7, was the man who had beheaded him, and was subsequently rewarded with the governorship of North Africa. Heraclian knew Constantius was hunting down Stilicho's killers. His first victim had been the former minister, Olympius, who had been the first to betray Stilicho. Constantius tracked him down and had him clubbed to death in a brutal fashion.

Heraclian knew he was next on Constantius' hit list. So, he decided attack was the best form of defence. He invaded Italy, hoping to raise a rebellion against Constantius and Honorius in Rome. Given the fragile state of the western empire, this might perhaps have worked. But Constantius was ready for him. He defeated Heraclian's soldiers, whereupon Heraclian fled back to Africa, only to be seized by his disgruntled subjects and beheaded in Carthage in 413. His head joined the others in Ravenna.

In an age when darkness was falling over the western empire, few would disagree it was to Constantius' credit he took revenge on Stilicho's killers, and showed there was still some honour left among the Romans.

10

The Hollow Crown

Sometime in January 414, an enormously extravagant wedding was celebrated in Narbonne in southern Gaul. Amidst the Roman buildings, a huge gathering of Goths outnumbered the surviving Roman citizens. But there was no tension in the air. Relations between the two races were strikingly cordial, for this represented an unprecedented union of Goth and Roman.

The groom was Ataulf, king of the Goths. His bride was none other than Galla Placidia, the beautiful Roman princess captured in the sack of Rome in 410. Apparently, all the gold and treasures which the Goths had taken from the Romans were spread out before her. How a Roman princess brought up in the luxurious courts of Ravenna and Constantinople reacted to being the wife of a barbarian king has not been recorded. However, there is no evidence she objected. More unexpected was Ataulf's declaration he wanted to restore the Roman name. He dressed as a Roman and gave a speech that the Roman writer, Orosius, has preserved for us.

> *At first, I ardently desired that the Roman name should be obliterated, and that all Roman soil should be converted into an empire of the Goths; I longed that Romania should become Gothia and Ataulf be what Caesar Augustus was. But I have been taught by much experience that the unbridled licence of the Goths will never admit of their obeying laws, and without laws a republic is not a republic. I have therefore chosen the safer course of aspiring to the glory of restoring and increasing the Roman name by Gothic vigour; and I hope to be handed down to posterity as the initiator of a Roman restoration, as it is impossible for me to change the form of the empire.*[36]

These words were probably crafted by Orosius but there is every reason to suppose that Ataulf said something similar. It was the first time the German invaders saw themselves not as the destroyers of Rome but as its inheritors. As time developed, that sentiment would grow not just among the Goths but among many other German invaders. Ultimately, some 400 years later, it would lead to Charlemagne's coronation as Emperor of the Romans in 800 in St Peter's Basilica.

But let's return to the fifth century. Ironically, Ataulf's wish to restore the Roman name began as a dispute with Ravenna. It was an unexpected consequence of Heraclian's rebellion against Constantius which sparked it. Until that moment, relations between Ataulf's Goths and Ravenna had been reasonably good since Constantius agreed to provide them with grain provided they left Italy. This was crucially important to the Goths since, throughout this period, they struggled to feed themselves. But when Heraclian revolted in Carthage, he cut the grain supply to Italy, and Constantius had no option but to renege on his agreement to supply the Goths.

It was this which prompted Ataulf to declare an independent Gothic state in Aquitaine and marry Galla Placidia. With his Roman wife, Ataulf felt he was now on equal terms with Honorius and proposed an alliance and the resumption of the grain payments. But Constantius refused. Not only were he and Honorius outraged by what they regarded as the forced marriage of Honorius' sister to a barbarian, but it transpired Constantius was bitterly jealous of losing Placidia to Ataulf, since he seems to have been in love with her.

Rejected by Ravenna, Ataulf focused on expanding Gothic interests in Hispania and set up court at Barcelona. There, Placidia gave birth to a son called Theodosius. This was a momentous occasion for an empire obsessed with dynastic legitimacy because Honorius had no children (many historians have speculated he was impotent), and his nephew, Theodosius, also had no children since he was still a child. Therefore, the astonishing fact was that Placidia and Ataulf's son was officially next in line to inherit the Roman Empire.

For a moment, it looked as if Ataulf and Galla Placidia might establish a new imperial dynasty. But it was not to be. Within months, Placidia's son died. And within months of that, Ataulf himself died at the hands of a vengeful follower of the Gothic general, Sarus, whom he had killed as described in the last chapter. The story goes that one night, Ataulf went to his stables to tend to his horses, which was his daily routine; but whereas he was normally accompanied by at least some of his followers, on this occasion he went alone, and the renegade follower of Sarus, Dubius by name, was waiting for him and jumped out of the dark to stab him to death.

His dying words were to send his Roman wife back to her own country where she would be happy. But this did not happen immediately. Indeed, for a week, a follower of Sarus seized power, and made Galla Placidia walk in the company of slaves behind her husband's funeral procession before he in turn was slain by another Goth, Wallia. Wallia respected Ataulf's wishes and offered to return her to Ravenna in exchange for a resumption of the corn supplies which the Goths so badly needed.

Constantius jumped at this opportunity. He recognised the Gothic possession of Aquitaine as *foederati* of the empire and renewed the grain supply. Immediately Galla Placidia returned, he married her. According to Roman sources, this was against her wishes. Apparently, she found him physically unattractive. Most historians have dismissed this as propaganda spread by Constantius' enemies. But there could have been a significant age gap between the two of them. We have no record of his age but we know he had been a senior soldier in Stilicho's army, and might have been old by Roman standards, in his fifties or sixties, while she was in her mid-twenties. But despite her apparent dislike of him, she married him and rapidly bore him two children, the future emperor Valentinian III, and his sister, Honoria.

Constantius' success was so great that not only did he win the hand of Galla Placidia, but on 8 February 421, he was even promoted to be *co-Augustus* with Honorius. This was an extraordinary recognition of his achievements. Meanwhile, the Goths' new-found alliance with Ravenna seemed to be a winning formula for both sides. Gothic rule in Aquitaine flourished and they also persuaded the Vandals and Alans in Hispania to declare their loyalty to Ravenna by becoming *foederati*.

Constantius was triumphant. Declaring the start of a new age for Rome, he convened a council of Gallic Roman administrators in 418 at Arles to mark the restoration of the Roman Empire in Gaul. But the reality was very different. It was attended by only a handful of Roman governors mostly from the south of Gaul. The rest of the country was in barbarian hands, even if those barbarians called themselves *foederati*.

For the truth was the western empire was slipping away from Roman control. Everywhere the barbarians settled, they seized the land. In Aquitaine, the land was allocated two-thirds to the incoming Goths, leaving one third for the original Roman landowners. A similar settlement was made with the Burgundians in eastern Gaul. Meanwhile, the Franks were simply taking whatever they wanted in the north-east of Gaul.

Constantius may have thought he was restoring the Roman Empire, but the reality was very different. His new crown was hollow.

11

New Rome

While the west was dying, in the east it was the opposite. New Rome was rising to take the place of its ailing western cousin.

Nowhere was this more evident than in the city of Constantinople. Possibly as early as 405, the praetorian prefect, Flavius Anthemius, began one of the most important defensive constructions in the history of the world – the mighty Theodosian walls of Constantinople (see Figures 13 to 15). Probably completed by 413, they extended about five miles from the Golden Horn to the Sea of Marmara, completely sealing off the land route into the city. Attackers were confronted by a triple set of walls. First, they needed to cross a moat and the first relatively small wall. But beyond that was a larger middle wall, and beyond that the gigantic inner wall. Attackers would have been trapped between the walls and bombarded by catapults and arrows. Not surprisingly, no army succeeded in scaling them until 1453 when the Ottoman Turks finally blasted a hole through them using cannons. Although the Fourth Crusade of 1204 succeeded in taking Constantinople, the land walls were never breached and the crusaders, with the help of the Venetian fleet, scaled the smaller sea walls.

And it was not just Constantinople's walls that provided a strong defence against barbarian attack. What we know today as the Turkish straits conveniently separated the Middle East from Europe. These comprise the Bosphorus Strait to the north, on which Constantinople was sited, and the Dardanelles or Gallipoli Strait to the south. The Sea of Marmara lies between the two straits. While the western empire suffered from having a hugely long frontier with Germania along the Rhine and indirectly along the Danube, the Sea of Marmara effectively blocked barbarian attacks into the eastern empire's prosperous Middle Eastern provinces. The Sea of Marmara can perhaps be compared with the English Channel, which prevented foreign conquest of England by many would-be invaders from continental Europe, with some notable exceptions such as the Normans. The history of the Goths is also a good example of the defensive capabilities of the Sea of Marmara. After winning the Battle of Adrianople in 378, they could not break into Anatolia because they simply could not cross the Turkish straits. This was the reason they finally headed west and eventually ended up sacking Rome in 410.

Behind the walls of Constantinople and the Turkish straits, the eastern empire flourished. In May 408, the eastern emperor, Arcadius, died and was succeeded by his seven-year-old son, Theodosius II. The praetorian prefect, Anthemius, capably ruled the eastern empire until his death in 414. We don't know what he died of, but the assumption is that it was natural causes rather than foul play. Another effective minister called Aurelian succeeded him.

At the same time, there rose to prominence one of the most interesting figures of fifth-century Rome politics: Theodosius II's older sister, Aelia Pulcheria, who turned 16 in 414 when Theodosius was 13. That year, she was proclaimed *Augusta* and took over as regent. She was a much tougher proposition than her brother and became the de facto ruler of the east. She was also religious and took a vow of virginity, although the motivation for this was probably to further her own ambition since, in patriarchal Roman society, she would have been expected to be subservient to her husband. Without one, she was better able to exercise power in her own right.

Theodosian women, such as Galla Placidia and Aelia Pulcheria, were far more formidable than their male counterparts. However, Theodosius II was not quite as useless as his father Arcadius had been. He was said to be intelligent, with an interest in books about religion and natural science. He was also said to be gentle and compassionate, something rarely heard of in the fifth-century Roman Empire. He was also getting older. In 421, he reached the age of 20 and was old enough to be emperor in his own right. This was a threat to Pulcheria. So, she played matchmaker and sought to find him a wife who would both dominate him and be controlled by her.

In this she was highly successful. It was not long before she found a suitable young woman called Aelia Eudocia. The story, told to us by the chronicler John Malalas, is that Eudocia appeared in Constantinople as the daughter of a wealthy Athenian who had disinherited her, giving his wealth to her brothers. She sought justice in Constantinople, and when Pulcheria heard her case, she was instantly impressed with her beauty, intelligence and excellent education. They became best friends and Aelia Pulcheria used her friend's devastating good looks to her advantage. One day, she told Theodosius to hide behind a curtain and take a peek at her gorgeous new friend.

It worked. Theodosius instantly fell in love and they married in 421. Our chronicler says that Eudocia was not just attractive but kind as well, as reflected in the treatment of her brothers. For when they heard she had married the emperor, they became worried she might take revenge for disinheriting her. But no, as the kind sister she was, she did not punish them but invited them to her wedding where she promoted them to prefects.

Otherwise, all was fairly quiet in the east. While the west was collapsing under the weight of barbarian invasion, the east had only one minor war with Persia in 421–2 occasioned by Persian persecution of the Christians.

When reading our sources on the two halves of the empire in the fifth century, I always feel we are looking at two completely different worlds. While law and order were breaking down in most of the western provinces, the east was flourishing. In the east, we hear about emperors peeping at pretty girls from behind curtains. In the west, we hear about the growing collection of severed heads on spears outside Ravenna.

In the east, life was lived at a sophisticated level, just as it had been for centuries in the ancient world. For example, while literacy was rapidly declining in the west, intellectual debate was as vibrant between pagans and Christians as it had been in the days of Julian the Apostate. However, in the east this debate was becoming more violent as Christians became more militant. Alexandria was an example of this. In the fifth century, it was still one of the great cities of the Roman Empire. Teeming with perhaps 600,000 inhabitants, it contained a highly educated elite who maintained a flourishing university.

However, an incident became famous indicative of the growing conflict between Christians, Jews and pagans. In Alexandria's university there was a woman called Hypatia, widely renowned for her intellect and beauty. She taught mathematics and philosophy and did not hold back from praising the pagan works of Plato and Aristotle. This infuriated the Patriarch of Alexandria, Cyril, who was, in the words of the historian JB Bury, 'an ecclesiastical tyrant of the most repulsive type'[37]. She became a target for his band of followers called the *parabalani*. These were fanatical Christians, whose official job was tending to the sick but who in fact preferred to beat up pagans and Jews. They particularly resented Hypatia, and one day when she was walking home from the university, they ambushed her, dragged her into a church and killed her. This outrage became a prominent and controversial subject among the chattering classes in the eastern empire and was much written about by chroniclers of the time.

I think this story serves to highlight the contrasting experiences of the two halves of the empire. In the east, Hypatia's death became renowned as an outrage against civilised behaviour. But in the west, how many massacres by barbarians went unrecorded? Entire cities were being destroyed and Roman citizens enslaved. For example, the island of Britain is famous for orbiting completely out of the civilised world at this time. After 409, there are no surviving records of what even happened there for the next hundred years. The last legionaries probably left for Gaul with Constantine III, sometime between 406 and 410. After that, the archaeological cupboard is bare suggesting people in Britain reverted to a prehistoric level of existence, without stone housing, roof tiles, coins, and even without pottery made using a wheel. These staples of Roman civilisation only start appearing again in the seventh century when the island was dominated by the Saxons.

The divergence between the two halves of the Roman Empire in the fifth century is staggering. The west was declining into barbarism while in the east all our evidence suggests it was more buoyant, economically and culturally, than ever before. While, as described, this was helped by the strength of Constantinople's walls and the geographic benefit of the Turkish straits, there was another critical reason I have not mentioned and this lay with Persia, Rome's traditional foe. For Persia was having its own problems with the Huns as we will now consider.

12

Persia and the White Huns

Persia had always been Rome's main enemy. In the third and fourth centuries, it inflicted some of the worst defeats on Rome in its entire history such as the defeat and capture of the emperor Valerian in 260, who was humiliated into becoming a human footstool for Shapur I to mount his horse. But this changed in the fifth century, when there was almost perpetual peace between Rome and Persia.

This was because for most of the fifth century Persia was itself beset by nomadic invaders on its eastern frontier – the White Huns (also called Kidarites and Hepthalites who were their successive ruling dynasties). The White Huns were similar to but quite separate from the European Huns who were pushing the German tribes west. The term 'white' is thought to denote geography rather than skin colour because the Huns colour-coded their compass with white signifying the west, black the north, red the south and blue the east. But before the White Huns arrived, when the European Huns raided through the Caucasus in 395, this alarmed the Persians sufficiently to make an alliance with the Romans to guard the Caucasus against further Hunnic invasions.

The result was not only peace between Rome and Persia at the beginning of the fifth century, but the two even became partners supporting each other against the encroaching barbarians. The Persian shahanshah, Yazdgerd I (399–420), regarded Rome as a useful ally, and relaxed the anti-Christian laws the Sasanians had previously instituted, recognising the 'Nestorian' Church as a tolerated Christian religion in Persia in 410. This rapprochement led to an extraordinary gesture of friendship when the emperor Arcadius asked Yazdgerd to be the guardian of his son, the future Theodosius II.

In contrast to the long and costly wars fought between Rome and Persia in the third and fourth centuries, the fifth was almost free of any conflict. There were only two short wars between the two great powers. The first in 421–2 occurred when Yazdgerd's son, Bahram V, began a persecution of Christians in Persia in revenge for alleged Roman attacks on Zoroastrian temples. This tit-for-tat war only lasted a few months and a Roman victory restored the peace. Another short war occurred in 440 over the Roman non-payment of gold to Persia to defend the Caucasus from Hunnic attack. The details are unclear but the Romans had stopped paying what might have been as much as 500 pounds of gold annually to the Persians, prompting Yazdgerd II to threaten war if the payment, which he termed tribute, was not made. Theodosius II was offended by the term tribute and hostilities broke out. However, as with the previous war nearly 20 years before, there was no enthusiasm on either side to pursue it aggressively. Distracted by the Vandal capture of Carthage, the Romans quickly sought an end to hostilities by agreeing to some sort of payment to the Persians, which has never been specified. In their turn, the Sasanians, still under pressure from the White Huns, were only too happy to restore good relations. As an indication of goodwill, both sides agreed to demilitarise their frontier in Mesopotamia.

The only other conflict was in Armenia which the Persians invaded in 451 when they defeated the Christian Armenians at the Battle of Avarair. Control of Armenia proved transitory. Although they tried to impose Zoroastrianism on the largely Christian population, this met with limited success, and in 484 the Armenians secured their independence and the right to Christian worship at the treaty of Nvarsak.

Persia became less and less of a potential threat to Constantinople in the second half of the fifth century as attacks by the White Huns increasingly dominated Sasanian military and political resources. In 484, matters came to a head when the Persian shahanshah, Peroz, was killed with most of the elite Persian cavalry in a Hunnic trap near Balk in modern Afghanistan. The Roman chronicler, Procopius, has left us with a detailed description of the battle in which the Huns dug a long trench concealed with shrubbery and wood. They then charged at the Sasanian army, only to wheel around and feign a retreat. The Huns fled and retreated over the trench using a path they had left raised. Completely unaware of this, the Persians galloped after the Huns along a wide front, hoping to outflank and surround them. Thousands of their elite armoured cavalry disappeared headfirst into the trench impaling themselves on wooden spikes buried there. The slaughter was immense. Almost all of the Persian cavalry were killed. Peroz and many of the Persian nobility also died. It was in many ways an equivalent of the Battle of Adrianople for the Persians. It broke Persia and reduced it for several decades to being an impotent vassal of the White Huns.

Persia's removal as a threat to the eastern empire offered Constantinople a huge opportunity to intervene in the west and save the western empire. But it didn't. This was essentially due to political incompetence. As described in the last chapter, Theodosius' son, Arcadius, and his son Theodosius II, were non-entities who relied on their ministers to run the government and army. In Arcadius' reign before the sack of Rome in 410, a series of three ministers ruled the empire: Rufinus, Eutropius and Anthemius. With the exception of Anthemius, who built the Theodosian walls of Constantinople, and had a more strategic vision of the empire's needs, the other two were more interested in preserving their own power than either saving the west or rebuilding the eastern army. In fact, they shrank the eastern army as much as they could since they were suspicious of generals who might use the army against them. For example, after Rufinus falsely claimed he had led the army to victory over the Huns when they invaded Mesopotamia in 395, a claim blatantly false since there was no battle and the Huns had simply withdrawn back to the north after concluding a successful raid, he reduced the army's size in case any of the generals posed a threat to him.

This demilitarisation continued after Arcadius' death in 408, when he was succeeded by Theodosius II who yielded power first to his elder sister, Pulcheria, then to his wife Eudocia and finally to his eunuch minister, Chrysaphius. During his reign, and until Attila crossed the Danube in 441, the army was purposefully kept to a minimum, not because the eastern empire was short of money, as in the west, but because Pulcheria, Eudocia and Chrysaphius were afraid of a strong army that could threaten their own authority.

This situation continued until the threat from Attila caused a remilitarisation of the eastern empire that would have profound implications for both east and west, as we will discuss in later chapters.

13

Empress of the West

Let us return from Constantinople to our narrative on the western empire. On 2 September 421, the co-emperor Constantius died unexpectedly. He died just when he had reached the pinnacle of his success – Honorius' equal and Galla Placidia's husband. The cause of death remains a mystery. We do not even know his age. As mentioned before, it is possible he was in his fifties or sixties and he probably died naturally. Certainly, no foul play was suspected by the chroniclers of the time. What he might have achieved had he lived, we shall never know. His death created a power vacuum, into which his capable young wife was only too willing to step. The next few years would be dominated by her.

As noted previously, Theodosian women tended to be far more effective than their male relations. Placidia was no exception. Her first task was to take the reins of power from her feeble-minded brother, Honorius, who was, of course, still emperor. Placidia was in a good position to do this. Not only had she been promoted to *Augusta* when her husband Constantius was made *Augustus*, but she also had a son, Valentinian, as the potential heir to the throne. Despite this, things did not go her way. Our principal source (Photius) says that she and her brother befriended each other causing onlookers to wonder if incest was being committed: '…their immoderate pleasure in each other and their constant kissing on the mouth caused many people to entertain shameful suspicions about them.' However, this friendship quickly turned sour: '…this affection was replaced by such a degree of hatred that fighting often broke out in Ravenna and blows were delivered on both sides.'

This bizarre account is difficult to interpret but the most plausible explanation is that Placidia hoped to dominate her brother by being affectionate, but when she overdid it, he smelled a rat and accused her of trying to control him. Or perhaps Placidia was a victim of her rivals at court. Theodosius was easy to manipulate, and no doubt her enemies were whispering in his ear that she was plotting against him. Whatever happened, in late 422, Placidia fled Ravenna, either exiled by Honorius or escaping his unwelcome advances, and arrived in Constantinople with her two children. Her timing could not have been worse. For within months, on 15 August 423, Honorius died of oedema, probably because of heart failure, a condition which ran in the Theodosian family.

If she had stayed in Ravenna, she would presumably have been able to assert the rights of her son, Valentinian, with herself as regent. But far away in Constantinople, there was now scope for someone else to seize power on the ground, which is exactly what happened. In Italy, the *magister militum*, Castinus, proposed that a senior minister called Johannes be made emperor. The Roman senate declared their support. As with most western usurpers, Johannes did not want to fall out with Constantinople and sent an embassy to Theodosius and Pulcheria, offering to work together. But Pulcheria, still regent in the east, took the bold decision to reject this proposal.

She was helped by the governor of North Africa, Bonifacius, who sided with Constantinople and not Rome. North Africa was a vitally important territory, not only because of its wealth, which had so far survived barbarian destruction, but also because it was the granary of Italy. When Bonifacius cut the grain supply, it put tremendous pressure on Johannes who responded by sending a fleet with troops, including Hunnic mercenaries, to Carthage. But Bonifacius defeated them and Rome was left to starve. Matters got worse for Johannes when the Visigoths in Gaul rejected him as emperor.

With Johannes in a weak position, Pulcheria decided to strike. She despatched an army and fleet for Italy, led by the general Ardabur and his son, Aspar, to put Placidia's son, Valentinian, on the throne. Interestingly, Constantinople had previously refused to recognise Placidia and her husband, Constantius, when they were promoted to being co-emperor and empress with Honorius in 421. The reasons for this have never been clear but presumably it was because they were suspicious of Constantius as an outsider who might usurp the throne. But Placidia's son, Valentinian, was a different matter. He had Theodosian blood in his veins and a dynastic claim to the throne despite being only six years old.

Of course, child emperors were not the best idea for a collapsing empire but, as the Romans faced the bankruptcy of their traditional value system, they clung on ever more desperately to the concept of dynastic legitimacy. Theoretically, this was not necessarily a bad thing. Roman history was plagued by civil war, normally between rival emperors, and allegiance to one imperial dynasty was a logical way of trying to prevent civil strife. For example, when Diocletian's tetrarchy failed, Constantine re-established the idea of having one imperial dynasty rule the empire. But theory and practice sometimes do not mix well, and the fifth-century Roman Empire was unlucky to have a dynasty of incompetents (the Theodosians) at just the moment it needed strong leadership.

In 424, Galla Placidia accompanied the eastern army, heading towards Italy through Illyria. It was far stronger than what remained of the western army, and had little difficulty taking Aquileia at the top of the Adriatic before marching towards Ravenna where the usurper Johannes was.

But then disaster struck the eastern expedition. Ardabur was sailing with the eastern fleet for Ravenna to make a joint naval and land attack on the western capital, when a violent storm blew up, wrecking many of the boats, including his own. He was shipwrecked close to Ravenna and captured. The usurper, Johannes, sensed his prisoner might enable him to buy some sort of settlement with Constantinople and save his life. So, he treated Ardabur well and offered to negotiate. This proved a big mistake. For when he heard of his father's capture, Aspar took a few regiments of eastern cavalry and galloped down the Adriatic coast as fast as he could for Ravenna.

Meanwhile in Ravenna, as Johannes was hoping to use Ardabur as a bargaining counter, Ardabur himself was busy persuading the Roman garrison commander that he should change sides. He promptly did just that as Aspar arrived with the cavalry. Johannes was seized and put in chains and Ardabur was released.

The unfortunate Johannes was despatched to Galla Placidia at Aquileia, who, as I mentioned, was no shrinking violet and chose to make an example of him. In the hippodrome, his right hand was first cut off; then he was paraded backwards on a donkey, and finally beheaded. This horrific treatment was clearly intended to show other would-be usurpers what happened if you dared to cross the house of Theodosius.

Placidia's six-year-old son was proclaimed emperor of the west as Valentinian III on 23 October 425, in Rome. He was betrothed to Theodosius II's three-year-old daughter, Licinia Eudoxia, thereby cementing relations between the eastern and western empires.

Galla Placidia probably took a moment to congratulate herself on a job well done. Perhaps she treated herself to a cup of vintage Falernian wine. She had come a long way from being the prisoner of the Goths. As regent to her son, she was now the de facto ruler of the west. Indeed, she was one of three women who effectively ruled the Roman Empire, with her niece, Aelia Pulcheria, and her sister-in-law, Aelia Eudocia, both firmly in the driving seat in Constantinople.

But being at the top of Roman politics was never easy. No sooner was one rival eliminated than another replaced them. Placidia would soon have to engage in a bitter fight for power with a more formidable opponent than Johannes. Chroniclers would later call him 'the last of the Romans'. His name was Flavius Aetius.

14

The Last of the Romans

Flavius Aetius' early life was far from ordinary. In 405, at about the age of 15, he was sent as a high-ranking hostage to the Goths for three years, and then to the Huns from around 408 to an unknown date. What might have broken a lesser man seems to have done the opposite in his case. He took full advantage of the opportunities presented to develop his skills as a soldier, learning techniques from the Huns that were revolutionising warfare at the time, in particular archery from the saddle. Gregory of Tours, quoting Renatus Frigeridus, described him as tough and capable:

> *Aetius was of medium height, manly in his habits and well proportioned. He had no bodily infirmity and was spare in physique. His intelligence was keen, he was full of energy, a superb horseman, a fine shot with an arrow and tireless with the lance. He was extremely able as a soldier and he was skilled in the arts of peace. There was no avarice in him and even less cupidity. He was magnanimous in his behaviour and never swayed in his judgement by the advice of unworthy counsellors. He*

> *bore adversity with great patience, was ready for any exacting enterprise, he scorned danger and was able to endure hunger, thirst and loss of sleep.*[38]

Aetius was a Roman aristocrat, the son of a Roman general and his high-born Roman wife. His father, Gaudentius, originally came from the Balkans, as so many of Rome's soldiers since the third century, and probably began his career in the eastern army before ending up on Stilicho's general staff as *magister militum* for Gaul, sometime after the sack of Rome in 410.

Although described by later chroniclers as 'the last of the Romans', Aetius was less like Aurelian or Diocletian, intent on restoring the classical Roman Empire to its former glory, and more like his eastern counterpart, the Alanic-Gothic general Aspar, a capable general intent on carving out his own power base. He never aspired to be emperor, or to control the eastern court, as Stilicho had done. His ambitions were limited to being the supreme general in the west.

His skill lay in using whatever resources he could muster, be they Hunnic mercenaries or by playing one barbarian tribe off against another. His forte was his knowledge of the Huns and Goths, acquired through his lengthy stays with them. Consequently, he was better versed in barbarian battle tactics than traditional Roman warfare. He was more adept at ambushes, feigned retreats and night attacks than pitched battles. He spent relatively little time in Ravenna or Rome and was to be found most often in the Gallo-Roman town of Arles or out on campaign in the Gallic countryside.

His years spent as a hostage with the Goths and Huns meant he had excellent contacts with the barbarians. His second wife, Pelagia, was a high-ranking Gothic princess, probably with her own Gothic retainers and she must have had valuable connections with the Gothic nobility. According to Gregory of Tours, she was devoted to Aetius and deeply worried for his safety when he went to fight Attila later in his career:

> *Soon afterwards the rumour reached Rome that Aetius was in great danger with the troops of the enemy all around him. When she heard this his wife was very anxious and distressed. She went frequently to the churches of the holy Apostles and prayed that she might have her husband back safe from this campaign. This she did by day and by night.*[39]

But his greatest asset, and the real cause of his rise to power, was his contact not with the Goths but the Huns. He was on good terms with the various Hunnic kings and nobility, and this made him invaluable to any Roman government. In 423, when Honorius died, he got his chance to rise from relative obscurity by throwing in his lot with the usurper Johannes who asked him to gather a Hunnic army to counter Galla Placidia's eastern army. He crossed the Danube to speak with Octar, the main Hunnic king.

Aetius returned with an army but not in time to save Johannes. According to one source, he arrived in northern Italy with 60,000 Huns; certainly a huge exaggeration, but whatever the size of his army it was nevertheless large enough to intimidate Galla Placidia. Although he arrived just three days after Johannes had been executed and should have met a similar fate, Placidia dared not offend the Huns. She made a deal with Aetius in which she paid the Huns to return home while giving him the position of *magister militum* in Gaul, the position his father had held. She may have hoped he was sufficiently far from Ravenna to do her any harm. But they were now sworn enemies.

To counter Aetius, Galla Placidia relied on the support of her two other generals (*magistri militum)* in the western empire, both apparently loyal to her. One, Bonifacius in North Africa, who had supported her from the beginning. The second, Felix in Italy, her replacement of the rebel Castinus, who had fled.

Meanwhile, Aetius threw himself into defending his new territory. In 426, the Visigoths, who had been settled in Aquitaine supposedly as Roman allies, were not behaving like allies at all. In fact, led by their king, Theoderic I, they were besieging Arles, the Roman capital of Gaul, situated on the south coast. Aetius took what remained of the Roman army in Gaul and rescued the city by forcing the Goths to withdraw.

Our sources are vague about what happened, and if we piece them together, I suggest it is unlikely Aetius defeated the Goths in battle. The Gothic king, Theoderic, was a savvy operator and he did not want an open war with the Romans. Technically he still had a treaty with Ravenna, and he also knew Aetius personally from the days when he had been a hostage. He opted for peace and made up the story that his attack on Arles had originally been done back in 423 to help the rightful emperor, Valentinian III, since Arles at that time was under the control of supporters of the usurping emperor,

Johannes. Both sides happily agreed to this fiction and renewed the peace of 418, exchanging hostages.

But this did not stop Aetius from claiming a victory. He wanted to put pressure on Placidia and returned to Ravenna in triumph, where he found that her two most senior generals, Felix in Italy and Bonifacius in North Africa, had fallen out.

Felix was the more senior and wanted to oust Bonifacius by sowing the seeds of discord between him and Placidia. A skilled deceiver, he lied to Placidia that Bonifacius was about to set up his own breakaway North African empire and recommended she recall him immediately. At the same time, he wrote to Bonifacius, telling him Placidia intended to execute him.

Bonifacius fell straight into the trap. He read Felix's letter first and then Placidia's command to return. Fearing for his life, he refused to go to Italy. This confirmed he was a traitor in Placidia's eyes. She thanked the wily Felix and instructed him to send an expedition to North Africa, which, however, Bonifacius defeated quite easily. It's worth mentioning that some of our sources say that it was Aetius, not Felix, who tricked Bonifacius. But historians are almost unanimous in thinking this was a later attempt to discredit Aetius because, although he was just as scheming and back-stabbing as any good Roman, at this stage he simply did not have the political credibility to be able to tell Placidia what to do.

Indeed, Aetius was still fighting the barbarians. He returned to Gaul to counter the Franks who were expanding their territory along the Rhine. It has to be said that Aetius' Gallic legions were nothing like the legions of old. As discussed in Chapter 5, the Roman army in the early fifth century was a shadow of its former self, especially in the west, where the Romans mainly used barbarians as mercenaries to fight their wars. So, his 'Roman' army was almost certainly small, maybe a couple of thousand Roman legionaries and cavalry, supplemented with hired barbarians. This meant he avoided large-scale battles with the Franks and used his limited resources to occupy strategic points like bridges and fortress hilltops.

Meanwhile, back in the cloisters of power in Ravenna, Felix's treacherous plans were about to detonate in his hands. Because, in 429, Placidia realised he was double-crossing her. Envoys from Bonifacius showed her the duplicitous letter Felix had written. The mist lifted from her eyes. She immediately reinstated Bonifacius. Yet she hesitated to arrest Felix since he was still very powerful with the Italian legions under his control. So, what could she do? She had no choice but to turn to Aetius.

15

Between a Rock and a Hard Place

Galla Placidia was nothing if not cunning. But her schemes were seldom successful. Her plan was to set her two most troublesome generals, Aetius and Felix, against each other. Because Aetius had been doing a good job in Gaul, it was easy to promote him from *magister militum* for Gaul to the next rung up the ladder, *magister militum praesentalis*, the position just below Felix but close enough to make him feel uncomfortable. She thought that by locking the two into conflict she could neutralise their threat.

But things didn't turn out as she planned. Aetius was by now a more formidable opponent than either Placidia or Felix realised. His string of minor victories in Gaul had made him into a war hero. In 430, this reputation was reinforced by defeating a renegade Goth called Anaolsus, who was ravaging Roman territory around Arles, and annihilating a tribe of Jutungi who invaded Raetia. When he went to Ravenna to celebrate his victories, he had many supporters.

Felix was waiting for him, ready to arrest his rival on

trumped charges of treason. But he woefully underestimated Aetius' popularity. Felix's own soldiers turned against him. Deciding they preferred Aetius to him, they seized him, his wife and his supporters and executed them. Aetius had triumphed.

Or had he? Because Placidia turned to her other general, Bonifacius, and recklessly recalled him from Carthage to Ravenna despite the fact the Vandals were advancing on the city (as we will cover in the next chapter). Without showing any consideration for the defence of this vitally important part of what remained of the western empire, yet again she tried to play her last two remaining generals off against each other to preserve her own power. Aetius was away in Gaul, fighting the Franks in the north, and since he was far away, Galla Placidia simply stripped him of his command, making Bonifacius the senior commander-in-chief of the western armies. Stabbed in the back in this way, Aetius had no choice but to gather his Gallic army and march on Italy. Placidia had sparked a destructive civil war.

Given Aetius' reputation on the battlefield, the smart money must have been on him defeating Bonifacius fairly easily. But that *didn't* happen. Bonifacius met Aetius near Rimini and defeated him. Our sources are silent about the battle but presumably Aetius did not have enough Huns. Whatever the cause of his defeat, it looked as if this was the end for him. But as fifth-century chroniclers noted, Aetius should never be underestimated.

To begin with, his defeat was softened by the news Bonifacius had been mortally wounded in the battle and could not follow up on his victory. He passed his position to his son-in-law, Sebastianus, who was not really up to the job. Aetius fled to his country estates where Sebastianus tried but failed to assassinate him.

Then Aetius played his tried and tested trump card by returning to his old friends, the Huns. In 433, Aetius arrived at the court of the Hunnic king, Rua. We have no record what agreement was made, but it was sufficient for him to return to Ravenna either with a force of Huns, or with the promise of one. Placidia caved in. Although Sebastianus tried to contact the Visigoths to secure their help, he was unsuccessful and Placidia reluctantly recognised Aetius as the new commander-in-chief of the western army. Her battle to maintain her own authority had failed. Aetius had won. He was now the de facto ruler of the western empire.

Let us pause for a moment and consider the implications of Aetius' success. I suggest his rise to power was not as positive as it might seem and indeed it undermined the longer-term future of the western empire for two reasons.

First, his entire career was built around an unsustainable alliance with the Huns. As already described, Placidia originally only gave him command of Gaul because he arrived with a Hunnic army to support the usurper Johannes. After Bonifacius defeated him at the Battle of Rimini in 432, he was again saved by the Huns. When he had the top job, he still depended on Hunnic support. A striking example was with the Burgundians, who were advancing into western Gaul. They were dangerous for Aetius because they could ally with the Visigoths. So, in 436, he again asked the Hunnic king Rua for help. Rua obliged with a series of Hunnic raids directly into Burgundian territory with such horrifying ferocity that one Gallic chronicler recorded: 'almost the entire people with their king were destroyed.'[40] This may have been an exaggeration but the Huns did kill the Burgundian king, Gundohar, who had been a major political figure ever since his people had crossed the Rhine in the mass invasion of Gaul in 406.

Aetius also used the Huns to fight the Visigoths. In 436, when the Burgundians threatened in the east, the Visigoths were advancing from the west. They reached the Roman port of Narbonne on the Mediterranean coast and laid siege to it. The Visigothic king, Theoderic, was keen to gain a Mediterranean port and Aetius was keen to stop him. There was heavy fighting between the Visigoths and Romans, which Aetius got the better of, again by using his Hunnic allies. Narbonne was saved, and the Visigoths were pushed back into Aquitaine where their king, Theodoric, agreed to reinstate the treaty of 418.

Aetius' main failing lay in his decision to use the Huns as mercenaries instead of rebuilding the Roman army. Admittedly, he may not have had much choice. In contrast to the eastern empire, which still had a larger tax base and could afford a large army (although as described later it did not build one until the 440s), tax revenues in the west had plummeted ever since Britain, Hispania and most of Gaul had been overrun by barbarians. Only Italy and North Africa were still paying tax which meant Aetius probably could not afford to rebuild a viable Roman army.

But the issue was that his policy of using Hunnic mercenaries only stored up problems for the future. For example, on top of paying the Huns, Aetius also had to give them territory. The best example was the Roman province of Pannonia, a large area including most of modern western Hungary and Slovakia. It was right next to where they lived on the Hungarian plains, giving them good access into Italy should they need it (and Attila used it very effectively in his Italian campaign of 452, as we will discover). More worrying was which territory Aetius would have to cede to them next? In short, he was effectively mortgaging the Roman Empire to the Huns to buy himself victories in the short term.

Aetius' second main failing lay with North Africa. As we shall hear in the next chapter, he did nothing to prevent the Vandals from taking Carthage (although neither did Placidia or Valentinian III). Instead, he focused on building his power base in Gaul, which was in practice his own personal fiefdom, while neglecting the western empire's wider interests. Strategically, this was a blunder of the first order and shows he had little vision for the recovery of the western empire.

But can we really blame Aetius for these strategic mistakes? In truth, he was a victim of a wider political failure. Since he was not emperor, he had to maintain his own power base in Gaul to survive. The real problem lay with the incompetent Theodosian dynasty who felt threatened by him (first Placidia and later Valentinian III, as we will discover in Chapter 28). They did their best to undermine him in case he tried to overthrow them. Perhaps that is exactly what he should have done. Yet he knew if he did, he would face the wrath of the eastern emperor Theodosius II. And he had witnessed how that might end when, in 423, his co-conspirator, Johannes, had been paraded backwards on a donkey, his hands cut off and then beheaded. Aetius was caught between the proverbial rock and a hard place. And that rock was about to become a real-life rock. For the Vandals were in fact massing not far from the rock of Gibraltar to make their crossing to Africa.

16

The Kingdom in the Sun

The Atlantic wind whips the sea through the Pillars of Hercules. Foaming waves shudder and splutter between the tall, gaunt mountains either side. Hispania to the north and Mauritania to the south. Travel there today and you will find an unforgettable landscape where you expect to see giants roaming. Go back nearly 1,600 years to 429, and on the furthest tip of Hispania, you would have found a Roman town, Mellaria, where Tarifa stands today. Small vessels pack its harbour. Long lines of tall, blond-haired and blue-eyed men, women and their children are waiting to embark on the vessels and sail across the strait. All day long, the vessels sail back and forth through the choppy water. The boats are ferrying a huge number of these people across to Africa, maybe 80,000.

On the opposite side, there is no resistance to this invasion. The locals have fled. The Roman army has withdrawn. Long sandy beaches beckon. The invaders set about building temporary accommodation to store food and provide shelter to the thousands who are arriving every day. These people are the Vandals, and they are crossing the eight-mile stretch of sea, known as the Strait of Gibraltar, that separates Hispania from Africa.

The Vandals' arrival in North Africa was a turning point in Roman history. The region was a crucially important part of the Roman Empire. Throughout all the turmoil that had afflicted the western empire it had remained safe. But in 439, Carthage fell to the Vandals led by their king Gaiseric. It was a mortal blow from which the western empire never recovered. So, how did it happen?

First, let us clarify the exact geography of the territory called Africa by the Romans for it can be confusing since, today, we refer to Africa as an entire continent. But in Roman times, Africa meant just the north-western edge of that continent, including the modern-day countries of Morocco, Algeria and Tunisia. Egypt was, of course, also part of the eastern Roman Empire but *not* regarded as part of North Africa.

It is also important to know that Carthage was not just Roman Africa's capital but also one of the most important and wealthiest cities in the entire Roman Empire, as its extensive archaeological remains still testify. It was the breadbasket of Rome, and the western empire's most prosperous province after Italy itself. It exported not only grain but also olives, wine and pottery. These were of course produced all over the empire but, in the days of the classical Roman Empire, African exports were helped by the state-subsidised shipping service which existed to support the grain trade but could craftily be used by merchants as cheap transport for other goods. Because of this vibrant trade, Carthage had grown to become one of the largest Roman cities with probably over

100,000 inhabitants and was famous for its wealth. Indeed, many Roman senators had vast estates in North Africa.

The story of the Vandal conquest began in Hispania. As described in Chapter 6, Hispania had been invaded in 409 by four barbarian tribes: two sets of Vandals, the Hasding and Siling tribes, and a group of Alans and German Suevi (shorthand for Marcomanni and Alemanni). By 418, these had formed one supergroup of barbarians led by the Hasding Vandals. In 428, a new leader called Gaiseric seized power. After Attila, he would become the Romans' worst enemy in the fifth century. The sixth-century historian Jordanes has left us with a description:

> *[He] was a man of moderate height and lame in consequence of a fall from a horse. He was a man of deep thought and few words, holding luxury in disdain, furious in his anger, greedy for gain, shrewd in winning over the barbarians and skilled in sowing the seeds of dissension to arouse enmity.*[41]

We don't know precisely when Gaiseric had a vision to create a Vandal kingdom in North Africa but the lure of palm trees and rolling fields of wheat (as we will discuss in the next chapter, North Africa was much more verdant in Roman times than it is today) had appealed to barbarians before, in particular to Alaric, who had wanted to take his Goths there after he sacked Rome in 410. The only obstacle for the Vandals was the same as for the Goths – their limited maritime skills. In the late 420s, the Vandals made up for this by gathering boats and raiding the Balearic Islands. By 429, Gaiseric felt ready to make the crossing. He occupied Roman Mellaria (modern Tarifa) and prepared for the eight-mile crossing to North Africa, aiming to land on the deserted beaches close to where the modern town of Tangiers is located (in Roman times there was nothing there). In May 429, some 80,000 Vandals and other Germans sailed across the strait, probably over several weeks, as only a few thousand could travel each day in a fairly small number of boats. Their invasion worked because there was no Roman army to meet them, since most of it was based in the east close to the major towns. Unfortunately for the Romans they were too preoccupied with their own internal squabbles to notice the Vandal invasion of North Africa. It was a crucial mistake.

The Vandals advanced slowly along the North African seaboard, meeting very limited Roman resistance, and taking about twelve months to reach the second largest Roman town in North Africa, Hippo Regius, where the renowned theologian Saint Augustine lived. Outside it, Bonifacius finally met them with his army but was defeated. However, as was true of so many of the German tribes, the Vandals lacked skills at siege warfare and settled down to a long siege. Then, in early 431, an eastern Roman fleet and army appeared to help the beleaguered western Romans. Constantinople had woken up to the Vandal threat and, worried that the Vandals might try to interfere with the prosperous maritime trade in the eastern Mediterranean – the 'mare nostrum' of the eastern empire – it sent a reasonable-sized force led by the capable general Aspar (a Goth) to prevent this happening. This intervention from the east was vital when the western Romans were weakened by a civil war in 432 between Bonifacius and

Aetius, as described in the last chapter. Indeed, in gratitude to Aspar, Valentinian III appointed him consul for the west. The position of consul was an anachronism dating back to the days of the Roman Republic, half a millennium before, but was still used even in this period as an honorary title conferred on important and successful people. What is interesting about Aspar's nomination is that it was extremely unusual for the western court to confer the consulship on anyone other than the eastern emperor. To confer it on an eastern general shows how critically dependent the west was on the east's military support.

But even Aspar could not defeat the Vandals and, in a second battle, sometime in early 432, the eastern Romans were forced to retreat. They abandoned Hippo, which Gaiseric took and sacked savagely in retribution for the protracted siege. However, although Aspar's eastern army could not defeat the Vandals it did prevent their further advance into what remained of Roman North Africa, which was in fact its most wealthy part – the province of Byzacena, approximately similar to modern Tunisia, with Carthage its capital.

So far, so good. Aspar had contained the Vandal threat. But in 434, he had to leave Africa to concentrate on the growing Hunnic menace to the eastern empire along the Danube. Although this looked to be Gaiseric's opportunity to take Carthage, he was prevented from doing this because Constantinople had left sufficient troops in Africa to defend the city. Gaiseric then did something completely unexpected – in 435, he made peace with the Romans.

This treaty is intriguing because the records on it are thin and insofar as they exist, they present a bizarrely contrasting view of events. The Romans presented it as a victory. They recognised the Vandals' seizure of African territory in exchange for their becoming Roman allies or *foederati.* In retrospect, we can see that Gaiseric, true to form, was playing the Romans along. He tricked them into thinking he was a convert to the Roman cause. He was serious enough to send his son, Huneric, to Rome as a hostage. In return, he was given a Roman military title, we're not sure which one, but something like *dux*.

These events are reminiscent of how Alaric duped the Romans in the run-up to his sack of Rome in 410. Yet again, the Romans thought they were dealing with an ignorant barbarian and underestimated how cunning Gaiseric was. It was only four and a half years (with his son safely returned) before Gaiseric suddenly launched a surprise attack on Carthage in October 439. Again, records are frustratingly thin about what happened, but it seems he took the city by tricking its defenders into opening the gates. Perhaps using his Roman position as *dux* of Mauretania and Numidia, he persuaded the Roman garrison to allow him entry into the city. Certainly, there was no siege of Carthage or a battle outside it. Some historians speculate that the city's fall might have been due to pro-Vandal sympathisers inside the walls. This line of argument rests on the view that many African Romans were disenchanted with rule from Italy. Absentee Italian landlords were common and a source of local resentment. Many Roman senators had extensive lands in Africa which they never visited but were happy to extract profits from. These were now given to the Vandal nobility. The poorer Romans were apparently not unhappy with this arrangement.

What influenced Gaiseric's timing? One suggestion is he was worried about a growing rapprochement between the Visigoths and Romans (Aetius made a treaty with the Visigoths in 439, the same year he attacked Carthage) since he had a feud with the Visigothic king, Theodoric. This seems to have been over his daughter, whose name has not been recorded. Our sources are clear that at some point (the dates are not apparent), there had been an important political union made between the Visigoths and Vandals when Theodoric's daughter had married Gaiseric's son, Huneric. For reasons that have never been adequately explained (one source claims the couple had fallen out over how to bring up their children), the marriage turned sour and Theodoric's beautiful daughter had been returned by Gaiseric to her father with her nose and ears cut off. The Vandal claim was that she had apparently tried to poison her husband. The whole incident is shrouded in mystery, and it is much more likely there was some political disagreement than a domestic row between the couple. But whatever it was, from that point onwards, the Visigoths and Vandals became sworn enemies.

The fall of Carthage was partly due to Gaiseric's cunning, but it was also due to Roman incompetence. As discussed in the last chapter, Aetius can be blamed for focusing too much on Gaul and too little on North Africa. But it was not just Aetius, for the eastern empire also took its eye off the ball. The eastern Romans had defended Carthage well to begin with, but were distracted by the Hunnic threat along the Danube.

The Romans would pay dearly for their mistakes. The fall of Carthage was a devastating blow for both halves of the empire. It particularly hurt the western empire which lost its grain supply and maybe as much as half of its remaining tax revenues. Meanwhile, the eastern empire's valuable maritime trade in the eastern Mediterranean was now vulnerable to Vandal piracy. Realising their mistake, the two sides of the empire rushed to assemble an expeditionary force to recover Carthage. Aetius sent as many soldiers as he could spare from Gaul (probably not many) south to Sicily to join a large army sent by Constantinople to the island. The eastern empire is said to have put together a fleet of 1,100 ships (almost certainly an exaggeration) to transport its army to Africa via Sicily.

But the expedition never sailed. In 441, the eastern empire recalled its troops from Sicily. There was something much more threatening on the horizon. The Huns had crossed the Danube. New Hunnic leaders had seized power. One of them was called Attila. A new age had begun.

PART III

The Scourge of God

17

A Lack of Rainfall

So far, we have not addressed one of the greatest mysteries in the story of the Huns. Why did they appear on the edge of Europe in the mid-fourth century?

Until recently, historians have largely ignored this vital subject. This is partly because the Romans themselves were silent on this topic. Other than blaming divine displeasure (which became especially common when Attila launched his ferocious onslaughts), none of our chroniclers ventured to speculate on the cause of the Huns' sudden appearance.

For many years, the only explanation was offered by Chinese sources.[42] These suggested that Han China's resurgence in the first century AD forced a group of breakaway Xiongnu (see Map 3) to move to the west of China to the Altai Mountain region (where modern Kazakhstan, China, Russia and Mongolia converge). Historians are now broadly agreed that these 'western' Xiongnu were probably the same Huns who invaded both Europe and Persia/India in the fourth and fifth centuries. However, there is a major problem with the timing of this migration. For there is a 200-year gap between the Chinese record of the Xiongnu's westward movement and the Huns' actual appearance on the edge of Europe (in modern Ukraine) in the AD 360s. This has become known as the 'missing 200-year interlude' and historians have struggled to explain what happened during this period. For example, if the Xiongnu were truly escaping the wrath of Chinese armies, why did they feel it necessary to flee all the way to Europe to find safety?

However, paleoclimatology (the study of previous climates in Earth's history) has come up with an explanation long suspected by a handful of historians. Recent studies analysing millennia-long juniper tree-ring records[43] – and yes, it might sound surprising that there are still trees dating back thousands of years, but they do exist – suggest that in the fourth-century Asian steppe-lands, there was a prolonged period of drought – what climatologists call a megadrought. The evidence suggests the drought was most intense between around AD 310 to 360. This type of prolonged drought would have caused nomads to search for more fertile ground on which to graze their flocks of goats and sheep. The timing of this megadrought fits perfectly with the Hunnic migration since it occurred just before the Huns appeared on the edge of eastern Europe.

Another interesting insight into the Huns' movements is offered by those anthropologists who believe that nomads prefer *not* to travel too far. The word 'nomad' comes from the Greek *nomas* and, contrary to its popular modern meaning, does not mean someone who likes to travel for the sake of it. Instead, it refers to a tribe that alternates grazing land between summer and winter, typically within a 100-mile radius. In the Asian steppe-land, this is required because it comprises two types of pasture. Upland summer pasture which provides abundant grass in summer but not in winter, and lowland winter pasture which has grass in winter but not summer. The Huns' priority was moving their flocks between upland and lowland pasture since these animals were their most precious asset, meeting all their needs in terms of milk, meat and leather for clothing. Therefore, the Huns did not enjoy wandering the globe, as some historians have thought. For them to have migrated thousands of miles to the west would have required some spectacular impetus, such as climate change.

Let us look briefly at the evidence for climate change in the fourth century AD aside from that provided by juniper tree-ring records. Again, paleoclimatology has more to offer. Separate evidence from that provided by the juniper trees exists suggesting the central Asian steppe suffered from prolonged La Niña-like conditions in the fourth century. El Niño and La Niña refer to the cycle of warming and cooling of water in the eastern tropical Pacific Ocean cycle. El Niño is warm and La Niña is cold. The effect of this cycle in the Pacific can have quite a profound and variable effect on the climates of other places on Earth. And for the Asian steppe, El Niño normally produces rain while La Niña produces drought. Climatologists are now fairly certain that in the fourth century AD there was a prolonged La Niña in the Pacific, which would have contributed to the aridity of the Asian steppe, supporting the juniper tree-ring evidence for a megadrought.

Before we move back to the political, military and economic consequence of the Huns' migration to Europe, let us briefly consider the broader impact of climatic change on the Roman Empire since it is probably the most exciting area of new research into the ancient world at the moment. One historian[44] has recently published groundbreaking new research suggesting Rome's history, from its earliest origins, was heavily influenced by climatic changes.

For example, in the early and middle Roman period, there is abundant archaeological and literary evidence suggesting the climate was more favourable in the Mediterranean Basin than it is today. Most striking was the exceptional fertility of North Africa. It is well known that Egypt and modern Tunisia (where Carthage was situated) were called 'the granary of Rome' by the Romans. Today, both countries are grain importers. Yet during the Roman period, from Morocco to Egypt, a line of coastal cities produced vast quantities of corn, wine and fruit, and bred horses as well. Wild animals also lived much closer to the Mediterranean than today, providing an abundant source of exotic creatures to be massacred in the Roman amphitheatres. For example, Pliny the Elder said that elephants roamed the Atlas Mountains. Today, they are long gone.

Aside from the agricultural fecundity of North Africa, the Romans have left copious records of Tiber floods. Roman Italy seems to have had far more rainfall than today. Pliny the Younger and Ovid recorded frequent Tiber floods during the summers. Pliny even described Roman furniture floating down the streets in floods during Trajan's reign. By contrast, in the Middle Ages, there is no record of Tiber floods. Another example is agricultural production. Pliny the Elder said that not only was Italian wheat excellent but that it was also grown in the mountains, suggesting warmer and wetter conditions than today. In Greece, ancient heavy olive-crushing installations have been discovered high above the modern levels of olive cultivation, again suggesting that Greece was wetter and more fertile.

So, there is plenty of literary and archaeological evidence to suggest the Mediterranean enjoyed a favourable climate for agriculture in the early and middle Roman periods. Historians have termed it the 'Roman Warm Period' or the 'Roman Climate Optimum', lasting from around 250 BC to AD 400. It is perhaps no coincidence that it was during this period that Rome rose to power and enjoyed its greatest prosperity. But worse was to follow. It was replaced by the 'Late Antique Little Ice Age', a widely recognised period of cooling that lasted from 536 to about 660, and which climatologists believe was caused by a series of major volcanic eruptions around the world, starting in 536. Volcanic eruptions tend to cause cooling because the ash, dust and gases they release into the atmosphere normally reflect the sun's rays. This proved catastrophic for the eastern Roman Empire and the wider ancient world, since it caused harvest failures and famine, and contributed to the great plague in Justinian's reign, which devastated not just eastern Rome but the entire population of western Eurasia. In a later book in this series, I will discuss this momentous time in more detail.

It was not just the Roman Empire that was susceptible to climate change. Historians increasingly emphasise the historical importance of the Medieval Warm Period,[45] between AD 800 to 1300, when there was a noticeable rise in surface temperatures that changed the climate worldwide.

While this benefited Europe, with longer summers and more bountiful harvests producing population growth and cultural flowering, in other parts of the world it did the opposite, bringing prolonged drought and famine. In particular, it led to droughts which are now widely considered to be the main killers of two great medieval civilisations – the Mayan civilisation in Central America, and the Khmer Empire in Cambodia.

The story does not end there. As part of the same Medieval Warm Period phenomenon, and in a close parallel to the Roman experience with Hunnic expansion, paleoclimatology increasingly suggests the great Mongol Empire created by Genghis Khan in the thirteenth century was partly a response to droughts in central Asia similar to those that may have caused the Huns to migrate west in the fourth century.

The Huns' appearance in Europe has long remained an enigma. As we will discover, when the fury of the Hunnic onslaught reached its zenith under Attila, the Romans could find no explanation other than divine punishment. Attila was, in their words, 'the scourge of God'. However, it may be more accurate to say he was ultimately the product of a lack of rainfall on the Asian steppe-land.

18

The Empire of Gold

Before Attila, we know very little about the Hunnic kings. When Stilicho was fighting to preserve the western empire, Roman sources mention only a couple of them, principally a king called Uldin, who helped Stilicho fight the Goth Radagaisus and who subsequently invaded Thrace in 408. Another king called Charaton is described as receiving an embassy from the emperor Theodosius II led by the Roman chronicler and diplomat Olympiodorus who wrote an extensive history of the early fifth century, now lost but thought to have been used by the sources we rely on like those of Zosimus and Sozomen. He was a colourful character utterly devoted to his pet parrot, who accompanied him everywhere. His parrot was apparently prodigiously talented and able to sing, dance and talk in Greek.

It is deeply frustrating Olympiodorus' history is lost to us, since it would no doubt have provided us with a useful description of Hunnic society before Priscus' vivid account of the court of Attila written half a century later. Without it, our sources are almost silent on the growth of the Hunnic Empire before Attila. The Huns themselves were illiterate and have left no written records. Aside from archaeological excavations, which we will discuss shortly, our knowledge of the fourth-century Huns is reliant on anecdotal Roman and Chinese sources.

This raises far more questions than answers. As mentioned in Chapter 1, no one really knows what they even looked like. Did they still look Mongolian or, in the 200 years after they left Mongolia and spread west, had they mixed with other races? Most historians think they had, and they probably looked more mixed race than purely Mongolian. This racial mixing seems to have developed further in the fifth century, especially with the Germanic nations they subdued.

The European Huns' early political history is almost as obscure. Uldin and Charaton are now regarded as only minor Hunnic kings, of which there were many before Octar and Rua merged the Hunnic confederation. During this time, relations between the Romans and Huns were mostly cordial because they shared a common interest in opposing the Germanic nations. The Huns were intent on subjugating the Germans and even regarded the Romans as allies against them, as shown by their alliance with Stilicho against the Goths. It was then that Aetius and other Romans were sent as hostages to the Hunnic court to improve relations and guarantee honourable conduct.

But the east Romans must have felt these amicable relations were fragile for, in the mid-400s, the praetorian prefect for the east, Anthemius, started construction of the famous Theodosian walls protecting Constantinople. This huge project was probably finished around 413, and it was a good thing for the Romans it was since in 422, Rua and Octar upped the stakes by demanding that the eastern Romans pay them 350 pounds of gold as tribute every year. The eastern empire was far wealthier than its western cousin and Theodosius II was happy to pay the gold if it brought him an easy life.

Thereafter, matters between the Huns and Romans carried on much as before, with Aetius using his connections to recruit Hunnic mercenaries. We know almost nothing about Hunnic politics in the 420s and 430s except that Octar died fighting the Burgundians in 430, leaving Rua to rule alone. Despite the Romans dutifully paying them 350 pounds of gold, the Huns' greed got the better of them, and in 434, Rua crossed the Danube and invaded Thrace, enticed by the prospect of plunder and an increase in the Roman tribute. As mentioned in Chapter 16, this caused the immediate recall of the eastern general, Aspar, who was defending Carthage from the Vandals.

Fortunately for Aspar, Rua died suddenly in 435 before any battle was joined. The eastern emperor Theodosius II was not slow to take the credit for this. He pointed out he had been doing a lot of praying recently, and, as emperor, had a direct line to the Holy Father. The Romans believed him and the official version quickly became established that, in answer to the emperor's prayers, Rua had been incinerated by a bolt of lightning. The bells rang out in every Roman church and the Romans sat back and thanked God they were Christian. Meanwhile, the Huns returned to the Hungarian plains in order to decide the succession, always a fraught occasion.

Again, our sources are silent about the Hunnic power struggle after Rua's death. All we know is that two hitherto unknown leaders seized power: Bleda and his brother, Attila. If Rua had children, they were presumably eliminated by Bleda and Attila. The only thing we know for certain is that Hunnic politics was brutal and bloody. For example, Priscus informs us that two royal relations, probably cousins of Bleda and Attila, fled to the east Roman Empire only to be returned at Hunnic insistence, whereupon they were immediately impaled, which was the typical form of Hunnic capital punishment. Being a senior Hun was not for the faint-hearted.

The silence in our sources from 435 until 439 has given rise to some unhelpful speculation by historians. In particular, you will read in some commentaries that the European Huns attacked Persia. However, there is absolutely no evidence of this in the primary sources. I suggest a misunderstanding has arisen because of a mention in Priscus' history that ambassadors from Aetius' western empire suggested to Attila that he *should* attack Persia. The idea was to distract him from attacking the Romans. However, a close reading of the text reveals that Priscus later says it made no sense for Attila's Huns to attack Persia since it was too far away from Attila's capital on the Hungarian plains. As mentioned in Chapter 12, the Huns who did attack Persia in the fifth century were not Attila's Huns but a completely separate group called the White Huns who approached Persia from the east through modern Afghanistan.

So, if the Huns were not attacking Persia in the 430s, what were they doing?

The answer lies almost certainly with Germania. The European Huns were probably busy in the 420s and 430s subjugating all the Germanic nations east of the Rhine and north of the Danube. Germania in ancient times was far larger than modern Germany, stretching from the Rhine to the Dnieper in modern Ukraine and from the Baltic to the Black Sea. As the Huns spread west, the Germanic response was either to flee into Roman territory (like Fritigern's Goths in the 370s) or to stay and become Hunnic subjects.

While our written sources are fairly silent about what life was like living under Hunnic rule, recent archaeology has helped us by suggesting it was not as bad as might be expected. For example, the excavation of hundreds of burial sites in Hungary and eastern Europe dating back to the fifth century has uncovered many more German graves than Hunnic ones.

Hunnic graves are distinguished by their unique type of bow, distinctive Hunnic cauldrons, and, most famously of all, by the elongated skulls caused by the Hunnic practice of binding the heads of babies. German graves often contain long, straight German swords and an abundance of Germanic decorative metalwork, including brooches, buckles and jewellery. But most revealing of all, those dating to the fifth century also contain an abundance of Roman gold used in highly prized Roman manufactured objects, from tableware to jewellery, armour and coins. In contrast, German graves dug before the Hunnic occupation of central Europe are strikingly bereft of golden objects.

These findings are crucially important in determining how the Hunnic Empire operated. For it suggests the Huns paid their German subjects large quantities of gold. By the 430s, the Huns were ruling a huge host of German tribes including Ostrogoths (as we call those Goths in the east who had *not* fled west), Gepids, Alans, Rugi, Suevi, Sciri, Heruli, Lombards, Thuringians, and some of the Alemanni and Franks not in western Roman territory. This meant the Hunnic army comprised many more Germans than Huns. Perhaps some 20,000 Hunnic horse archers were supplemented by tens of thousands of German infantry and cavalry. It was not as large as the half a million men that Jordanes attributed to Attila, but it was certainly well over 50,000. And the Germans, as the contents of their graves show, were paid in gold. A lot of gold. And there was only one source for that. The Roman Empire.

This meant the Hunnic Empire, created in the mid-fifth century, began an entirely new relationship with Rome. Previously there had been almost no direct contact between the Huns and Romans. As discussed in Part I, in the fourth and early fifth centuries, the Huns had had a major *indirect* impact on the Romans through encouraging German migration into the empire. This stopped as they extended their dominion into central Europe, ruling the Germans directly rather than pushing them west. The influential Irish historian JB Bury, writing over a hundred years ago, thought the creation of a Hunnic state in central Europe (see Map 6) was 'good' for the Romans since, after the Germanic onslaught across the Rhine in December 406, it stopped any more German invasions of Roman territory. What he ignored was that this Hunnic-German empire was not self-sufficient. It needed Roman gold to survive. And this meant war. The time was now ready for the second phase of the Huns' interaction with the Romans. Direct invasion. As Edward Gibbon wrote: 'In the reign of Attila, the Huns again became the terror of the world.'[46]

19

Attila

Jordanes, the Gothic historian, has left us with a description of Attila:

> *He was a man born into the world to shake the nations, the scourge of all lands, who in some way terrified all mankind by the dreadful rumours heard abroad concerning him. He was haughty in his walk, rolling his eyes hither and thither, so that the power of his proud spirit appeared in the movement of his body. He was indeed a lover of war, yet restrained in action, mighty in counsel, gracious to supplicants and lenient to those who were once received into his protection. He was short of stature, with a broad chest and a large head; his eyes were small, his beard thin and sprinkled with grey; and he had a flat nose and a swarthy complexion, showing the evidence of his origin.*[47]

While Attila seems to have looked reasonably Mongolian, he was not born on the steppes. He was probably born around 400 on the Great Hungarian Plain where the Huns settled in the late fourth century. His father was called Mundiuch and his mother is unknown. Mundiuch had been brother to Octar and Rua, who were the joint kings of the Huns in the late 420s and 430s, and with whom, as mentioned previously, Aetius had established good relations when he was sent to live with the Huns as a hostage.

Other than this we have no information on Attila's early life. The first mention of him in Roman sources comes when he was co-ruler of the Hunnic Empire with his brother Bleda. Together, they were turning the screw on Rome to extract more gold. In 439, they demanded a meeting with the eastern Romans outside the Roman city of Margus on the Danube, the border demarcating the two empires, an event vividly described by the Roman chronicler Priscus.

According to Priscus, the Huns were on horseback and refused to dismount so that the Roman delegation had to climb back onto their horses and listen to the demands made by the new Hunnic leaders. First was a doubling of the annual tribute from 350 pounds of gold to 700. Second was the subject of political refugees. The Huns were obsessed with finding and eliminating dissident members of the Hunnic royal families who had fled into the Roman Empire, and the Romans replied by promising to return all those they could find. In addition, the Huns said they needed to set up some trading agreements between the two empires. And finally, just to show they were not all bad, they offered to return some Roman prisoners.

Back in Constantinople, the Roman response was to cave in. They agreed to double the gold subsidy and all the other demands, not least because news arrived that the Vandals had taken Carthage. At least initially, the east Romans appear to have thought this was a bigger threat than the Huns since Gaiseric could build a fleet to challenge Roman domination of the Mediterranean. The eastern Roman army assembled to sail for Africa thinking the Hunnic bully had been bought off.

But the bully was getting bolder. Not much more than a year later, the Huns were back. This time, their complaint was they had not received all the refugees they wanted. There was also an altercation in the city of Margus over the new trading agreements. We can only imagine what it must have been like dealing with Hunnic 'merchants' if such existed. Several Roman merchants were killed. Then the Huns accused the bishop of Margus of crossing over the Danube to steal valuables from the Hunnic royal tombs. They demanded he was delivered to them for punishment.

This turned out to be a cunning pretext. For the terrified bishop, anxiously awaiting the footsteps of Roman soldiers coming to arrest him, did a deal with the Huns to open the city gates in return for dropping the charges. Although the treacherous bishop's fate is unknown, the Huns walked into Margus and took control of a major Roman fortified city controlling a broad stretch of the Danube. They also occupied several other Roman forts along the river, including one at Viminacium.

Their next destination was a huge Roman strongpoint, the city of Naissus (modern Nis in Serbia), considered the gateway to the Balkans, and famous for being the birthplace of Constantine the Great. The city had gigantic walls which had easily fended off the Goths in the previous century. Its inhabitants no doubt thought they would be safe. After all, every Roman knew barbarians were terrible at siege craft. But the Huns were not like other barbarians. They were actually good at siege warfare. Priscus has left us with a vivid description of the fall of the city.

> *...battering rams were brought up. They were large machines. A beam is suspended by slack chains from timbers which incline together, and it is provided with a sharp metal point and screens for the safety of those working it. With short ropes attached to the rear, men vigorously swing the beam away from the target of the blow and then release it ... From the walls the defenders tumbled down wagon-sized boulders ... Some rams were crushed together with the men working them, but they could not hold out against the great number of machines. Then the enemy brought up scaling ladders ... The barbarians entered through the part of the circuit wall broken by the blows of the rams and also over the scaling ladders and the city was taken.*[48]

How did the Huns gain the siege skills which had eluded all the Germanic barbarians? Historians have put forward many theories, from ancient knowledge dating back to when they had been part of the Xiongnu Empire that had devastated so many Chinese cities, to their working with and copying Aetius' Roman army. While both of these may be at least partly true, another possibility is simply that their organisational skills were superior to those of the disorganised Germans.

The fall of a great city like Naissus transmitted shock tremors to Constantinople. As described in Chapter 16, the eastern Roman army was immediately recalled from Sicily, ending any hopes of crushing the Vandals. This had enormous strategic consequences. North Africa would remain in Vandal hands for nearly a hundred years. The western empire lost its richest province outside Italy. Indeed, from here on it would be confined to just Italy, some of Gaul and Illyria.

Meanwhile, Constantinople could not wait for its army to return from Sicily. Afraid that Attila and Bleda would march on the imperial capital, Theodosius' government sued for peace. The Huns humiliated the Romans. They doubled the tribute from 700 pounds of gold to 1,400.

But despite this, the eastern empire was far from finished. Indeed, I suggest Attila's threat sparked a revolution that would have far-reaching consequences. For, while Theodosius II himself was incompetent, he was surrounded by capable ministers and generals who were quick to react to the new reality that was Attila. Foremost among these was Anatolius, made consul in 440, who had effectively been running the eastern empire during the 430s in his position as *magister militum* for the eastern army. Another highly competent individual was the Gothic general, Aspar, recently returned from Sicily. Yet another capable minister was Flavius Constantinus, who we will hear more about in the next chapter.

It was these men who rose to the Hunnic challenge. They refused to concede defeat to the Huns by organising a massive increase in the eastern army. The number of field armies was probably increased from two or three to five as has been suggested in a recent publication (2023) by Anthony Kaldellis and Marion Kruse.[49] These field armies are recorded in the *Notitia Dignitatum*, a surviving ancient list of the legions and vexillations (as the units smaller than the legions were called) in the late Roman army in both east and west. It says that two of the five field armies were based in the western provinces, the armies of Illyricum and Thrace, while the eastern frontier had its own army, the army of the *Oriens*. There were also two praesental armies based in and around Constantinople itself, so called because they were *in praesenti*, meaning 'in the emperor's presence'.

The research recently presented by Kaldellis and Kruse places the increase in the number of field armies to five firmly in the 440s. This is important because it rejects the previous scholarly consensus that the eastern empire had five field armies from 395 onwards. This was based on the erroneous view that the *Notitia* was written around 395, the year when Theodosius I died. The rationale for this was always flimsy, based on little more than a perception that 395 was a watershed year for the Roman Empire when Theodosius reunited it and supposedly left it stable and safe. This never made sense, in my view, since most written sources suggest 395 was a low point for the Roman army when Theodosius' civil wars had all but destroyed the elite regular Roman regiments and left the Goths as the Romans' main military force but a mercenary one (see Chapter 5).

This new dating of the *Notitia* not only supports the theory for the remilitarisation of the eastern empire in the 440s in response to Attila's campaigns but it also helps to explain another question that has long perplexed historians –

why did the eastern empire *not* come to the aid of the west in the crisis of 406–410 that led to the sack of Rome? The most it did was to send 4,000 soldiers to Ravenna in 408 to help Honorius. The answer lies in the fact it only had two or three field armies before the 440s, meaning it simply did not have the resources available to send to the west.

As to the size of the enlarged eastern army, the *Notitia* suggests a field army had about 20,000 men. In reality, I suspect there were fewer than this, perhaps 10,000. This means, in the 440s, Constantinople might have increased its field army troops from as little as around 20,000 (two field armies with 10,000 men) to as much as 50,000 (five with 10,000). In addition, there were stationary border units called the *limitanei*, as described in Chapter 4, since the Roman army was divided between border troops (*limitanei*) and central field armies (*comitatenses*). The *limitanei* were distinctly inferior to the field armies but the *Notitia* suggests they were more numerous, so perhaps there could have been some 50,000 or more of them. Therefore, in the 440s, the total strength of the eastern army could have risen from perhaps around 70,000 (20,000 field army and 50,000 *limitanei*) to 100,000 (50,000 field army and 50,000 *limitanei*).

One important question is how the increase in the army was funded? Frustratingly, we have no detailed answer to this, but most historians think the eastern empire was undergoing a period of general economic prosperity in the fifth century which would have translated into greater state revenues, so it seems reasonable to assume that the growth of the eastern Roman army in the 440s was facilitated by a buoyant economy. In contrast, the western economy had all but collapsed, as had the western Roman army.

The result was something truly remarkable. In 443 or 444, the eastern Romans felt bold enough to stop paying the annual tribute. While not specifically mentioned in any sources, most historians accept this happened as, later on in 447, Attila demanded a back payment of 6,000 pounds of gold, implying the annual payment of 1,400 pounds agreed in 441 had not been paid for a little over four years.

Constantinople had thrown down the gauntlet to Attila. And, no doubt to its surprise, it got away with it, at least for the time being. Why? Because Attila was busy playing politics. As with so much of Hunnic history, we know virtually nothing about what happened. But in 444 or 445, Roman sources say that Attila had his brother, Bleda, murdered. Whether true or not, Bleda disappears from history. Attila emerged as the sole leader of the most powerful Hunnic Empire that had ever existed west of Mongolia.

Once he had seized supreme power, Attila turned his attention to the eastern empire. He must have been painfully aware that the eastern Romans were openly defying him by not paying their tribute. He was also no doubt aware they had rebuilt their army. In 446, he prepared for war. But he was an opportunist. As Jordanes said: '[He] fought with craft before he made war.'[50] He wanted the right opportunity to attack the east. Then, in early January 447, as if by divine providence, the perfect opportunity arose. An earthquake hit Constantinople's great walls.

20

The Battle for the East

On 26 January 447, during the second hour after midnight, an earthquake severely damaged Constantinople's gleaming new walls, built to protect it from the Huns. Fifty-seven towers collapsed. The next day, the emperor Theodosius II, walked barefoot, dressed in a simple white tunic, seven miles from the Great Palace at the eastern end of the city to the military parade ground at the Hebdomon outside the city. There he prayed to God to show mercy upon the Romans. A great crowd, including all the dignitaries of the eastern court and a multitude of citizens, joined him to chant the Trisagion, the invocation still in daily use in the Greek Orthodox Church today, to appeal to God for mercy.

> *Holy God, Holy Mighty One, Holy Immortal One, have mercy upon us.*

This was the moment Attila had been waiting for. Immediately, a massive Hunnic army crossed the Danube heading straight for Constantinople. Fortunately for the inhabitants of the city, the highly capable praetorian prefect of the east, Flavius

Constantinus, had no intention of waiting for God's help. Instead, he was a man of action, typical of the ministers in the east and so unlike those in the west, who was determined to save the city before Attila reached it. In a show of astonishing logistical organisation, he marshalled all the resources of the capital to rebuild the walls within two months. Not only was every single skilled stonemason, artisan and labourer immediately summoned but he also harnessed the energies of the two dominant factions in the city, the Blues and the Greens.

These were chariot racing associations, whose fans were as fanatical as those of any modern football or baseball team. Normally they were locked in conflict, which would often turn violent, and after a brief attempt to make them work together – which failed miserably – he had the brilliant idea of making them compete. He gave them different sections of the walls to repair and set them competitions as to who could finish first. The result was that for sixty days most of the city's inhabitants worked literally around the clock to rebuild the walls. Thousands of flaming torches burned throughout every night as the multitude of workers cut and laid stones.

Today, we can still see an ancient commemoration of this astonishing achievement in modern Istanbul. Beside the bus station, at the Mevlevihane Kapisi (as the gate is called in Turkish) is a marble slab cemented into the stonework of the ancient wall (see Figure 14) that reads:

> *By Theodosius' command, Constantinus triumphantly built these strong walls in less than two months. Pallas Athene could hardly have built such a secure citadel in so short a time.*[51]

Pallas Athene was the goddess of Athens and the guardian of the Acropolis. I cannot help smiling that, in their hour of need, the nominally Christian population of Constantinople honoured a pagan goddess as the model against which they measured their own efforts.

Meanwhile, the new Roman army was mobilising to meet the Huns in battle and either stop them in their tracks, or at least buy time for Constantinus to rebuild the city walls. I should mention at this point we have very limited commentary on this critical campaign in 447. Indeed, until recently historians even disputed the number of campaigns Attila fought against the eastern empire. Some thought there were three wars, in 441, 443 and 447.[52] Now the scholarly consensus believes there were two, in 441 and 447. The second campaign in 447 was, I believe, just as critical as Attila's more famous onslaught against the western empire in 451, which culminated in the Battle of the Catalaunian Plains.

The Huns crossed the Danube close to Naissus, which was a blackened ruin after its sacking in 441. They took the forts along the way, including the most important one, Ratiaria, without too much difficulty, and then advanced into Thrace. This was where the Romans were waiting for them. Beside the River Utus, just below the Danube in modern-day Bulgaria, a significant section of the eastern Roman army met the Hunnic juggernaut. It was probably the largest Roman army seen in Europe for some time. Its commander-in-chief, Arnegisclus, was determined to break the Huns. We have frustratingly limited information about the battle. It is only mentioned in three sources, all of which suggest a great conflict was fought.[53] Jordanes says Arnegisclus died when his horse was killed beneath him.

> *Against him (Attila), Arnegisclus, magister militum, marched from Marcianopolis in Mysia and fought bravely. He was obstructed by his horse when it fell beneath him, and thus unable to fight, he was killed.*[54]

Marcellinus Comes has left us with another insight:

> *The general (magister militum) Arnegisclus was killed in Dacia Ripensis near the River Utus in a fierce battle against king Attila, in which many of the enemy were slain.*[55]

These last eight words '*in which many of the enemy were slain*' are the most revealing. For it is certain Attila crossed the Danube in 447 with a large army, including not only Huns but also a formidable collection of German tribes from east of the Rhine and Danube – Goths, Gepids, Sciri, Rugi and many more – since Attila ruled approximately half of ancient Germania. Just to challenge this army was brave. To slay many of them was a huge achievement. Yes, Attila defeated the Romans but he received a bloody nose. It was a lesson he would not forget. The Battle of the Utus River marked a turning point. But it did not save Constantinople. As mentioned, earlier this was done by the city's inhabitants themselves who worked day and night to repair the walls.

Attila stopped to sack Marcianople, which was probably unwise since it delayed him further, and when he came within striking distance of Constantinople, the walls had been repaired and were well manned. He did not even stop to besiege the city. Instead, he headed south to see if there was any way of crossing the Dardanelles into Asia.

There he met another Roman army. Constantinus had mustered whatever regiments he could from the Persian frontier, and in the Chersonesus, close to modern Gallipoli, these confronted the Huns in another reportedly bloody battle. We have even less detail than about the Battle of the Utus River but again the Huns defeated the Romans. However, Attila abandoned any hope of crossing into Asia and turned west through Thrace into Greece. He sacked cities along the way but the most important ones survived, in particular Thessalonika and Adrianople, and if Athens was his aim, he never got there for he was held up in the pass at Thermopylae just as the Persian armies of Xerxes had been over 900 years before.

Unable to take Constantinople or to cross the Dardanelles, and with his army probably weakened by heavy casualties, Attila decided to settle with the Romans and head home. The general Flavius Anatolius travelled to the Hunnic camp to negotiate a new peace. Attila insisted on an increase in the annual tribute from 1,400 pounds of gold to 2,100 as well as the payment of 6,000 pounds of arrears to cover the non-payment of tribute for the four years since 443. Anatolius accepted.

Historians have tended to see Anatolius' treaty as a capitulation by Constantinople. This is influenced by Priscus' condemnation of the tribute paid to Attila. Priscus says:

> *The Romans pretended that they made these arrangements voluntarily, but because of the overwhelming fear which gripped their commanders they were compelled to accept gladly every injunction, however harsh, in their eagerness for peace.*[56]

Priscus also says the tribute paid to the Huns crippled the finances of the eastern empire: 'Even senators contributed a fixed amount of gold ... They paid only with difficulty ... so that men who had once been wealthy were putting up for sale their wives' jewelry and their furniture. This was the disaster that happened to the Romans after the war, and the result was that many killed themselves either by starvation or by hanging. The imperial treasuries were also emptied.'

However, for once I would not pay too much attention to Priscus' record, which is otherwise one of our most reliable sources. For Priscus was an outspoken critic of the Theodosian dynasty (with good reason) and, writing years after the event, he wanted to present the treaty of 447 in a harsher light than it deserved. There are, I suggest, several reasons to suppose it was not that bad for the Romans.

First, on closer inspection, the actual cost of the tribute seems less onerous than Priscus claims. Indeed, it was only 3 per cent of the eastern empire's total tax revenues, according to one historian,[57] who has estimated the total annual tax revenue of the eastern empire at around 66,000 pounds of gold (2,100 of 66,000 is 3 per cent). The combined hit with the 6,000 pounds of arrears at the end of 447 would have been 12 per cent (8,100 of 66,000) – significant but not catastrophic.

It's also worth bearing in mind the tribute paid to Attila was similar to that paid to Alaric when he held Rome to ransom 40 years earlier. In 408, the Roman senate had paid Alaric 4,000 pounds of gold to buy him off. In 409, they paid 5,000 pounds of gold and 30,000 of silver as well as huge consignments of silk, pepper and other items to prevent him from sacking the city.

Priscus' focus on the tax burden borne by the senators may also reflect the fact they were under-taxed previously. In contrast to the western empire, Constantinople seems to have had a relatively efficient tax system which was crucial to its success.

Finally, there is an interesting aspect of this treaty which is overlooked. Attila demanded the creation of a no-go zone south of the Danube, up to one hundred miles deep and three hundred wide. This unusual request sounds defensive. It suggests Attila was looking to bolster his defences against a possible eastern Roman counter-attack into his territory. It is another reason to think Attila was wary of fighting the new eastern Roman army again.

The battle for the east was over. I suggest it had not been a resounding victory for Attila. Yes, he had restored the payment of tribute. The Hunnic army had also suffered heavy casualties.

Attila returned to his palace north of the Danube to ponder his next campaign. His gaze turned westward. The conventional view is that he was looking to triumph over the western empire just as he had done over the eastern. I disagree with this. I think the campaign of 447 raised doubts about both him and his army. He had not come close to taking

Constantinople. Nor had he taken any of the other major cities. Unrest must have been growing among his German subjects. I suggest there was far more pressure on Attila than most historians think. He needed an easy victory. And Gaul offered him that possibility with its weak Roman army and its fragmented political situation.

But before we get to that, let us hear what I consider one of the most extraordinary tales recorded in the entire fifth century – the journey of two young Romans to have dinner with Attila.

21

Dinner with Attila

Flames from the oil lamps flicker, as if they might go out. The air is disturbed by the long robes of the courtiers as they sweep down the colonnaded hallway.

We are in the Great Palace in Constantinople. Almost a city in itself, and testimony to the wealth of the Eastern Roman Empire, in contrast to its dying cousin in the west. Leading them is a tall, overweight man, his breasts bulging through his tunic like those of a woman. He turns to speak to those scurrying along beside him. His voice is high pitched like a young boy's. He is Chrysaphius: a eunuch and the emperor's chief minister. Theodosius II trusts him implicitly. Chrysaphius knows everything that happens in the palace. He is the emperor's eyes and ears.

They enter a dark room overlooking a grand courtyard. The eunuch turns to a gaunt- looking man wearing a fur-lined cloak and leather jerkin. The man is deeply tanned in contrast to the eunuch's pale, florid complexion. He has the dark eyes and squat nose of a Hun. Chrysaphius bows before him, as if looking for a favour. Then he talks in hushed, secretive tones, pausing to allow a translator to convert his Greek into the

Hunnic language. The man nods. Servants bring in a chest of gold coins and place it on the table.

This is a true story. In 449, Theodosius' chief minister, the eunuch Chrysaphius, devised a plan to assassinate Attila. As I mentioned in the introduction to this book, the Roman chronicler, Priscus of Panium, has left us with a unique record of this bizarre event. The tale goes that two years after the Roman-Hunnic treaty of 447, Attila sent two ambassadors to Constantinople to complain that the Romans had not kept to the terms of the treaty. Yes, the gold had been paid, but they had not returned enough of the Hunnic fugitives that were such an obsession for Attila. The Romans had also been farming the land in the agreed no-go zone south of the Danube. The emperor Theodosius received the Hunnic ambassadors, heard their demands, and was more than happy to promise he would rectify these complaints.

But then Chrysaphius, his eunuch minister, had an idea. Why not bribe one of these ambassadors to kill Attila? The ambassador they approached was one of Attila's bodyguards called Edeco. Chrysaphius held a secret meeting with him in the Great Palace and offered him fifty pounds of gold if he would slay his master. Edeco agreed, and the Romans assembled an embassy to travel north to the Hunnic king's palace.

As mentioned in my introduction, Priscus' account of this embassy is a vivid and surprising picture of the man and life at the Hunnic court that captivated me when I first read it. It's a thrilling tale. Let me summarise it now.

First, who were the two central characters? Priscus came from Panium, a town on the shore of the Sea of Marmara, close to Constantinople. We don't know exactly when he was born but it was probably in the 410s, putting him in his thirties when he visited Attila's camp. He was clearly well educated and moved in the highest circles of eastern Roman society. Perhaps he was a lawyer working for highly ranked officials. A close friend of Maximinus, who, he says, 'with earnest entreaty persuaded me to accompany him'[58] on this expedition. He went on to write a history that has been lost in the sense that there is no manuscript containing any of the eight books with which he is credited. However, there are plenty of excerpts and references to it included in the writings of authors that have survived. The best preserved is the story of his visit to Attila which was included in a reference library created by the tenth-century Byzantine emperor, Constantine VII Porphyrogenitus. In a remarkable attempt to save classical literature from being lost, Constantine VII commissioned scholars to copy all the texts written by Greek historians from the fifth century BC to the ninth century AD and to divide them into 53 categories, such as 'on letters', 'on military victories', 'on religion' and the like. Priscus' account of Attila survives in the categories on 'embassies of Romans to barbarians' and 'on embassies of barbarians to Romans'. Not all the categories have survived but at least Priscus' embassy has.

In addition, we have numerous references to Priscus' wider history of the fifth century from other chroniclers whose works have survived, especially Jordanes, John of Antioch, as well as from a Byzantine encyclopaedia called the *Suda*. We do not know why Priscus wrote his history, but it was famous in his own day and for centuries to come.

His friend Maximinus was a high-born eastern soldier, who had served as an officer in the short war with Persia in 422–24, then as the head of the expedition to Attila in 449, and thereafter was promoted to one of the emperor Marcian's main ministers and later made governor of Egypt, where he died. How he met Priscus is unknown, but they were firm friends and Priscus travelled to see him when he was governor of Egypt.

Maximinus led the embassy as it worked its way across the lands south of the Danube, devastated by the Huns, and into the wilds of the Hungarian plains where the Hunnic capital was located. What makes the story especially gripping is that neither Maximinus nor Priscus had been told it was an assassination attempt. They were innocents walking straight into a trap. The only person who knew, aside from the would-be assassin Edeco, was their translator, Vigilas, who was fluent in Hunnic and Latin and Greek and had met Attila before.

To cut a long and fascinating story short, on reaching Attila's camp in the Hungarian plains, Edeco turned out to be no traitor and immediately told Attila he had been offered a bribe to kill him. Attila could have had them all impaled on the spot. But when he discovered Maximinus and Priscus were innocent and knew nothing of the plot to kill him, he seems to have taken a liking to these two young Romans.

What followed was quite unexpected, not least to Maximinus and Priscus. Attila was astonishingly generous to them. He let them spend a couple of weeks accompanying him as he went about the business of ruling the Hunnic Empire. He invited them to dinners and official functions. The Romans were on best behaviour and Priscus says they were careful not to get carried away at the festivities and drink too much. They were even offered attractive women for the night, which they politely but resolutely turned down. Attila made a point of letting them toast his health at a sumptuous banquet which they attended, and he seems to have enjoyed giving them a unique and privileged insight into life at the Hunnic court.

Attila also had the last laugh over the emperor Theodosius. After allowing Priscus and Maximinus to return home unharmed, he sent two more Hunnic ambassadors to Constantinople to rebuke the treacherous emperor. These Huns marched into the imperial chamber in front of hundreds of Roman dignitaries. Instead of falling to their feet in front of the Roman Emperor and crawling to kiss the hem of his purple robe in customary fashion, they walked up to him and threw at his feet the bag of gold intended for his would-be assassin. Then one of them reprimanded Theodosius, telling him this was no way for a slave to treat his master (i.e. Theodosius was Attila's slave). The Huns turned on their heels and left. No one had ever spoken to Theodosius in this way in his life. Let alone in front of his courtiers. If Priscus and Maximinus saw it they must have smiled.

Priscus' history has left us with a unique picture of Attila. Let us look in more detail at what we can draw out of this.

Figure 1: With gaunt faces and hands gripping swords, these four co-emperors (the Tetrarchs) provide our best insight into the mentality of the late Roman Empire. Now in Venice, it was originally in Constantinople. (Author's Collection)

Figure 2: This head of the emperor Constantine was originally part of a colossal statue in the Roman Forum. Striking for its sense of authority, it reflects Constantine's position as sole ruler of the Roman Empire. He embraced Christianity and made the early Christian church into a formidable institution. (Author's Collection)

Figure 3: The Column of Constantine in Istanbul originally had a statue of Constantine at its top. It was the taller than Trajan's Column in Rome and as tall as the Colosseum. A strong gale in 1106 knocked the statue and its topmost cylinders down. The Byzantine emperor, Manuel Komnenos, replaced the statue with a cross. (Author's Collection)

Figure 4: Ivory diptych possibly representing Stilicho wearing the clothes typical of a late Roman soldier with a long sword, spear, and oval shield. (Wikimedia Commons, Public Domain)

Figure 5: The emperor Aurelian built walls around Rome during the 'crisis of the third century'. Running for 12 miles, they comprise a single set of walls, unlike the triple walls of Constantinople, and proved inadequate to fend off the Goths, who sacked Rome in 410 or the Vandals who sacked it in 455. (Author's Collection)

Figure 6: The Aqueduct of Valens in Istanbul. Probably started before Valens' reign and completed in AD 368, it was 167 miles long and brought water from Thrace into Constantinople to be stored in underground cisterns. Constantinople had 33 aqueducts, of which five were of a monumental size like that of Valens. (Author's Collection)

Figure 7: Aqueducts brought water to several hundred cisterns in Constantinople. The Basilica Cistern in Istanbul, pictured here, was the largest in the city. (Author's Collection)

Figure 8: Marble columns in the Basilica cistern were taken from pagan temples, such as this head of Medusa. (Author's Collection)

Figure 9: Theodosius I placed this obelisk of Thutmose III at the centre of the hippodrome in Constantinople in c. 390. It asserted Constantinople's position as 'New Rome', copying the tradition begun by Augustus of moving obelisks to the empire's capital. (Author's Collection)

Figure 10: Theodosius I gives a laurel wreath to the winner in a chariot race, flanked by his two sons, Honorius and Arcadius. Despite this show of imperial power, within 15 years of Theodosius' death, Rome was sacked by the Goths. (Author's Collection)

Figure 11: These mosaics in Galla Placidia's Mausoleum in Ravenna are among the most beautiful of all Roman mosaics. Galla Placidia effectively ruled the western empire from 425 to 433 as regent for her young son, Valentinian III. (Author's Collection)

Figure 12: Painting of Attila by Eugène Delacroix (1798-1863). Although highly stylised, it conveys the terror Attila inspired in his enemies. (Wikimedia Commons, Public Domain)

Figure 13: The Theodosian walls of Constantinople (modern Istanbul). Comprising three walls, the tallest tower in this photo is part of the inner wall, which was larger than the first and second walls. Because of these defences, Attila did not even try to take Constantinople. No enemy breached them until 1453, when the Ottoman Turks used cannons. (Author's Collection)

Figure 14: Part of the inscription in the walls of Constantinople at the Mevlevihane Gate, which records in Latin the rebuilding of the walls in just two months after the earthquake of 447. This helped to prevent Attila from taking Constantinople. (Author's Collection)

Figure 15: Another section of the walls of Constantinople, this time above the Mevlevihane Gate, showing the inner wall (unrestored) on the left and the middle wall (restored) on the right. (Author's Collection)

Figure 16: The Column of Marcian in Istanbul. The eastern emperor Marcian (450-457) stopped payment of the annual tribute to Attila in 450. Attila attacked the western empire instead. (Author's Collection)

Figure 17: Mediolanum (modern Milan) was sacked by Attila in 452. The Columns of San Lorenzo, shown here, are one of the few Roman remains that survived. (Author's Collection)

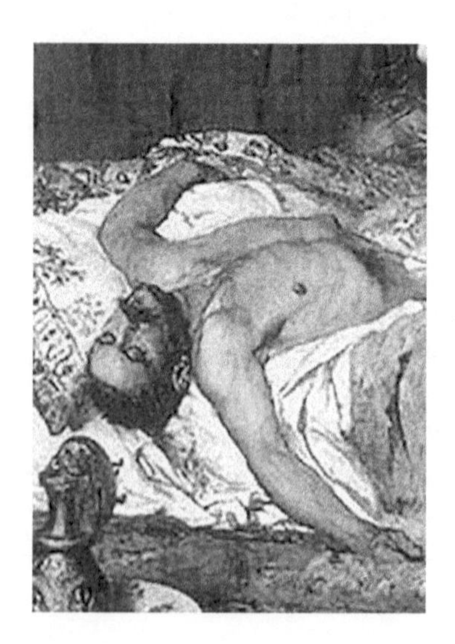

Figure 18: Attila died in early 453 as portrayed in this painting by Ferenc Paczka (1856-1925). Our main sources say he died from a nose-bleed while sleeping intoxicated on his wedding night to a German princess. However, assassination or suicide may also have been possible. (Wikimedia Commons, Public Domain)

22

In Search of the Real Attila

The name Attila is synonymous with brutality and destruction. His legend is remarkable for its longevity, which has survived intact to this day. In origin, this was probably cultivated by Attila himself to intimidate his opponents but, after his death, it was amplified in the fifth century by Christian chroniclers who liked to portray Attila as the Antichrist in order to emphasise God's victory over a heathen enemy. For example, we will discover in Chapter 24 that his epithet 'the scourge of God' derived from just such a source.

Yet our only eyewitness account of Attila does not bear out the legend. In Priscus' many vivid descriptions of him, we find a man who despised ostentation, was thoughtful and respectful of others, and showed love and affection to his family. This does not mean that Priscus' account is entirely consistent. Indeed, in some areas he raises more questions than answers. Let us examine in more detail what he says.

One of Priscus' most striking scenes shows Attila eating and drinking from wooden cups and plates, in contrast to the golden and silver ones he gave his guests, at a feast the Romans attended.

> *First Attila's servant came in carrying a platter of meat. After him everyone's waiters placed bread and cooked food on the tables. For the other barbarians and for us lavish meals had been prepared, placed on silver trays, but for Attila there was nothing more than meat on a wooden platter. He showed himself moderate in everything else too. Gold and silver goblets were given to the feasters, but his own cup was wooden.*[59]

Attila clearly saw no need to show off his wealth and power. His clothes were frugal but strikingly clean as described below. He also disdained the display of jewels and gold about his horse and weapons, as was customary with both barbarians and Romans.

> *His clothing too was frugal, since it cultivated no quality except cleanliness. Neither his sword, hanging beside him, nor the fastenings of his barbarian shoes nor his horse's bit, like the other Scythians', was adorned with gold or jewels or anything else that marks honour.*[60]

While Priscus observed a strict etiquette at Attila's court it was less oppressive than that of the emperor Theodosius II, who required his followers to prostrate themselves on the ground before him, crawl to his feet and kiss the hem of his purple robe. Priscus shows the Hun leader honouring his chief followers with ceremonial drinking toasts.

> *Once everyone was sitting in order, a cupbearer came in and gave Attila a wooden cup of wine. He took it and*

welcomed the man first in order. After Attila so honoured him, the man rose, and it was not right for him to sit until he sipped from the wooden cup or drank it down and gave it back to the cupbearer. As he remained seated, everyone present honoured him in the same way: receiving their cups, offering a greeting and taking a sip. For each diner, there was one cupbearer, who had to enter in a line when Attila's cupbearer departed. After the second man and the rest were honoured in turn, Attila greeted us in like manner according to the order of our seats.[61]

While Attila may have been more easy-going than you might expect, he was also a driven man. This is shown in a revealing legend concerning the discovery of a mystical sword discovered by a herdsman. The sword seems to have had magical powers.

He dug it up and took it straight to Attila. Attila rejoiced at this gift and, since he was majestic, he thought he had been appointed ruler of the whole world, and the sword of mars had granted him omnipotence in war.[62]

Priscus' mention of the popularity of this tale suggests Attila had carefully nurtured it to strengthen his reputation. Like most great dictators, Attila was not just a warlord but also a skilled performer and political operator. To rule the hitherto disparate and lawless Huns would have required a strong personal brand. Attila cultivated this so well that it has survived to this day.

Attila also had a subtle sense of humour unusual in tyrants. He certainly liked to mock the pompous Roman emperors. As mentioned in the last chapter, he made fun of the emperor Theodosius II by sending him ambassadors reprimanding him for trying to assassinate his master (his master being Attila). Put-downs like this recur throughout the last years of his life. We have not reached the story of his western campaigns yet, but when we do, we will discover he liked to make fun of Valentinian III by sending him messages telling him to prepare his palace for his arrival. When Attila sacked Milan, he was outraged to see paintings of Roman emperors triumphing over Huns. He hastily ordered them to be repainted showing the opposite: 'When [he] saw a painting of Roman emperors sitting on golden thrones and Huns lying dead at their feet, he sought out an artist and ordered him to paint Attila upon a throne and the Roman emperors with sacks on their shoulders pouring out gold at his feet.'[63]

His humour was subtle and not grotesque in contrast to that enjoyed by most Huns, as vividly described by Priscus in the context of a deformed dwarf who was a court jester. The dwarf, Zerkon, was a favourite with his brother, Bleda, but his inane antics irritated Attila beyond belief.

Zerkon, called a Hun, was in fact a Maurosian (Moorish) by race. The deformity of his body caused laughter, as did his lisp and appearance. He was short and hunchbacked, his feet were twisted, and his nose was visible only as nostrils because of its excessive snubness...Attila could not bear the sight of him, but Bleda very much enjoyed not just his hilarious remarks, but especially the way he walked and the extraordinary way he moved his body.[64]

You can't get away from the fact Priscus warmed to Attila. He was witty and subtle. He exuded confidence but not arrogance. He was courteous when he wanted to be, yet cruel when he felt it necessary.

Yet in some areas, Priscus' account raises more questions than answers. A striking example is with Attila's family. On the one hand, Priscus tells us that, when they were travelling with him, Attila departed for a village to marry the daughter of a chieftain called Eskam, explaining that 'the Huns practise polygamy'. Yet despite this, Attila's Hunnic wife, Kreka, is a central figure in the chronicle, and very clearly his 'main' wife who seems not only to have wielded authority herself but to have acted independently of Attila, even inviting the Romans to dinner: '…Kreka, Attila's wife, invited us to dinner at the house of Adames, the man who oversaw her affairs. We joined him along with some of the nation's leading men.' How this portrayal of a formidable wife fits with his alleged polygamy is never explained.

After his death, it was his three sons born to Kreka who inherited his empire. There is absolutely no mention of other children, legitimate or not. Priscus dwells on Attila's close relationship with his three sons. For example, at one of the feasts Priscus attended, Attila was getting bored until he spotted one of them:

…he (Attila) was not saying or doing anything resembling laughter, except that he pulled the youngest of

> *his children closer by his cheek (his name was Ernach). He had come in and was standing nearby, and Attila looked at him with serene eyes. I was amazed that he might be slighting his other children by paying attention to that son, but the barbarian sitting next to me, who understood Hunnic and told me to repeat nothing of what he was going to tell me, said that prophets had predicted to Attila that his nation would fall but that it would rise again under this son.*[65]

Priscus has provided us with a rare insight into this remarkable man. But, even through the lens he provided, the real Attila remains enigmatic. I have left a postscript at the end of this book with my translation of the main highlights of Priscus' journey to meet Attila. I leave it to you to read it and decide for yourself what sort of man he really was.

23

Attila's Bride

Theodosius II's minister, Chrysaphius, was quick to make amends when he knew his plot to kill Attila had gone awry. He despatched another embassy laden with gold to placate the Hun leader. Attila was willing to be placated. For now, it looked as if the Theodosian court could relax.

But six months later, in July 450, everything changed. Theodosius, then in his late forties, was out riding when his horse threw him. He suffered a serious spinal injury and died two days later. This marked the end of the Theodosian dynasty in the east since Theodosius had no son to succeed him. His cousin in the west, Valentinian III, was entitled to inherit the throne and unite the two halves of the empire. But true to his feeble Theodosian genes, he did nothing. As we know, Theodosian women were normally more forceful than their male relatives, and it was Theodosius' elder sister, Aelia Pulcheria, who seized this opportunity to reassert her authority.

Pulcheria had dominated her brother for the first half of his reign, but had lost her influence over him when he had fallen under the spell of his beautiful wife, Eudocia, who had, of course, originally been Pulcheria's protégé as described in Chapter 11. But Pulcheria and Eudocia, originally such good friends, had fallen out and become enemies. Eudocia even accused her erstwhile friend of giving her brother a contract to sell her into slavery, which he had signed, in his usual absent-minded manner, only for his furious wife to tear it up. Perhaps linked to that or not, their marriage became unhappy and relations between them soured so that they separated and she moved to Jerusalem. Theodosius never remarried and spent the rest of his life under the sway of his eunuch minister, Chrysaphius.

With Theodosius' death, the barbarian-born general, Aspar, could have tried to seize the throne with the army's support since he was the most senior general in the army and the most powerful man in the empire. But, suspecting that his Alanic-Gothic heritage would prove unacceptable to the people, he preferred to be the power behind the throne and sponsored an army officer for the job, well-liked in military circles, called Marcian. While an unremarkable figure, according to one source: 'a tall man with lank grey hair and swollen feet',[66] Marcian quickly established himself as a formidable and independent-minded emperor – indeed, more so than Aspar had bargained for. To settle some old scores, Aspar executed Theodosius' eunuch minister, Chrysaphius, who was no friend of his. Attila would have approved.

To confer legitimacy on Marcian, Theodosius' sister Pulcheria agreed to marry him. The only problem with the marriage was that Pulcheria had taken a vow of chastity thirty-seven years before. However, she either revoked her vows or Marcian accepted theirs was to be a platonic relationship. All we know is that coins were struck, showing the two of them shaking hands. In August 450, in front of the assembled ranks of legionaries in Constantinople, Pulcheria crowned Marcian emperor and placed a purple cloak on his shoulders. It was the first and last time that a woman crowned a Roman emperor.

However, women continued to dominate Roman politics that year for Valentinian III's sister, Honoria, booked her place in history in a most spectacular and bizarre fashion by appealing to Attila to save her from a marriage arranged by her brother. He wanted her to marry a Roman senator called Herculanus, whose key attributes were inherited money and a lack of ambition. Honoria's response was that he might be called Herculanus, but he did not exactly look like Hercules. Honoria had always been a feisty sister. She had taken various lovers and got pregnant with one of them, whereupon Valentinian sent her to Constantinople to give birth out of the limelight. There she was, no doubt, scolded by the virtuous Pulcheria. Indeed, this may have been the last straw which drove her to the extreme recourse of contacting Attila.

She sent her servant, a eunuch called Hyacinthus, to Attila's camp on the Hungarian plains, just as Priscus and Maximinus had journeyed there the previous year. Roman eunuchs tended to be overweight and have high-pitched voices, so we can only guess at how the stern-faced Attila and his battle-hardened warriors might have reacted to this entreaty. Hyacinthus told the Huns that Honoria was being forced into a marriage against her will and that she would pay Attila gold if he would stop her brother from behaving so cruelly. As a sign this was a genuine request, he gave the Hun king Honoria's signet ring.

There can have been few embassies like this before, and Attila must have wondered just what the Romans were up to. Was this another of their bizarre attempts to assassinate him? It is to his credit he quickly spotted a political opportunity. He told Hyacinthus that not only would he like to help the distraught princess, but that he would like to marry her himself. He said he accepted her ring as an engagement for marriage and that he would now wait to hear from his new fiancée about their wedding plans.

Hyacinthus returned to Ravenna, no doubt troubled by what had happened. The news of his secret mission was quickly leaked. Valentinian was appalled. The unfortunate eunuch was hauled before the emperor where he confessed under torture to what he had done and was then beheaded. Valentinian was in no mood for frivolities. He told his sister to pack her bags and to join her new husband. Honoria protested that had never been her wish, and she had only wanted her brother to treat her better. She agreed to marry Herculanus or even go to a convent. Valentinian insisted that this time she had gone too far and that she must now join Attila. At that moment, their mother, Galla Placidia, in the last political intervention of her life, told her son to behave himself and allow his sister to stay. Valentinian could stand up to his sister but not his mother. Honoria was allowed to remain and married Herculanus.

The court at Ravenna must have been quietly hoping that Attila had a short memory, or that perhaps he had been joking. But their hopes were dashed when, a couple of months later, in the autumn of 450, a Hunnic delegation arrived at Ravenna saying they had come for Attila's bride.

Not only did they want to celebrate the marriage, but they had a special message from the great Hun. Honoria's dowry was to be half the western empire, although there is no record of precisely which territories Attila wanted.

Priscus has recorded Valentinian's strained reply. Expressing his surprise at Attila's request, the emperor said his sister was now happily married to another man, and that men not women ruled Rome, so there could never be a dowry like that. The Hun ambassadors must have struggled to stifle their laughter and returned home.

More Hunnic embassies followed in quick succession. One had Honoria's signet ring which was given to Valentinian as evidence of his sister's genuine wishes. Again, the Huns were politely told that there had been a huge misunderstanding and that, although the emperor had the greatest respect for the king of the Huns, he really could not go along with these suggestions. A final Hunnic embassy arrived in early 451 and delivered a stark message to the emperor. If he refused to honour his sister's pledge to Attila, then it would be war. Priscus has recorded Attila's laconic wit in his ambassador's communication to the distraught emperor: 'Through me, [the ambassador said] the great Attila – my lord and your lord – has instructed you to prepare the palace for him.'[67]

It is clear throughout all of this that Attila was having a bit of fun with Valentinian. And Attila was playing games with everyone. At the same time that he despatched his romantic embassies to Ravenna, he also sent an embassy to the new eastern emperor, Marcian. There the Hun delegation told the new emperor that they hoped he would be a good Roman and pay his tribute on time.

They didn't expect his reply. Marcian was no weak Theodosian. He was an experienced soldier not afraid to challenge Attila to another war. According to Priscus: 'The eastern Romans said that they would not undertake to pay the tribute agreed by Theodosius and that if Attila remained at peace, they would give him gifts, but if he threatened war, they would bring against him men and equipment no less powerful than his own.'[68]

With this response, Marcian threw down the gauntlet to Attila. The gold tribute was cancelled. No gift was made to appease the Huns. This was a staggeringly different approach from that of the feeble western empire and a clear sign the eastern army had been rebuilt and was now ready to risk another round with Attila. It was also a direct challenge to Attila's authority. As described in Chapter 18, Attila's empire depended on a plentiful supply of gold to buy the loyalty of its German subjects. No gold meant no Hunnic Empire. But Attila chose not to take on the eastern army again. Instead, he turned west.

It is extremely doubtful he ever seriously believed Honoria would marry him or that Valentinian would simply donate half of the western empire as her dowry but nevertheless he spotted an opportunity. He knew what a mess the western empire was in. The western Roman army was feeble compared with the one in the east. We hear almost nothing about it from any sources, suggesting it was a small and unremarkable force, probably little more than a handful of the old frontier legions – the *limitanei* – and a central field army of perhaps a few thousand strong at most.

Valentinian was also a pushover compared with Marcian. But most intriguingly of all, Attila must have known the key to unlocking the west was not the Romans but the Germans. They had overrun most of the western empire. Since most of his army was German, this also presented a dilemma for him. Did he need to control those Germans who had so far escaped Hunnic domination? Was he afraid of the growing power of the Visigoths? Might they encourage his Germanic subjects to rebel against him? We know Attila was clever. As Jordanes said of him: 'he fought with craft before he made war.'

His first step was to sow discord between the different German factions and tribes. The Franks were a good example. They had divided loyalties between the two sons of a recently dead Frankish king (whose name has never been identified) who had no love for each other, with one joining Aetius and the other favouring Attila. Indeed, one historian[69] thinks it was this Frankish dispute which drew Attila's gaze west. But Attila was interested in more than the Franks, for he sent delegations to the Visigoths and the Vandals proposing alliances against the Romans. And to sow the seeds of discord more effectively, he also offered the Romans an alliance against the Visigoths.

The one mistake Attila made was to underestimate Aetius. Jordanes says he had a great deal of respect for Aetius although they had probably never met. Aetius would have been about sixty years old in 451, and Attila forty-five, so Attila was probably too young to have met him when he was a hostage with the Huns. Nevertheless, he would have been familiar with Aetius' good relationship with previous Hunnic kings.

As for Aetius, he was fully alert to the threat Attila posed and had been busy securing alliances with as many of the barbarians in Gaul as he could. He made alliances with those Franks already on his side, as well as the Alans and the Burgundians, the latter having no love for the Huns after the savage attack they had suffered back in 437, although they seem to have forgotten it was orchestrated by Aetius. He even contacted the Saxons in long-forgotten Britain. But the sticking point lay with the most powerful group in the whole of Gaul. These were the Visigoths, led by Theodoric. They refused to join a Roman alliance.

In desperation, Aetius persuaded Valentinian to write to Theoderic, begging him to join with the Romans in resisting the Huns. For the first time, the Roman emperor referred to them as equals: 'Bravest of nations, [wrote the emperor] we are well advised to unite against this universal despot who wishes to enslave the whole earth.'[70] Imperial etiquette had previously required the emperor to address the Visigoths as his vassals. No more. And with good reason. For in March 451, Attila was ready to strike west. A vast Hunnic army, mainly comprising his Germanic subjects, was moving west. Its target was Gaul.

24

Blitzkrieg in the West

In early 451, the Huns crossed the Rhine. The first major city to fall was Metz, ninety miles west of the Rhine. It was completely destroyed apart from a chapel dedicated to Stephen, the first Christian martyr. A legend quickly developed that God saved the chapel but punished the rest of the population since they were sinners.

This is typical of our few surviving sources on Attila's march into Gaul which are nearly all stories of Christian miracles, making it almost impossible to know what really happened. For example, Paris, or Lutetia as the Romans called it, was reputedly saved by a young peasant girl, Genevesa, who took a vow of chastity and led the city in what one historian has described as a prayer marathon. She subsequently became Paris's patron saint, renamed Genevieve, and the modern-day Pantheon in the city, a huge neo-classical edifice, was originally dedicated to her before being converted in the French Revolution into a secular monument.

A tradition quickly sprang up, which dominates the surviving historical sources, that Attila was the 'scourge of God' bringing punishment for the sins of the Gallo-Romans.

The phrase was coined at the Gallic town of Troyes when its bishop went out to meet Attila and asked him who he was, whereupon the Hun apparently replied, 'I am the scourge of god.'[71] The humble bishop told Attila to take his life but to spare those of his congregation. According to the legend, this act of self-sacrifice prompted a miracle and '[the Huns] were blinded by heaven and they passed straight through, in one gate and out by another, neither seeing nor harming anyone.'

In Rheims, ninety miles west of Metz, another legend relates that the Huns were met by the bishop whom they promptly decapitated as he read from the Bible. But his head kept on talking as it rolled down the steps of the cathedral, causing them to flee in terror. Closer to the truth is probably that many Gallic towns survived not because they were populated by pious virgins and virtuous bishops, as the early Christians would have us believe, but because they had massive Roman fortifications built by the late Roman emperors, Aurelian and Diocletian, back in the third century. Some of these are still visible today. The modern French town of Sens is a good example where its enormous Roman walls that defied Attila have stood for over 1,500 years.

Meanwhile, as the Hunnic juggernaut smashed its way west, in the sunshine of southern Gaul at his court in Toulouse, Theodoric, king of the Visigoths, was still pondering what to do.

Aetius was of course desperate for his help. Our sources say he called on the help of a prominent Roman senator called Avitus, a friend of Theodoric's, to meet the Visigothic king and argue for an alliance. Avitus is an interesting figure because he was highly regarded by both the Visigoths and the Romans. A Gallo-Roman aristocrat and a former soldier before becoming a senator, he held various senior positions in the western Roman government. We don't know what Avitus said to Theodoric, but his counsel does not seem to have swayed the Visigothic king.

More important than Avitus' pleas may have been a diplomatic blunder made by Attila before the invasion. For one of Attila's numerous embassies had travelled to Carthage to ask Gaiseric, king of the Vandals, for a treaty against the Romans. This would have displeased Theoderic since he and Gaiseric were sworn enemies. As mentioned in Chapter 16, the cause of this feud lay with Gaiseric's cruel treatment of Theodoric's daughter.[72] When her marriage to Gaiseric's son, Huneric, broke down, her ears had been clipped and her nose slit, and Theodoric's once beautiful daughter was left disfigured. She was returned to the Goths but never seen in public again. Ever since then, Theoderic had sworn to take vengeance on the Vandals. As Attila's army approached, Theodoric might have been reminded that a friend of the Vandals was no friend of his.

Another reason for Theodoric to fight was that Attila's army already included a huge force of eastern Goths, or Ostrogoths as historians call them, and the very last thing Theodoric would have wanted was to become a vassal of the Ostrogoths.

As Theoderic pondered what to do, he heard news of the sack of Metz and Rheims. The Hunnic advance seemed unstoppable. He also heard that in the spring of 451, Aetius had crossed the Alps with a small Roman army from Italy and headed north to meet up with his allies, including the Burgundians, some of the Franks, the Alans and some of the *bagaudae* (Gallic peasants). But everyone knew this Roman coalition was nowhere near strong enough to defeat Attila's great army. Theodoric must have wondered what would happen if the Huns appeared victorious on Visigothic borders. Would they be next in line for subjugation?

Theodoric left it to the last minute. But he made his decision. Yes, he would join the Romans. Jordanes has left us with a vivid description of his change of heart.

Romans [so Theodoric spoke to the Roman envoys], you have attained your desire; you have made Attila our foe also. We will pursue him wherever he summons us, and though he is puffed up by his victories over many races, yet the Goths know how to fight this haughty foe. The nobles shouted assent to the reply and the multitude gladly followed. All were fierce for battle and longed to meet the Huns, their foe. And so a countless host was led forth by Theodoric, king of the Visigoths…[73]

At a stroke, the war was transformed. In the late spring, the Roman roads from Aquitaine were choked with tens of thousands of Visigothic warriors as they poured north to join the Romans. Finally, Aetius' hope for a grand coalition had come good. Now for battle.

25

The Siege of Orléans

By early June 451, the Huns were in central Gaul. They reached the large Gallo-Roman city of Orléans, or *Civitas Aurelianorum* meaning the city of the emperor Aurelian, who had re-founded it after its destruction in the crisis of the third century and endowed it with huge fortifications. Indeed, Orléans was one of the best examples of the late Roman fortification network in Gaul. It was also still prosperous, benefiting from its central position in Gaul as a trading hub. For example, it was much larger than Paris which had never really recovered from its sack in the third century. This made it a magnet for Attila who hoped it would provide the plunder necessary to keep his heterogeneous army happy.

In addition, a group of Alans close to Orléans, led by Sangibanus, promised to join Attila. The Alans were normally Roman allies but the lack of any meaningful Roman opposition to Attila's advance made them decide to join him rather than fight him.

The events at Orléans proved to be a turning point in Attila's campaign. We have two different versions of what happened. One comes from an essential historical source called the *History of the Franks*, left to us by Gregory of Tours, a famous Gallo-Roman chronicler and bishop of Tours, who lived a hundred years later. This focuses on the development of the Frankish nation, most of which took place some decades after Attila's Gallic campaign, but it does also contain a vivid description of the Huns' assault on the city.

Being a fervent Christian, Gregory has left us with another miracle story which says that the bishop of Orléans, Anianus, had sent messengers begging for Aetius to come to the city's aid. Nothing happened, and the Huns battered the city's gates. Anianus called on his congregation to pray fervently for God to save them. 'If you pray with conviction, God comes with speed,'[74] he exhorted the citizens.

Confident God would hear his prayers, he sent his priests up to the ramparts to look for signs of Aetius' army. At first, there was nothing visible. As the Huns' battering rams splintered the city gates and the heathen barbarians poured into the city, he sent his followers to the ramparts one last time. Suddenly, they saw a vast cloud of dust on the horizon. It was Aetius' army. Anianus, who was made a saint for his piety, proclaimed, 'It is the help of the Lord.'[75] Seeing the approaching Romans, the Huns took fright and fled from the city.

While this is another vivid story from the early Christian Church, the other and more likely account is that left to us by our trusted Gothic chronicler, Jordanes. His version is that Aetius and Theoderic reached Orléans before Attila, whereupon they built an extensive network of ditches and earthworks to protect the city. Because of this, Sangibanus, the Alan leader, switched sides and joined Aetius. Reinforcements also arrived with Franks from the north and Burgundians from the west.

Aetius' grand coalition had come together in the nick of time. Jordanes says that it was the Visigoths who troubled Attila the most. 'Attila, king of the Huns, was taken aback by this event [the Visigoths joining Aetius] and lost confidence in his own troops, so that he feared to begin the conflict.'[76]

Even the legendary conqueror of the world decided to retreat. He knew the Visigoths were no pushover. He abandoned the siege of Orléans and retreated ninety miles east. He even reconsidered the entire campaign. According to Jordanes, he resorted to the well-practised recourse of taking omens.

> *…they [the Huns] examined the entrails of cattle and certain streaks in bones that had been scraped, and these foretold disaster to the Huns. Yet, as a slight consolation they prophesied that the chief commander of the foe they were to meet should fall and mar by his death the rest of the victory and the triumph. Now Attila deemed the death of Aetius a thing to be desired even at the cost of his own life, for Aetius stood in the way of his plans. So although he was disturbed by this prophecy … he began the battle…*[77]

Jordanes was writing nearly a century later, and his account is full of poetic licence. It's unlikely Attila joined battle just because he thought Aetius would be killed. But it makes a good story. Most likely is he had little choice but to fight the Roman/Visigothic alliance. Abandoning the campaign completely would have resulted in too much loss of face. His priority was to find a location that had the wide-open spaces in which he could use his Hunnic cavalry to maximum effect.

So, he retreated through the forest of Orléans to the Catalaunian Plains. There was a skirmish between the Franks in the vanguard of Aetius' army and the Gepids in the rearguard of Attila's. One source says this left 15,000 dead which must be a gross exaggeration. It bought time for Attila to reach his destination. Once in the open of the Catalaunian Plains, the Huns regrouped. Aetius' allied army caught up with him, and on 20 June 451 the two armies prepared for battle.

26

The Battle of the Catalaunian Plains

Historians have long been divided over the significance of the Battle of the Catalaunian Plains. Some regard it as one of the most pivotal battles in history when the fate of western Europe was decided. Others regard its outcome as immaterial since the Hunnic Empire was unsustainable; as JB Bury put it: '…there is no reason to suppose that the course of history would have been seriously altered [by a Hunnic victory]. For the rule of the Huns in Gaul could only have been a matter of a year or two; it could not have survived there any more than it survived in Hungary the death of Attila, on whose brains and personal character it depended.'[78]

However, one point on which all are agreed is that it was a very large battle. As Edward Gibbon said: 'All the nations from the Volga to the Atlantic took part.'[79] Jordanes says that Attila's army comprised half a million men, but this is clearly a huge exaggeration. Most historians think there were somewhere between 20,000 to 40,000 on each side, but this was still an astonishingly large number for that time, and must have been the largest military engagement fought in Gaul since Caesar's Gallic wars nearly 500 years previously. On Aetius' side was an army of Romans, Visigoths, Alans, Franks and Burgundians. By far the largest contingent would have been the Visigoths. On Attila's side was an army of Huns, Ostrogoths, Gepids, Franks and other German tribes.

Jordanes has left us with the best description of the conflict. He begins by saying: 'The battlefield was a plain rising by a sharp slope to a ridge, which both armies sought to gain; for advantage of position is a great help.'[80] The location was identified in 1885 by a local historian as being the area around modern Montgueux, close to the ancient town of Troyes, whose bishop, as recounted in the last episode, was the one who had asked Attila his name, only to be told he was 'the scourge of God'. Today, the ridge is clearly identifiable and, rather remarkably, the modern names of some areas still reference this battle fought over 1,500 years ago, with one area called 'L'enfer' ('hell') and another called 'La rivière de corps' ('the river of dead bodies').

On 21 June 451, the two armies drew up opposite each other. Jordanes describes the allied side with the Visigoths on the right wing, and Aetius with his Roman and barbarian forces on the left. Rather unusually, the centre was given to the Alans led by Sangibanus, since they were the least trustworthy, according to Jordanes, and by surrounding them with Visigoths and Romans, Aetius hoped to make it difficult for them to defect to the Huns. This proved a clever move.

On Attila's side, the line-up was more conventional, with the Hun leader and the primary group of Huns in the centre.

The Germans were on both wings. The two main German contingents were the Ostrogoths led by Valamir and the Gepids led by Ardaric. Jordanes has left us with a description of the two German kings, emphasising Attila's high regard for them: 'For Attila ... prized him [Ardaric] and Valamir, king of the Ostrogoths, above all the other chieftains. Valamir was a good keeper of secrets, bland of speech and skilled in wiles, and Ardaric ... was famed for his loyalty and wisdom.'[81]

The size of the Hunnic host is emphasised by Jordanes' description of the rest of the German tribes in his army, and the lowly positions they occupied in the Hun hierarchy. 'Now the rest of the crowd of kings ... and the leaders of various nations hung upon Attila's nod like slaves, and when he gave a sign even by a glance, without a murmur each stood forth in fear and trembling ... Attila alone was king of all kings...'[82]

The king of all kings was ready for his crowning glory – the destruction of all military resistance to the Huns in the west. But perhaps he was still nervous about taking on the Visigoths for he made an uncharacteristic tactical mistake. In the early morning of 21 June, he ignored the strategic significance of the ridge of Montgueux until it was too late. Both sides made a rush to take the highest part of the ridge. The Visigoths and Romans got there first. Attila sent his men to take the hill, but a substantial Visigothic force led by Thorismund, Theodoric's son, routed them and established command of this high ground.

The effect of losing the first skirmish seems to have demoralised the Hunnic army. Jordanes has left us with a long speech attributed to Attila designed to rouse his army into action in true Shakespearian fashion, which is almost certainly fiction, and from which I will quote a short extract.

> *Here you stand, after conquering mighty nations and subduing the world … Let us then attack the foe eagerly … Despise this union of discordant races! … You know how slight a matter the Roman attack is … Attack the Alans, smite the Visigoths! … I shall hurl the first spear at the foe.*[83]

Attila responded to this setback by striking first. There was little subtlety in his tactics. He took his best troops – the Hunnic cavalry – and let them loose against the centre of the coalition army. They smashed into the Alans in the centre who seem to have retreated since Jordanes says the Visigoths lost contact with them. The Alans were horsemen and, unlike the Romans on the left wing, would not have been able to form an infantry shield wall to resist the Huns. Jordanes says the fighting was exceptionally fierce.

> *Hand to hand they clashed in battle, and the fight grew fierce, confused, monstrous, unrelenting – a fight the like of which no ancient time had ever recorded. There such deeds were done that a brave man who missed this marvellous spectacle could not hope to see anything so wonderful all his life long.*[84]

In true Homeric fashion, Jordanes describes a stream that became gorged with blood: '…a brook flowing between low banks through the plain was greatly increased by blood from the wounds of the slain.'[85] Thirsty warriors found they were drinking blood not water. 'Those whose wounds drove them to slake their parching thirst drank water mingled with gore.'[86] As mentioned earlier, in modern France, the stream is still called 'La rivière de corps'.

Attila may have thought that victory was his when the Alans in the centre retreated. But he was mistaken. The Romans were holding their own, presumably using *testudo* formations to hide from the rain of Hun arrows. Their German allies, the Franks and Burgundians, probably mainly on foot, were in their shield walls. The Hunnic cavalry would have unleashed their barrage of arrows but the Romans and Germans would have replied with a storm of javelins, arrows and the Frankish throwing axes for which they were famous. The result was a stand-off.

Meanwhile, on the allied right wing, the Visigoths were fighting fiercely against their Gothic cousins, the Ostrogoths. Both sides would have comprised a mix of cavalry and infantry hacking at each other with swords, spears and axes in what must have been a horrific contest. Then disaster struck the Visigoths. According to Jordanes: 'King Theodoric, while riding by to encourage his army, was thrown from his horse and trampled underfoot by his own men, thus ending his days at a ripe old age. But others say he was slain by the spear of Andag of the host of Ostrogoths…'[87]

Theodoric's death could have broken Visigothic morale, but the opposite happened. They were whipped into a frenzy against the Huns. Unfortunately, Jordanes is disappointingly brief about this vital part of the battle. Having spent two pages of his account describing Attila's speech to his troops before the main assault, he gives us only one sentence on the most important part of the battle: 'Then the Visigoths, separating from the Alani, fell upon the horde of Huns and nearly slew Attila.'[88]

So, what really happened? Most historians think Theodoric's son, Thorismund, charged down from the ridge where he had repulsed the Huns earlier that day, and drove into the flank of the Ostrogoths. But at what point in the battle did this occur? Was it before or after Theodoric's death? Some popular accounts of the battle describe Thorismund seeing his father fall and then launching his attack, and, in his fury, breaking through the Ostrogothic lines in an attempt to slay Attila. But this is pure fiction. Would Thorismund have actually seen his father fall? Almost certainly not. Theodoric would have been too far away to see exactly what had happened to him among thousands of warriors, even if his approximate location was identifiable by royal standards.

The most plausible explanation is that Thorismund was waiting on the hill for the right opportunity to attack the oncoming Ostrogoths. At some point, he led a charge down the hill and into the Ostrogothic flank. Since Jordanes says the Visigoths fell upon the Huns and nearly slew Attila, the ferocity of this charge must have been immense, taking them right through the Ostrogothic ranks and into the Hun centre where Attila himself was leading the assault.

This was when the battle was won. Somehow, the Visigothic cavalry broke the Huns who fled back to camp. Jordanes says: 'But he [Attila] prudently took flight and straightaway shut himself and his companions within the barriers of the camp, which he had fortified with wagons.

A frail defence indeed; yet there they sought refuge for their lives, whom a little while before no walls on earth could withstand.'[89]

How did the Visigoths achieve this victory? This has to be the single most important question in the entire battle. I suggest the answer lies in Attila's failure to use the advantage that had won him so many battles – the manoeuvrability of his excellent Hunnic cavalry. The Huns were skilled horse archers. They could taunt their enemies into charging by showering them with arrows and lead them into well-prepared traps. They were especially good at feigned retreats and ambushes. But they were less good at pitched battles. At the Catalaunian Plains, Attila did not let them use their unique skills. Instead, he forced them into a slogging match where they had no particular advantage. This was a crucial mistake, unusual for such a skilled military commander. As mentioned before, his army had many more Germans than Huns. Therefore, on the Catalaunian Plains, the traditional Hun tactics seem to have been hardly used at all and the bulk of the fighting was conventional – infantry lined up in shield walls and cavalry used to make high-impact charges. This favoured the mailed Visigothic cavalry more than the Huns. In short, this was why the Visigoths defeated the Huns.

With Attila now lodged behind his fortified camp of wagons, the battle carried on into the evening, according to Jordanes, in a fairly chaotic way. Indeed, he says it was so chaotic that both Thorismund and Aetius lost their way and ended up unsure exactly where they were. It is worth quoting in full Jordanes' passage describing this since it is so unusual that it rings true.

But Thorismund, the son of king Theodoric, who with Aetius had seized the hill and repulsed the enemy from the higher ground, came unwittingly to the wagons of the enemy in the darkness of the night, thinking he had reached his own lines. As he was fighting bravely, someone wounded him in the head and dragged him from his horse. Then he was rescued by the watchful care of his followers and withdrew from the fierce conflict. Aetius also became separated from his men in the confusion of the night and wandered about in the midst of the enemy. Fearing disaster had happened, he went about in search of the Goths. At last he reached the camp of his allies and passed the remainder of the night in the protection of their shields.[90]

This passage is one of the most convincing descriptions of the battle. It is entirely credible it degenerated into a chaotic muddle after Attila withdrew to his wagon citadel. The battle took place on nearly the longest day of the year and in the late evening light, there must have been groups of Germans wandering about and colliding with each other, some allied to the Huns and some with the Romans. Tolstoy famously said that in the advanced stages of a battle few people have a clue what's going on, least of all the generals. It was probably the same here. Thorismund was wounded in the head, perhaps after randomly meeting a group of Ostrogoths or Gepids. Jordanes says Aetius wasn't sure what had happened and went looking for the Visigoths to find out. It all has a ring of truth to it.

But despite the confusion, one thing was clear. Attila had been defeated. The next day, both sides looked warily at each other, as Jordanes recounted: '…the Romans saw the fields were piled high with bodies and that the Huns did not venture forth, so they thought the victory was theirs…'.[91] Meanwhile, Attila '…did nothing cowardly, like one that is overcome, but with clash of arms sounded the trumpets and threatened an attack.'[92]

But he did not attack. He was, according to Jordanes, like a wounded lion '…pierced by hunting spears, who paces to and fro before the mouth of his den and dares not spring, but ceases not to terrify by his roaring'.[93] His defiance could not disguise his despair. He told his men to heap up a great funeral pyre of horse saddles, so that if the Romans and Visigoths attacked and broke into the wagon circle, he would die in the flames rather than be captured alive. As an aside, this suggests the Huns had wooden saddles suitable for burning, not like the leather ones used by the Romans, and still used today. Hefty wooden saddles were used by the steppe nomads to give them stability on horseback before stirrups came into widespread use. The availability of saddles for burning also suggests heavy casualties.

As the saddles burned and smoke rose into the sky, there was silence. We can picture the scene: corpses everywhere, riderless horses grazing, smoke rising from campfires on both sides as the hungry warriors snatched a moment to eat something. Both sides exhausted.

On the Roman side, Aetius met Thorismund. They decided not to attack the Hun wagon circle. Instead, they chose to starve the Huns out. Placing their bowmen in front of the Hunnic camp, they tried to hinder movement. Attila's army was dependent on foraging and there must have been skirmishes as groups of Huns and their German allies left to find provisions. Meanwhile, the Visigoths sent out search parties to scour the battlefield for Theodoric's body which had not been recovered. Jordanes says: '…they found him where the dead lay thickest, as happens with brave men, and they honoured him with songs and bore him away in the sight of the enemy.'[94]

What happened next was one of the most intriguing aspects of the conflict. Jordanes says that Thorismund was keen to attack the Huns and finish them off, not least because he was '…eager to take vengeance for his father's death…'.[95] But Aetius dissuaded him and suggested he should return to the Visigothic capital at Toulouse to stake his claim to be king against his untrustworthy brothers. Jordanes is clear Aetius was afraid of a complete Hunnic defeat because he thought it would leave the Visigoths as the most powerful force in Gaul. Yet again, Aetius is portrayed as a cunning politician, playing off the different factions against each other. Jordanes adds: 'Aetius feared that if the Huns were totally destroyed by the Goths, the Roman Empire would be overwhelmed.'[96] Aetius needed both Visigoths and Huns to survive the battle so they would continue to hold each other in check.

There is one final twist to this story from the seventh-century Burgundian chronicler, Fredegar, who says that the night after the battle, Aetius went secretly to Attila's camp and persuaded the Hun to pay him 10,000 gold solidi (about 140 pounds of gold) to persuade Thorismund to withdraw. He then went to Thorismund and told him that Hun reinforcements were on the way and he needed 10,000 gold coins from the Visigoths to persuade Attila to leave.

But this story of Aetius' double-cross doesn't ring true. More likely is that, with Attila's defeat, Aetius had got what he wanted. So had Thorismund. Although he seems to have been genuinely remorseful about his father's death, he was the hero of the battle and well placed to wrest power from his brothers (fraternal conflict was rife among the Visigoths). As for Attila, his casualties were high enough for him not to want to resume the conflict. All three of the main protagonists preferred a stalemate to further fighting. The battle for the west was over. The Hunnic wagons rolled back east from whence they had come.

27

The Italian Job

Back on the Hungarian plains, Attila needed to make up for his defeat in Gaul. Most of all, he needed gold. So, he sent messengers to Constantinople to demand the unpaid tribute 'or else threatened war',[97] according to Priscus. But he had little joy from that quarter. When he was at home in his wooden palace a visitor came knocking. This was an ambassador from the eastern empire, Apollonius, a general said to be one of the bravest men in the empire.

And he needed to be brave, for he brought Attila bad news. Constantinople had no intention of paying the gold tribute to the great Hun. It hadn't paid this for two years since Theodosius II died in July 450, and the hard-line military government led by the new emperor Marcian had taken over, as described in Chapter 23.

Now Apollonius repeated what Marcian had said two years before. The most Attila could expect was the occasional gift from the emperor, and that was conditional on his good behaviour. If he wanted anything more, it would be war. No doubt Apollonius carried the customary gifts of silks, spices and pearls but that was all. There was no gold from Constantinople.

At first Attila refused to see him. Priscus records Apollonius told Attila that if 'the Huns welcomed him as an ambassador, then what he had brought would be given to them as gifts, but if they killed him, then what he had brought would be taken from them as spoils'[98] – meaning the eastern army would defeat the Huns and recover the gifts as plunder. This was bold indeed. Priscus does not tell us Attila's reply. Perhaps he was impressed with Apollonius' bravery, for he was not impaled for his impudence, and returned home unharmed to Constantinople.

Apart from this embassy, we don't know what Attila did over the winter of 451 to 452. He must have been worried about his heterogeneous empire fragmenting, especially as those German tribes who were vassals of the Huns eyed their western cousins' triumph. Did they dream of their freedom? Although we have no record of their dreams, I think the answer was very likely to have been yes.

Because of this, Attila needed a show of strength to maintain his authority and he needed it quickly. But where to strike? In the west, he faced the Visigoths. In the east was Marcian's revitalised army. He needed an easy victory. Something to show his German subjects he was still the boss. Something that would allow him to reward them with the gold trinkets that he himself so despised.

His gaze moved south towards Italy. One major attraction was its proximity. It was closer to the Hun encampment on the Hungarian plains than Gaul. Admittedly, it was protected by the Alps. But it could still be approached from the south-eastern corner. And there were no Visigoths in Italy. Marcian's army was too far away to rush to the defence of the eternal city. Of course, there was still Aetius to contend with, but did he really care about Italy? Gaul was his personal fiefdom, and he was untested in defending Italy, which was home to the ineffective emperor, Valentinian, and his wayward sister, Honoria. To use Winston Churchill's phrase, Italy must have seemed like the soft underbelly of Europe to Attila. It was time for the Italian job.

In the summer of 452, a Hun army made a lightning march from Hungary, across Illyria and into Italy. We have no details about this army but it was almost certainly smaller than the host that marched on Gaul the year before. It may also have had a higher proportion of Huns and fewer Germans. Yet it was still a powerful force, and its first target was the well-defended city of Aquileia at the top of the Adriatic.

This was large and prosperous, famous for its glass production and containing massive walls attached to a long-established legionary fortress. Attila's army laid siege to it but, unlike his success in taking Naissus south of the Danube, and Metz and Rheims west of the Rhine, it could not break through its stout defences. Perhaps, after all, Italy was not the soft underbelly of Europe? According to Jordanes, Attila was considering bypassing the city when he spotted an omen that the city was about to fall.

> *Attila chanced to be walking around the walls, considering whether to break camp or delay longer, and noticed that white birds, namely storks, who built their nests in the gables of houses, were bearing their young from the city and, contrary to their custom, were carrying them out into the country. Being a shrewd observer of*

> *events, he understood this and said to his soldiers: You see the birds foresee the future. They are leaving the city sure to perish and are forsaking strongholds doomed to fall by reason of imminent peril.*[99]

Trusting to his superstition, the Huns made one last furious attack, and '...bringing to bear all manner of engines of war, they quickly forced their way into the city...'.[100] The storks were proven right, and Jordanes says Aquileia was subjected to a sack so brutal that scarcely a trace of the city was left. Tradition has it that a small group of survivors fled by boat and struggled ashore, sixty miles away, on the shores of a sheltered lagoon. There they stayed and founded a community that came to be called Venice.

While Jordanes says that Aquileia was utterly destroyed, in fact an impressive set of mosaics was preserved in its main basilica under a protective layer of ash which can still be seen today. Centuries later, they were uncovered and used as the floor for first a church, and then the modern cathedral. But this was of little consolation to the Romans of the time. The destruction wrought in Aquileia struck fear into the hearts of every Roman in Italy.

Most of the inhabitants of the prosperous northern Italian towns seem to have fled before the Huns. As Attila marched west into the Po Valley, he found them deserted, and their gates open, with the Romans cowering in the surrounding woods and countryside. Almost no details of this part of his campaign have survived but it seems likely that he occupied the principal cities spread out along the River Po, including Concordia, Altinum, Patavium and Verona (see Map 7).

Aetius appears to have done nothing to stop him. The Roman army completely failed to defend Italy in 452, just as it had failed to defend it from Alaric some forty years before. This reflected its impoverished condition. In effect, it seems there was virtually no Roman army left in Italy. Just a collection of second-rate garrison troops (the remains of the *limitanei*) and some barbarian mercenaries. According to one chronicler, Prosper of Aquitaine,[101] this did not trouble Aetius much since he only cared about Gaul, and even recommended Valentinian flee from Italy to Gaul. But Valentinian was not taking advice from Aetius. Having spent his life in his shadow, the inept emperor was becoming rebellious. He packed his bags and fled from Ravenna to Rome. There he joined Leo, the bishop of Rome, and prayed for God to deliver them from Attila's wrath.

Meanwhile, Attila reached the gates of Milan, the erstwhile capital of the western empire which boasted an imposing imperial palace, a hippodrome, a monumental bath complex, and grand colonnades along its wide streets, although none of these have survived to this day. There was no battle outside Milan's walls, and we are not sure if the city was besieged or whether its fleeing inhabitants surrendered it. According to Maximus, a fifth-century bishop of Turin, it was violently sacked in the fashion so familiar to the Huns: '…what once seemed to be ours was despoiled by looting or was destroyed by the sword and consumed by fire…'.[102] But whether this was true or not is anyone's guess.

In Milan, Attila showed he had at least retained his sense of humour. As I recounted in Chapter 22, according to Priscus, as he strode down the long hallways of the empty imperial palace, he stopped to look at a painting showing Roman emperors with dead Huns at their feet, whereupon he ordered an artist to repaint it with him in the centre surrounded by prostrate Roman emperors pouring out gold at his feet.

The Huns stopped at Milan. Aside from an expedition to sack the nearby town of Ticinum, Attila was content to watch the paint dry on his new and more accurate picture. He did not give the order to march south and sack Rome. Why has never been entirely clear but many reasons have been offered.

Priscus says the Huns were superstitious about sacking Rome because Alaric had died so soon after his sack of the city in 410. But the most famous version of all, and one which has become firmly enshrined in the canons of the Catholic Church, involves the bishop of Rome, Leo, who travelled to Attila's camp near Mantua with two prominent companions, Trygetius, a former prefect of the city of Rome who had earlier negotiated a peace settlement with Gaiseric, the Vandal king, and the former consul, Avienus, one of the most prominent senators in the city.

It should be remembered Attila had demanded Honoria, along with her dowry of half the western empire. Instead, he got the formidable Leo. Meanwhile, the emperor, Valentinian, was conspicuously absent from the proceedings. It was a brave move by Leo since Attila might have held them all to ransom or simply executed them. Instead, according to the chronicler, Prosper of Aquitaine, Leo worked a miracle. He maintains that the Hun leader '...was so impressed by the presence of Leo, that he ordered the war to be halted, and having promised peace, retired beyond the Danube'.[103]

What are we to make of this? There may be a grain of truth in it, for Leo was truly impressive. He was a Roman aristocrat who did not fear risking his life in political negotiations. He persecuted heretics, like the Manichaeans, and resisted Aetius' attempts to impose his authority over the praetorian prefect of Italy, Albinus. A favourite of Theodosius II, who at least had a bit more sense than Valentinian III, he was recognised by the eastern emperor as the Patriarch of the West, meaning he was superior to all the other bishops in the west. This would later translate into the title of Pope. As such, the Catholic Church today remembers him as the first Pope.

Given that he was a brave man, Attila may have taken a liking to him. Jordanes says that he held brave men in high esteem, such as the German kings, Valamir and Ardaric, and he also admired Aetius. We know from Priscus that, contrary to his terrifying reputation, Attila could be civilised and courteous to his guests, as he had been to Maximinus and Priscus. So, it is possible the great Hun really did take a liking to Leo. And many historians suspect his plea to spare Rome was sweetened with gold. But that cannot be the whole story. There must have been another reason, and the most likely explanation comes from the pen of Hydatius, a contemporary Roman bishop and chronicler from Hispania, who says that 'they [the Huns] were struck through divine providence by heaven-sent disasters, some with hunger and some with a disease.'[104]

Italy was suffering from famine in 452. The previous year, harvests had failed in many parts of Italy and the crops were little better in 452. The Huns had no logistical support whatsoever and depended on living off the land. Food would have been hard to get, even when it was a Hun who was doing the asking. The disease Hydatius mentioned was almost certainly malaria. At this time, and until the twentieth century, the northern Italian plains were home to malaria-carrying mosquitoes in summer which caused many invading armies to falter. The most significant casualty in this era was a Frankish invasion in 540, when a third of the army was said to have been killed by malaria.

Hydatius also mentions the eastern emperor Marcian coming to Rome's rescue. He says: 'In addition, [the Huns] were slaughtered by auxiliaries sent by the emperor Marcian and led by Aetius…'.[105] Although the mention of Aetius is suspect and unsupported by any other source, Prosper also says that while Attila was in Italy, the emperor Marcian attacked across the Danube into Hun territory. This is supported by another source, the official minutes of a conference of five hundred bishops held at Chalcedon, on the opposite bank of the Bosphorus from Constantinople, in the summer of 452. These minutes say the conference was delayed to October because the emperor was required to take command of troops along the Danube. We have no more details but it seems almost certain that the revitalised eastern army helped to save Rome.

For all these reasons, and also perhaps because of a pay-off by Leo, Attila chose to abandon the campaign and return home. The Italian job had been completed. It had been more successful than the disastrous invasion of Gaul. But was it sufficient for Attila to maintain his authority?

The jury is out on this question. I suspect unrest was growing. He had come nowhere near taking either

Constantinople or Rome. He had been defeated in Gaul. Compared with Alaric the Goth, his accomplishments were disappointing indeed. No doubt fully aware of this, Attila spent the rest of 452 pondering what to do. Jordanes describes his irritation at returning home: 'So, Attila returned to his own country, seeming to regret the peace and to be vexed at the cessation of war.'[106]

Clearly, the next step was to punish Constantinople. Marcian was not paying the tribute essential to keep the Hunnic Empire afloat. Attila sent an embassy '…threatening to devastate the provinces, because that which had been promised him by Theodosius … was in no way delivered, and saying that he would show himself more cruel to his foes than ever.'[107] Attila was apparently gearing up for round three with Constantinople.

Then one night the emperor Marcian had a dream.

28

The End of Attila's Empire

On a cold winter's night in Constantinople in 453, the emperor Marcian was sleeping fitfully. His mind was filled with the clamour of battle. Soon, he would face Attila's army to decide the fate of his empire. Then, in his dream, the noise subsided and an angel appeared beside his bed with a broken Hunnic bow.

So Jordanes began the strange story of Attila's death. When Marcian awoke from his dream, he was unsure what it signified. But two days later, messengers arrived from the army in Thrace. Attila was dead. Throughout the eastern and western empires, church bells rang out and people celebrated in the streets. Rome was free of its greatest enemy.

How did Attila die? The story has passed into legend based on the account left to us by Jordanes, copied from a lost part of Priscus' history. In early 453, Attila '…married an exceedingly beautiful girl, Ildico by name, the last of his innumerable wives, as was the custom of that nation. After the excessive partying at his wedding and weighed down by wine and sleep, he was lying on his back. He often had nosebleeds, but his blood now flowed backwards, since it was prevented from following its accustomed course, and spilled down a deadly journey into his throat, killing him.'[108]

The next morning, he did not emerge from his bedroom. His bride was too scared to raise the alarm, and his servants '... broke through the doors and discovered Attila's unwounded corpse'. Jordanes said that his new bride was found cowering beside their bed, no doubt terrified for her life. Jordanes, who was an abstemious monk, said in reproving tones that it was a 'shameful death'. An alternative version quickly developed and became a popular Germanic legend that Ildico had killed him. She later became something of a national heroine and is meant to have inspired Wagner to invent Brunnhilde, the fiery warrior princess, in his operas.

According to Jordanes, the Huns' immediate reaction was to perform a rite reserved for the deaths of great kings; called a *strava*, it's one of the very few Hunnic words to have survived to modern times. This involved a wild celebration around his body which was placed in the middle of a field surrounded by silk tents – according to Jordanes, '...a solemn and wondrous sight to behold'. The Huns paraded their horses, recited accounts of Attila's great deeds, and finally placed his body within three coffins, made of gold, silver and iron respectively. The outer coffin of iron reflected his iron rule, while the gold and silver ones reflected his wealth. One historian[109] has suggested Jordanes probably made this up since three metal coffins would have been extremely impractical, not least because of their weight.

Whatever the truth, Jordanes says his body was buried in a secret location in the middle of the night, filled with trophies from his victories, and then the slaves and servants who had dug the grave were killed, in a grim reminder of how brutal the Huns could be, although it should be remembered the same fate befell those who had buried Alaric the Visigoth.

The next day, the Huns awoke to discover that the world looked a very different place without Attila. The great leader had been just that: a great leader. And, according to Jordanes, without him, his empire immediately fractured due to a civil war between his sons.

As discussed in Chapter 22, despite Attila's alleged polygamy, only three sons are mentioned in our sources, all born to his main Hunnic wife, Kreka. These were Ellac, Dengizich and the youngest, Ernach. Jordanes says that instead of uniting after their father's death, they did the opposite and war broke out between the three of them: '...for the minds of young men are wont to be inflamed by ambition for power – and in their rash eagerness to rule they all alike destroyed his empire.'[110] Despite saying this, he provides no evidence of a Hunnic civil war. All he says is that, within a year of Attila's death in 454, a great battle was fought beside the River Nedao in Pannonia. The river has never been identified and Jordanes is vague about exactly who was fighting whom. He says it was the Gepids who, under their king Ardaric, first revolted against the Huns. He then describes a battle in which all the nations under Attila's sway fought each other: 'And so the bravest nations tore themselves to pieces ... One might see the Goths fighting with pikes, the Gepids raging with the sword, the Rugi breaking off the spears in their own wounds, the Suevi fighting on foot, the Huns with bows, the Alans drawing up a battle line of heavy-armed warriors and the Heruli of light-armed ones.'[111]

Attila's son, Ellac, was slain and his brothers fled east. This was the end of Attila's empire but not of the Huns. Jordanes says, rather vaguely, that the Gepids' rebellion against the Huns freed not just them but many other Germanic tribes. Historians think that Attila's empire imploded into at least nine different states. One of these was the remaining Huns who occupied the eastern half of what is today modern Romania. But to the west of them were at least eight Germanic groupings, including the Gepids, who occupied what had been the centre of Attila's empire on the Hungarian plains, followed by, moving west in a sort of arc, the Sarmatians, Ostrogoths, Sciri, Suevi, Heruli, Lombards and Rugi (see Map 8).

Jordanes' history is confusing, a subject I will come back to in a moment, but he says the Ostrogoths defeated the Huns '…who came at them as though they were seeking to recapture runaway slaves…'.[112] Apparently, the Goths also scored another victory over the Huns in around 468 at the Battle of Bassianae, when the Huns seem to have been trying to re-establish their authority north of the Danube.

It is at this juncture that Priscus provides us with the most detailed account we have of what happened to the Huns. He says Attila's two surviving sons, Ernak and Dengizich, wanted to re-establish relations with the eastern Romans and restore the Huns' trading rights along the Danube. Accordingly, Dengizich sent an embassy to the new eastern emperor, Leo, probably around 466, demanding concessions and perhaps tribute. But how were the mighty fallen. This time the Huns terrified no one. There was no question of the Romans paying tribute to them, or even giving them trading concessions. In response, Dengizich invaded Thrace and was defeated by an eastern Roman army led by Anagastes, the son of the general Arnegisclus, who had been defeated and killed by Attila at the Battle of the Utus River back in 447. Revenge must have been sweet for Arnegisclus' son who defeated and killed Dengizich and, according to a seventh-century source, took his severed head back to Constantinople where it was '…carried in procession through the Middle Street (the *Mese* which was the main road in Constantinople) and fixed on a pole at the Wooden Circus. The whole city turned out to look at it'.[113]

Meanwhile, Ernak, Dengizich's brother, did not participate in this attack on the eastern empire since he was distracted by the appearance of new enemies on the Huns' eastern borders. These were probably the Oghurs, steppe nomads and cousins of the Huns and ancestors of the tribes that would later be called Turkish. Ernak then disappears from history. This would have been disappointing for Attila since Priscus described how, at the dinner he attended with him (described in Chapter 22), the great Hun was especially fond of Ernak since it had been foretold that the Hunnic nation would fall and rise again led by this son. But the prophets had got it wrong. Not only did Ernak disappear but so too did the Huns.

So, what are we to make of this confused jigsaw puzzle of history with only a few fragments left to us by a handful of chroniclers? There's no doubt our sources are potentially unreliable. Our main source, Jordanes' *The Gothic History* (or *Getica*), is very simplified. Unlike Priscus of Panium, Jordanes was writing about a hundred years after Attila's death, with no personal experience or recollection of what he was recording. His account is based on another history, now lost, written by Cassiodorus, a Roman chronicler, and written a few decades after Attila's death, also called *The Gothic History*. But Cassiodorus was not writing objective history. His account was designed to flatter Theodoric, king of the Ostrogoths, as he sat in his pseudo-Roman palace in Ravenna in the early sixth century, fifty years after Attila died. Cassiodorus seems to have painted a heroic account of how the Ostrogoths, together with the Gepids and other German tribes, revolted against the Huns and defeated them. But historians have long suspected this is an oversimplification of a more complex story, especially when it comes to Attila.

One historian[114] has recently come up with a plausible interpretation. The first point is that the Battle of Nedao was shorthand for a number of separate battles fought between individual German tribes probably both against the Huns as well as against each other. This represented a more complex fracturing of Attila's empire immediately after his death or even, I suspect, before he died. There then followed ten years of fighting between these various groups, during which time the Ostrogoths moved south across the Danube and into Roman territory. The core Hunnic group remained along the Danube in what is now modern Romania, but after Dengizich's defeat in the 460s they fell under the sway of the Bulgars, new arrivals and distant cousins from the steppes, after which they disappeared from history as an independent entity.

Did Attila's empire start to fragment before his death? I suspect so. As discussed in Chapter 18, it was an unsustainable protection racket on a massive scale. Victory on the battlefield was a prerequisite to keeping the protection racket going and to maintain the flow of gold. No victories and no gold. And in the early 450s the supply of gold had run out. Marcian had cancelled the tribute. Aetius had defeated Attila. Surely Attila's grip over his many subjects was faltering? Indeed, was his well-publicised death on his wedding night in fact a disguise for something else – assassination perhaps, or even suicide? Jordanes says Attila considered suicide after his defeat at the Battle of the Catalaunian Plains. We will never know the answer, but after Attila's death the Huns faded into the mists of time as mysteriously as they had first appeared.

PART IV

The Last Days of an Empire

29

Cutting Off Your Right Hand

The city walls stood tall in the flat countryside. In the distance, a group of horsemen were trotting towards the main gate. The guards saluted them. Covered in dust, the riders dismounted and announced who they were. One of the guards went to announce their arrival.

Leading the horsemen was Flavius Aetius, the man who had vanquished Attila. Now at the height of his power, he was ushered into a small chamber where the emperor Valentinian was seated. Aetius bowed. The emperor acknowledged him but seemed tense and nervous. In the shadow was the chamberlain Heraclius.

Aetius decided to carry on anyway. He had left his sword and dagger outside and carried only some papyrus scrolls listing the army's expenditure and tax receipts. Aetius normally did not consult the emperor about his actions, but this was a tricky matter and he wanted to explain he was going to make a special levy on the wealthy senators. He knew they would appeal to the emperor against him and wanted to head off trouble. The army was running out of money. Tax revenues had dwindled to next to nothing.

Suddenly, he was aware the emperor was not listening. His eyes were fixed on him like a maniac. Aetius stopped talking. He looked up at Valentinian. Was he ill? Silently, the emperor rose from his seat. Then he pulled his sword from its scabbard. He did it awkwardly so that Aetius almost smiled at his childlike incompetence. He had never seen him use a sword in his life.

Valentinian's voice was shaking. Aetius could not believe his ears as the emperor accused him of being a traitor. He said he wanted his throne for his son. Aetius stepped back. Was this some sort of joke?

Then he saw Heraclius jump to his feet. From his cloak he pulled a meat clever. Aetius had no weapons and was wearing no armour. The room was small. He raised his hands to ward them off as they rushed at him. Valentinian swung his sword at his head. Too astonished to duck, the blow caught him and sliced through the side of his face. Heraclius brought the meat cleaver down on the back of his head. Aetius collapsed, blood spurting from his wounds.

This event stands as one of the most extraordinary and shocking in Rome's entire history. On 21 September 454, Aetius, the man who had defeated Attila, was hacked to death by Valentinian III, the feeble western emperor and his chamberlain, Heraclius. The reasons were essentially twofold: first, Valentinian's paranoia that Aetius was about to displace him and, second, Attila's death.

Aetius and Valentinian had begun to fall out when the eastern emperor Theodosius II died in 450. Valentinian, in a rare moment of self-confidence, said he wanted to go to Constantinople to claim the eastern throne. Aetius told him not to. His opposition was sensible. Valentinian had no friends in Constantinople. Although Pulcheria, Theodosius' sister, was his cousin, she had her own designs on the imperial throne, and had no time for her dim-witted relation in the west. As for the eastern army, who were the real power brokers, they had no respect for Valentinian, who, everyone knew, was only Aetius' puppet. But Valentinian was offended by Aetius' clear disregard for him, and this grew into a festering resentment against him.

Resentment turned to fear when Valentinian realised the implications of not having a son and heir to the throne of his own. The emperor was married to Theodosius II's daughter, Licinia Eudoxia, and the couple had two daughters, Eudocia and Placidia, born in the late 430s. Thereafter, no further children were born, and for whatever reason, whether infertility or something else, by the 450s it was pretty clear there would be no son to succeed him.

Yet Aetius had a son, Gaudentius, born to his wife Pelagia, a Gothic princess (see Chapter 14). Aetius had persuaded Valentinian to betroth Gaudentius to his younger daughter, Placidia. It's important to note for our story that Valentinian's eldest daughter, Eudocia, was already pledged to Gaiseric's son, Huneric, as part of the peace deal with the Vandals in the early 440s, which meant in Roman eyes at least she would not be an empress. Therefore, Placidia was the empress apparent and Gaudentius the emperor apparent. This was hugely significant. For Valentinian, it meant Aetius' power would be unstoppable after the wedding. Indeed, when his son married Placidia, would Aetius assassinate Valentinian and place his son on the throne? This started to prey on Valentinian's mind, especially since the wedding was fast approaching as Placidia would soon be fifteen and old enough to marry.

Enter two new characters in our story: Petronius Maximus and Heraclius. Petronius Maximus was a high-ranking Roman senator and Heraclius was Valentinian's eunuch chamberlain. They both wanted to get rid of Aetius but for very different reasons.

The most intriguing reason lay with Maximus. According to the chronicler, John of Antioch, he actually had no gripe with Aetius but he needed to remove him so that he had access to Valentinian who was the one he really wanted to kill. This was because the emperor had raped his wife. The story was that Maximus and Valentinian liked to play dice for money. Maximus lost and was in debt to the emperor who had always lusted after his beautiful wife, Lucina. Maximus' gambling bankrupted him and Valentinian demanded Maximus' ring as security for the debt, and then sent the ring to Lucina, summoning her to the palace. Lucina thought it was her husband who needed her help and rushed to the palace only to be confronted by Valentinian who forced her to have dinner with him and then raped her. She went home, furious with her husband, thinking he had offered her to the emperor in settlement for his debt. That was the end of their marriage, and Maximus swore he would kill Valentinian. But he knew he could not get close to the emperor so long as Aetius was alive to protect him. So, he thought up a plan to kill first Aetius and then Valentinian.

While this convoluted romantic story has all the hallmarks of a great Hollywood movie, and delighted Edward Gibbon who retold it as the version he believed in, our far more reliable fifth-century chronicler, Priscus, doesn't mention this amorous entanglement at all and merely says that both Maximus and Heraclius wanted to kill Aetius to seize power for themselves.

The opportunity arose when Attila died. This was because so long as Attila was alive, Aetius was untouchable because he had been Attila's nemesis. But with Attila dead, Aetius lost his special position. Petronius Maximus and Heraclius persuaded Valentinian now was the time to strike. And he did – on 21 September 454. Priscus has left us with an account of what happened.

> *As Aetius was explaining the finances and calculating the tax revenues, with a shout Valentinian suddenly leaped up from his throne and cried out that he would no longer bear being the victim of so many drunken depravities. By holding him responsible for the troubles, he said, Aetius wanted to deprive him of power in the west just as he had deprived him of the eastern empire, insinuating that it was Aetius' fault he did not go and expel Marcian from office. As Aetius was marvelling at this unexpected outburst and was trying to divert him from his irrational charge, Valentinian drew his sword from his sheath and rushed at him with Heraclius, who was also carrying a knife under his cloak … Both men repeatedly struck Aetius' head and killed this man who had accomplished many manly deeds.*[115]

According to Edward Gibbon, it was probably the first and only time that the emperor used a sword.[116] John of Antioch, drawing on the lost account of Priscus, wrote that when Valentinian proudly boasted to the Roman senate of his actions, saying, 'Did I not perform the killing of Aetius well?', a senator replied: 'Whether well or not, I do not know. But I know that you cut off your right hand with your left.'[117] Even if no one actually said these words there can be no doubt it was what everyone thought.

Valentinian was certainly triumphant in his treachery. He rounded up Aetius' sympathisers and put them to death. The most prominent was the praetorian prefect of Italy, a senator by the name of Boethius, grandfather of the famous philosopher. But Valentinian quickly found that ruling in his own right was very different from being a puppet protected by Aetius. He was as naïve as he was incompetent. And nearly six months after killing Aetius, on 16 March 455, he was himself killed.

And the man behind it was the same Petronius Maximus who originally instigated Aetius' assassination. As described earlier, he either did this as a way of getting at Valentinian to avenge his wife, or, according to Priscus, because Heraclius tried to prevent his attempt to supplant Aetius:

> *Maximus visited Valentinian, after Aetius' murder, to be promoted to consul. Failing in this, he wanted to become a patrician, but Heraclius did not grant him this rank either. Heraclius was pursuing the same course as Maximus and did not want to have any power counterbalanced to his own. So he beat back Maximus' efforts by convincing Valentinian, who was now free from Aetius' influence, that he did not need to transfer Aetius' power to others.*[118]

The scheming Maximus decided to get rid of both Heraclius and Valentinian. He contacted two guards' officers, Optila and Thraustila, who had been Aetius' retainers, or *bucellarii*, as the members of the personal armies of late Roman generals were called, and persuaded them to kill both men. This happened in Rome, where Valentinian had moved after he murdered Aetius, to try to win popularity with the Roman senate, and the troops based in the city.

Valentinian certainly made a monumental mistake when he allowed Optila and Thraustila to join his own imperial guard. Indeed, Thraustila is claimed by one source to have been Aetius' son-in-law, having married an unnamed daughter of his. Both men were eager to take revenge on their master's murderer. How Valentinian was blind to this is hard to understand. Equally foolishly, he had taken to attending the military training sessions at the Campus Martius in the city, in a vain attempt to prove that he was not the idle fool most people thought him. It was there, Priscus tells us, that Optila and Thraustila were waiting for the emperor and Heraclius. Priscus tells us the gory story:

> *When he [Valentinian] dismounted from his horse and was walking off to practise archery, Optila and his followers attacked him. Drawing the swords hanging at their sides, they advanced. Optila struck Valentinian on the side of the head and, as he turned to see who had assaulted him, Optila struck a second blow, against his eye, that killed him. Thraustila then killed Heraclius.*[119]

So died the last of the Theodosian emperors. No soldiers at the Campus Martius lifted a finger to stop the killing and not a tear was shed for him.

On 17 March 455, Maximus was proclaimed emperor by the Roman soldiers in the city, almost certainly helped by a donative of gold. The first thing he did was to pay a visit to Valentinian's new widow, Eudoxia, where he forced her against her will to marry him, perhaps in revenge for Valentinian's treatment of his wife, as John of Antioch claimed in his salacious tale.

His next step was to despatch the highly regarded senator, Avitus, to persuade the Visigoths to back him (Avitus was influential with the Visigoths and had previously helped persuade them to join Aetius against Attila as discussed in Chapter 24). This shows what a hollow shell the western empire had become. Maximus desperately needed the support of the Visigoths if he was to survive because the western Roman army was no longer a serious military force. The Roman poet and chronicler, Sidonius Apollinaris, has left us with a lengthy description of Avitus' embassy to the Visigoths, and although he does his best to dress it up as a mission to force submission from them, in fact it was the exact opposite. It was an appeal for military aid from the most powerful barbarian group in continental Europe.

But while Maximus was begging the Visigoths for help, he ignored the Vandals by betrothing his son, Palladius, to marry the empress's eldest daughter, Eudocia. This was a colossal mistake since she had been betrothed to Gaiseric's son, Huneric. For the Vandals, there was only one answer to this. War.

30

The Sack of Rome Part II

It is often overlooked in accounts of this period that during most of the 440s and up until Valentinian's death in 454, there was a long period of peace between the Vandals and Rome. Surprisingly, it was the Vandals who wanted this most for three reasons.

First, peace with Rome was profitable. The supply of grain to Italy, which had always been a staple of the North African economy, resumed. In addition, Africa had long been an exporter not just of grain but of pottery, wine and olive oil. And during the 440s some of this trade continued, enriching the Vandal court and nobility.

Second, Gaiseric wanted to deflect the gaze of Constantinople. The eastern fleet that had speedily set sail in 440 for Carthage, only to be forced to return to face Attila, showed that the eastern empire was alert to the threat the Vandals posed in the Mediterranean. And at this point, Gaiseric preferred peaceful co-operation with the eastern Romans rather than confrontation.

The third and most intriguing reason is Gaiseric's apparent desire for acceptance by the imperial court at

Ravenna, and indeed more than just acceptance, for he seems to have harboured ambitions to join the imperial family. This centred on his son Huneric's betrothal to Valentinian's eldest daughter, Eudocia, which was agreed as part of the seminal treaty of 442. Our sources are vague about it but piecing together the meagre evidence we have, as mentioned in Chapter 16, we think that Huneric was originally married to an unnamed daughter of Theodoric, king of the Goths, at some point in the 430s, cementing a Vandal-Gothic alliance. However, this marriage ended when Theodoric's daughter was returned to him, disfigured, on the grounds that she had tried to poison Huneric. The timing of this is unclear but presumably it happened before the treaty of 442 when it is recorded that Huneric was sent as a hostage to Ravenna and betrothed to Eudocia. We don't know how long Huneric stayed at Ravenna but he was certainly back in Carthage by 455. Because of the lack of information about Huneric's activities, historians have come up with a host of different theories. One[120] that sounds plausible is he went as a hostage in a swap, with Eudocia going to Carthage. But when she did not appear, in order to keep the peace, it was agreed that they would be betrothed instead, and Huneric returned to Carthage.

Whatever the truth, the key point was that this betrothal was taken seriously by Gaiseric. And the key question is why?

The most convincing answer lies with the fragile position the Vandals occupied in North Africa. They must have been heavily outnumbered by the indigenous Romans. There were somewhere between one to three million Romans in Africa compared with only about 100,000 Vandals. So, the

Vandals were worried they would be overwhelmed. And we have some evidence of this because they tried hard to get the support of the ordinary Romans. For example, when they took Carthage, our sources suggest they appealed to the mass of ordinary Romans to rise up against their masters. Their request apparently met with approval since many of the poorer Romans disliked the western government which taxed them without returning any benefits, and they also resented the Roman senators, who were often absentee landlords owning much of the land in North Africa but not investing the income in the local economy and instead expropriating it to Italy where they lived.

The Vandals wanted to keep the African Romans on their side, and to do that they kept most of the apparatus of Roman administration and government unchanged. We know this from the accounts left to us by the sixth-century Roman chronicler, Procopius, who recorded in great detail the Roman reconquest of North Africa under the emperor Justinian and his general, Belisarius in 533. When the eastern Romans reconquered it they found that the province of Africa had not been reduced to rubble. Quite the opposite. It was still very prosperous. The only difference was at the top. It was ruled by Vandals not Romans.

One way of selling Vandal rule to the Roman population was to boost the Vandals' status by marrying into the imperial family. And this wasn't just impressive with the local Romans, it was also an important status symbol within the Vandal social hierarchy. Historians[121] believe the Vandals were relatively democratic. Hence there were plenty of nobles vying to be king. It was not guaranteed that Huneric would automatically succeed Gaiseric. However, if he was married to Eudocia this prestigious union would be a fairly compelling reason to make him king.

But there is another theory behind the Vandals' decision to declare war on Rome. This lies with the empress herself, Eudoxia (both mother and daughter were confusingly called Eudocia although the mother spelt her name with an 'x' instead of 'c'), who hated Maximus for forcing her to marry him. Indeed, two of our main sources say that it was she who, in her fury against Maximus, secretly appealed to the Vandal king for help, reminiscent of the way Honoria had appealed to Attila. In Priscus' words: 'Eudoxia, the wife of Valentinian, out of distress at the murder of her husband and her forced marriage, secretly summoned Gaiseric, who crossed from Africa to Rome with a large fleet.'[122]

Whatever the true reasons for the Vandal decision to go to war, there were also signs Maximus' reign was not going to last long. First, the eastern emperor Marcian would not recognise him. Second, the chronicler Sidonius says that the senate and the Roman mob started to turn against him, sensing that he was not up to the job: '...this man [Maximus], once made emperor, became imprisoned in the palace walls, rueing his own success before the first evening fell.'[123]

Maximus' problems were exacerbated by the lightning speed with which Gaiseric acted. Within weeks of Maximus seizing the throne in March 455, the Vandal king was ready to sail with his army. He probably thought speed was of the essence since what little remained of the western army was not concentrated in Rome and instead seems to have been dispersed around Italy and southern Gaul. Consequently, Rome was an easy target. Gaiseric may also have been worried by Avitus' embassy to the Goths. As mentioned before, the Vandals and Goths had been sworn enemies ever since Huneric had disfigured Theodoric's daughter. Gaiseric may have been concerned that a Roman-Gothic alliance was in the offing and wanted to pre-empt this.

Too late Maximus realised his mistake. There was no Roman army to fight the Vandals who docked at the Roman port of Ostia in June 455 just two months after Maximus seized the throne. Panic seized the city. And the man who panicked the most was Maximus. According to Priscus:

> *He [Maximus] mounted his horse and fled. The imperial bodyguards and the freemen he used to trust the most deserted him; when they saw him riding away, they mocked him and berated his cowardice. Just as he was about to leave the city, someone threw a stone at the side of his head and killed him. Arriving at the scene, a mob tore his corpse to pieces and, carrying his limbs on a pole, they sang songs of victory. And so he met the end of life in this way...*[124]

Rome was now an open city and Gaiseric reached the Aurelian walls on 2 June. Without an emperor or a general to defend it, the remaining inhabitants turned to the man who had allegedly saved the city from Attila the Hun in 452. This was Leo, the bishop of Rome, who went to meet the Vandal king in front of the city walls. It is hard to know how much to believe of what the Christian writers wrote about Leo, but he certainly seems to have been a courageous man. Prosper of Aquitaine recorded:

> *Holy bishop Leo met Gaiseric outside the gates and his supplication mollified him through the power of God to such an extent that, when everything was given into his hands, he was held back from burning, killing and torture.*[125]

The Vandals occupied Rome for 14 days and it seems they were true to their word and avoided wanton destruction and violence. There's no archaeological evidence that the city was damaged in the way that Attila meted out destruction to Aquileia and Milan. This is understandable because the Vandals thought of themselves as quasi-Romans. They didn't want to destroy Rome. They wanted its wealth. Anything worth stealing was taken, according to the chronicler Malchus, 'even the bronze statues'.[126] They took away as many valuables from the city as possible, including, we are told, the gold-plated copper roofing of the temple of Jupiter, which they had mistakenly thought was solid gold.

But most important of all was their human treasure trove. This included some senators and, most significantly, the empress Eudoxia and her two daughters, Eudocia and Placidia. Gaiseric literally stole the imperial family. This was the best proof of his wish to join the Roman world rather than to destroy it.

When the Vandals returned to Carthage, Huneric finally married Eudocia, and she rapidly gave birth to their first child, a son named Hilderic. Naturally, this was cause for celebration in the Vandal court. But not so at Ravenna or Constantinople. The Romans in both east and west refused to recognise either Huneric's marriage to Eudocia or the existence of their offspring. In particular, no Roman wanted to admit that Hilderic, and any further sons Eudocia bore to Huneric, would have a strong claim to the throne of the western empire.

And to make matters worse just at that moment, there was no emperor in the west at all. Maximus was dead and chaos reigned in Italy. But the western empire was not quite finished. And its last years would witness some of the most bizarre events in its entire history.

31

Out of the Ashes

When the Vandals left Rome and returned to their ships in June 455, they left a city that had been humiliated for a second time and a western empire that was a shell of what it had once been. It had no army. It had no wealth. It even had no emperor. Petronius Maximus' body was floating down the Tiber, ripped to pieces by the Roman mob.

So, surely this must be the end? But no, in just under two years, the western empire would stage a recovery under a new emperor called Majorian. But before that, a period of chaos followed the second sack of Rome. By late June 455, Gaiseric was back in Carthage, leaving a power vacuum in what remained of the western empire. However, this did not last for long since, almost immediately, the influential Gallic senator, Eparchius Avitus, was proclaimed emperor in Arles in Gaul in July 455. Why not in Ravenna or Rome? This was the key point. For in the absence of any obvious imperial candidates in Italy, Avitus was supported by his friends the Visigoths, and in particular the new king, Theodoric II, as well as the Roman Gallic senators. In itself, this was something of a revolution. The last time a barbarian group had created their own emperor was when Alaric had persuaded the Roman senate to make Priscus Attalus emperor in defiance of Honorius. That had not worked then, but now the western empire was crumbling like never before, and power was firmly in the hands of the barbarians.

Probably for this reason, Avitus was viewed apprehensively by the Romans in Italy. Although the Roman senate accepted his nomination as emperor in Gaul in July, by the time he reached Rome at the end of the year, opinion had rapidly turned against him for two reasons.

The first was discontent in the city at the lack of grain from North Africa. Gaiseric had again cut off the grain supply and, although Avitus had almost certainly organised grain to be transported from Gaul, this was not enough to keep the citizens happy. In addition, Avitus had brought with him a large Visigothic bodyguard, meaning not only that there were more mouths to feed, but that he was also paying them a handsome wage which the city could ill afford. According to one source, he was forced to remove the bronze fittings from the statues and friezes throughout the city to sell them to merchants as scrap metal to raise money to pay the Visigoths. Apparently this provoked the discontented citizens into a full-scale riot, causing him to flee the city with his Visigoths.

The second reason for his downfall was the rise to power of a Germanic soldier called Ricimer. One historian has written that Ricimer was 'a cold, calculating, sinister man who hesitated at no crime, no murder, no treason or perfidy to maintain himself securely in power'.[127] Henceforth, he will be one of the main players in the last years of the western empire.

We know little of his origins. His father was apparently a member of the Suevian royal family (the Suevi being shorthand for a collection of German tribes that had migrated across the Rhine in 406). His mother was a daughter of Wallia, king of the Goths from 415 to 419. So, his lineage was of a distinctly aristocratic Germanic type and he certainly was not Roman. He had fought in Aetius' army, where he distinguished himself as a capable soldier. This caused Avitus to appoint him a *comes*, or count, probably before he arrived in Rome in late 455, and to give him command of the defence of Sicily against the Vandals who were raiding the island after their sack of Rome. There he was successful, and he surprised and defeated a Vandal raid outside the town of Agrigentum in mid-456, which he used to promote himself as a general capable of opposing the Vandals.

What happened next was that, as Avitus fled Rome, Ricimer spotted an opportunity to seize power. With his reputation boosted by his recent victory over the hated Vandals, he rushed to Rome where he was welcomed as a hero. The senate deposed Avitus who fled north back to Gaul. Our sources are vague, but it seems Ricimer first seized Ravenna and killed Avitus' *magister militum*, a Visigoth called Remistus, before tracking down Avitus at Piacenza, where he attacked and defeated his Visigothic bodyguard and captured him. Ricimer would earn a reputation for brutality in future years, but on this occasion he was surprisingly lenient, and instead of executing Avitus he allowed him to abdicate and retire as the bishop of Piacenza.

This clemency was probably because Ricimer did not want to be seen as a regicide in the eyes of Constantinople.

The eastern emperor Marcian had been watching events in the west with concern but he died in January 457, having given Avitus neither his approval nor disapproval. Thereafter, the eastern empire was too concerned with its own increasingly fraught politics, as Leo I took power with the backing of the general, Aspar, to take much notice of what was happening in the west.

Another reason might have been a call for clemency by a rising star called Majorian. Similar to Ricimer, Majorian had been a senior commander in Aetius' army. But there the similarity ended. Just as Ricimer was firmly of barbarian descent, so Majorian was a blue-blooded Roman. His grandfather had been a *magister militum* under the emperor Theodosius I, and his parents were both Roman aristocrats. He had joined the army and distinguished himself fighting in Gaul for Aetius. He had even been selected by Valentinian III as a possible husband for his daughter, Placidia, in a move to counter Aetius' growing power. This had infuriated Aetius, who, as discussed in Chapter 28, wanted his own son to marry Placidia. Despite his obvious liking for Majorian, he had dismissed him from the army.

Majorian was recalled by Valentinian after Aetius' murder because he was still popular with Aetius' soldiers whom Valentinian wanted to win over. When they murdered Valentinian instead, Majorian became one of the next in line to succeed him. It was at this point that Majorian's and Ricimer's paths crossed. Ricimer knew he would never be accepted as emperor by either the Roman senate or Constantinople because of his Germanic lineage. Therefore, he supported Majorian as emperor, thinking he could control him.

For a year there was no emperor in the west. Majorian focused on defending Italy from the Vandals and Alemanni. He scored a success against the Vandals in Corsica, ridding the island of the invaders, as well as defeating a minor incursion by the Alemanni. Meanwhile, Ricimer won a major victory against a Vandal raid on Campania in southern Italy, in which Gaiseric's son-in-law was killed. It was against this background of a modest Roman resurgence that, on 1 April 457, near to Ravenna, some Italian regiments hailed Majorian as emperor. No doubt this had been carefully orchestrated by Majorian and Ricimer but it was still met with approval by the senate. It was further endorsed by the new eastern emperor, Leo (who succeeded Marcian in 457). All seemed set for a revival in the west.

32

The Last Action Hero

Edward Gibbon said of Majorian that he 'presents the welcome discovery of a great and heroic character, such as sometimes arises, in a degenerate age, to vindicate the honour of the human species.'[128] In its final hour, Rome found in Majorian a hero worthy of Aurelian, the 'man of steel', who had saved it in the third century. Yet by this time, it was too late to save the western empire. The clock was counting down to midnight and darkness was about to engulf it. Majorian's tale would be short and tragic.

One of the many things that made Majorian different from Ricimer was that he had a vision to restore the western empire. Essential to this was the ejection of the Vandals from North Africa. To achieve this, he needed to strengthen what little remained of the western Roman army and navy, and to do that he needed money. So, he began by reforming the hopelessly ineffective taxation system. As Gibbon said: 'The private and public actions of Majorian are very imperfectly known.'[129] But fortunately we have a unique record of a small part of his tax reforms preserved by the Visigoths in their own compendium of Roman laws.[130] One of these published in March 458, entitled *De indulgentiis reliquorum*, or 'On the Remission of Past-Due Accounts', remitted all the tax arrears of the landowners and explicitly prohibited public administrators from collecting taxes.

You might well ask how this would help increase tax revenues? But Majorian hoped to buy the co-operation of the senators rather than oppose them. First, the public administrators had a bad record of keeping the collected tax money for themselves. By writing them out of the equation, he hoped to remove what had become a gross inefficiency in the system. Second, by wiping the slate clean with the senators, he hoped to win them over to pay their fair share of tax going forward. Coming from the Roman senatorial class himself, we can only assume that Majorian knew what he was doing. Certainly one of the western empire's greatest weaknesses appears to have been the egregious tax avoidance by the Roman aristocracy. A full study of the late Roman tax system has not been written and probably won't be because of the lack of source material but whatever it was Majorian did, he was able to raise enough money first to recruit numerous foreign mercenaries, and then later to build a reasonably large fleet.

It's also worth noting that Majorian's reforms did not end with tax. Details of several other reforms have survived which show a wish to confront a whole range of challenges facing fifth-century Italy, including one entitled *De sanctimonialibus vel viduis et de successionibus earum* ('Holy Maidens, Widows, and Their Succession'), which forbade women from entering holy orders until they were at least 40 years old. This was aimed at reducing celibacy among women of child-bearing age, which the Romans regarded as one of the main reasons for population decline in Italy. Another condemned adultery and yet another imposed fines on anyone pillaging stone from the great Roman public buildings like the Colosseum and the many temples which had fallen into disrepair. Majorian seems to have been a genuine reformer, keen to preserve Rome's heritage and to put a stop to its decline.

Although the Vandals were his ultimate target, his first focus was on securing Gaul. It's worth pausing for a moment to consider the complex political situation that had developed there. The Visigoths were now the most powerful entity in Gaul based in Aquitaine. The Franks occupied the north-eastern corner. The Burgundians were in the west, in modern Burgundy and Switzerland. In the north-west, were the peasant rebels called the *bagaudae*, and the Amoricans in Brittany. However, central and southern Gaul was still Roman. The traditional heartland of Roman Gaul lay in the south-east in modern Provence, based around still fairly large Roman towns like Arles, Lyon and Narbonne where the Gallic senators lived. But there was also a Roman province in the north around Soissons, Paris and Orléans that reached to the English Channel. This latter territory had been carved out by Aetius and contained what was probably the last remnants of the old Gallic Roman army which had once defended the Rhine, and was under the command of one of his generals, called Aegidius. It was this territory which proved to be the longest-lasting Roman possession in Gaul, even outliving the formal end of the western Roman Empire in 476 when it was ruled by Aegidius' son Syagrius. Historians have called it the kingdom of Soissons after its main city (see Map 8).

Majorian had strong connections with this northern

territory since he had fought with Aetius, and he and Aegidius were friends. However, the southern Gallic Romans opposed him. They had supported Avitus and it seems there was even a rebellion in Provence against him suggested by an inscription found in Lugdunum (modern Lyons), dating to 458, which omits to mention the fact that he was elected consul that year alongside the eastern emperor Leo I. In the same year, Theodoric II, king of the Visigoths, also attacked Roman Narbonne, the possession of which had always been a long-held Visigothic aim.

It was against the Visigoths that Majorian won his greatest victory. Leading a newly recruited force of mercenaries across the Alps, which was said to include many of the German and Hun tribes previously in Attila's army, he joined up with Aegidius' Roman army, marching south from Soissons. They met and together defeated Theodoric's Visigoths in a battle outside Arles. The Roman victory was such that Theodoric even agreed to become a Roman *foederatus*, or vassal. This rapprochement with the Visigoths enabled Majorian to move into Hispania, where he recovered territory from the Suevi. He also drove the Burgundians back from Lyon, whereupon they agreed to return to federate status. Finally, he won the southern Gallic Romans to his cause, not only because of his victories but also because he wrote off tax arrears for the Gallic senators in just the same way as he had with the Italian ones.

To cap it all, the Roman governor of Illyria, Marcellinus, who had broken away from Ravenna in disgust at Valentinian's murder of Aetius, pledged his loyalty to Majorian. In its last years, the western empire seemed to be making a remarkable recovery. It looked as if Majorian was unstoppable.

Marcellinus promised to move his troops to Sicily to prepare for an attack on the Vandals in North Africa. But despite this offer, Majorian built a fleet based in southern Hispania rather than Italy. His aim was to construct enough transport ships to take his army across the Strait of Gibraltar which was not defended by the Vandals.

This has attracted criticism from historians because an attack from Sicily, using Marcellinus' troops, might have made more of an impact. But the western Roman navy was almost non-existent and it was entirely logical for Majorian to favour a simple crossing of the Strait of Gibraltar. An apocryphal story has survived from the pen of the sixth-century Roman chronicler Procopius, who greatly admired Majorian, that the emperor, pretending to be a Roman envoy, dyed his fair hair black to disguise himself as he travelled to Carthage so that he could get a first-hand impression of the state of the Vandal kingdom. Gaiseric showed him warehouses filled with weapons. When these began to shake, Gaiseric realised Majorian was no ordinary Roman but a mortal threat to the Vandals.

Gaiseric prepared for war. Displaying all his characteristic resourcefulness, he laid waste the region around the Strait of Gibraltar, so that if Majorian should succeed in crossing to Africa, he would find a barren land unable to support his army. Meanwhile, Majorian built a fleet with 300 ships and kept it concealed at anchor in the port of Elche, near to Cartagena in southern Hispania.

But Gaiseric was never to be underestimated. He planned a surprise attack on Majorian's fleet. It is frustrating that we have no details whatsoever of the battle, but out of the blue the Vandal fleet descended on the Romans as their ships were at anchor. The entire Roman fleet was captured or destroyed. One Roman chronicler says traitors disclosed the position of the fleet to the Vandals. It would not surprise me if Ricimer was behind this. For, just as Majorian's star was in the ascendancy, so Ricimer's was in danger of being eclipsed. He had started as Majorian's equal but now he was very much the junior partner being only one of three generals reporting to the emperor, the other two – Aegidius in Gaul and Marcellinus in Illyria – both having stronger claims on Majorian's patronage.

Such a view would be supported by what happened next. After the loss of his fleet, Majorian was forced to make peace with Gaiseric. Although we have no details of what terms were agreed, according to Priscus he made a shameful treaty with the Vandal king. Whether this involved paying Gaiseric gold or giving him territory, Majorian's prestige suffered a serious blow. The Roman senate was furious that the taxes they had paid were now at the bottom of the ocean. Majorian set off for Rome to explain his position and restore his authority.

But he never got there. Priscus says:

> *Now as he [Majorian] was crossing to Italy, Ricimer plotted death for him. Majorian dismissed his army after the defeat and returned to Rome only with his bodyguard. But Ricimer's men arrested him and removed his purple cloak and his diadem. They beat him and then they beheaded him.*[131]

It was a sad end for such a brave emperor. Having killed his former friend, the treacherous Ricimer would now lead the western empire towards extinction.

33

Disintegration

The historian JB Bury saw Ricimer as the link between Stilicho and Odoacer. Stilicho was the barbarian general who tried to save Rome (see Chapters 5 and 6) while Odoacer was the barbarian general who drove the last nail into its coffin (which we will cover in Chapter 36). Ricimer lived between these two extremes, at that interim stage when the whole of western Europe was changing beyond recognition but no one knew how it would end up.

This uncertainty divided the senate into two factions. One wanted to restore the western empire to its former glory, and the other wanted to recognise that life had changed irreversibly, and new solutions were needed, such as siding with the new powers, i.e. the Germans. Although our sources are extremely limited, and we have very little insight into the machinations of the senate, this would explain why, at first, Majorian received the senate's backing for his projected imperial restoration, and then suddenly lost its support as the pro-German senators gained the upper hand and opted to support Ricimer. For when Ricimer brutally killed Majorian in August 461, the surprising truth is that many senators seem to have backed him.

This was because the meagre evidence we have suggests the pro-German faction within the senate was normally stronger than the imperialist one. The writings of Sidonius Apollinaris suggest most Roman senators were quite good at pandering to their new German masters. In Gaul, this normally took the form of the wealthy landowners giving up a third, or sometimes two-thirds of their estates to the Germans. In Italy, the surrender of senatorial property came later than in Gaul, and was one of Odoacer's vote-winning promises to his German mercenaries. But the Roman landowners didn't lose everything even after the end of the western empire, when the Ostrogoths invaded Italy and set up their own Italian kingdom. The senate remained in place, playing an important role in government and politics. A thorough analysis of the history of the late Roman senate is still to be written (if such is possible given the limited source material) but, in my view, what evidence we have suggests the short-term and selfish interests of most senators was a major factor in hastening the end of the western empire. It was not something the great republicans of old, like Cicero, would have been proud of.

Although the Roman senate was happy to go along with Ricimer's brutal deposition of Majorian, the other remnants of the western empire were not. And there were two very significant remnants, probably militarily more powerful than the battered remains of the legions in Italy. These were Gaul and Dalmatia. Majorian's supporters controlled both, and it is no surprise that both rejected Ricimer. As mentioned in the last chapter, the *magister militum* in Gaul was Aegidius, who had played a key role in Majorian's victory over the Visigoths in 458 at the Battle of Arles, and who vehemently opposed Ricimer.

Meanwhile, the Dalmatian *magister militum* was Marcellinus, who had broken away in 454 in disgust at Valentinian III's murder of Aetius. As mentioned in the last chapter, he had supported Majorian and taken his troops to Sicily to support the planned attack on North Africa. Given Dalmatia's proximity to the Italian mainland, Marcellinus posed the most immediate threat to Ricimer, who responded by bribing his army to defect, shortly after his murder of Majorian in 461. This was easily done since they were mostly Hunnic mercenaries and open to the highest bidder. This forced Marcellinus to return to Dalmatia, which was too far away to pose much of a threat to Ricimer.

Before Ricimer turned his attention to Gaul, he decided to create his own puppet emperor. On 19 November 461, three months after murdering Majorian, he proclaimed a new emperor at Ravenna: a man named Libius Severus, an undistinguished senator about whom we know almost nothing except for two sources that say he was given the nickname 'Serpentius', meaning serpent or snake. While the reasons for this reptilian epithet are not immediately apparent, we have no reason to believe that Severus was anything other than completely servile to Ricimer. Severus was recognised by the Roman senate but that was all. In Constantinople, the emperor Leo took no notice of him and neither did Aegidius nor Marcellinus. Ricimer ruled Italy but only as a virtual king.

Why was Constantinople not taking more interest in Ricimer's antics in Italy? The answer was simple. The emperor

Leo was too busy dealing with the challenges caused by Attila's imploding empire, in particular a large group of Ostrogoths who had crossed the Danube and demanded tribute from the eastern empire, as well as the rump Hunnic state led at this point by Attila's sons, Dengizich and Ernak.

But there was someone else keenly interested in developments in Italy. And that was Gaiseric, king of the Vandals. By this time, Gaiseric was the grand old man of late antiquity. He was at least 75 years old and had been king for nearly 40 years. Having sacked Rome in 455 and taken a group of imperial women back to Carthage, he was intent on ousting Ricimer and fancied taking up residence himself in the imperial palace on the Palatine Hill in Rome. Not only did he have a grandson, Hilderic (Huneric and Eudocia's son), whose claim to the western throne was strong, but he was also holding as effective prisoners the former empress, Licinia Eudoxia, and her other daughter, Placidia. Placidia was of interest to Gaiseric because she offered yet another route to the western throne since she was betrothed to a senator called Olybrius, who had fled to Constantinople when the Vandals sacked Rome. This gave Gaiseric an opportunity to offer the hand of friendship to the eastern emperor Leo by sending Placidia to her husband, whom she had not yet met.

So, in 462, he sent Licinia Eudoxia and Placidia to Constantinople in a gesture of goodwill. Placidia duly celebrated her marriage with Olybrius. Meanwhile Eudocia the younger stayed with her husband and son. Gaiseric was as cunning as a fox, and to keep alive as many claims on the western throne as possible, he now supported Olybrius as another potential contender. Why would Olybrius and his wife, Placidia, support Gaiseric if they ever donned the purple? The surprising truth is that Placidia seems to have formed a bond with Gaiseric, maybe since she was Eudocia's sister (who was still in Carthage) and also perhaps because of her good treatment in Carthage.

Meanwhile back in Ravenna, Ricimer was getting worried. He knew Gaiseric wanted to depose him but of more immediate concern was Aegidius in Gaul. Aegidius had a reasonably powerful army that, as mentioned before, probably contained the best troops left in the western empire. With Majorian's barbarian mercenaries, he had even defeated the Visigoths in 458. It was quite possible he would now march on Italy to oust Ricimer. Ricimer's response was to make a man named Agrippinus *magister militum* of Gaul.

Agrippinus had been Avitus' deputy when he had been the hero of both the Gallic senators and the Visigoths. Agrippinus was rushed to the Visigothic court at Toulouse where a deal was done. In exchange for giving the Visigoths the port of Narbonne, they pledged to support Ricimer against a possible attack by Aegidius. Ricimer was willing to cede what little remained of Roman Gaul to buy his own safety. Matters got even more desperate for the last Romans in Gaul when Agrippinus disappeared in 463 (our sources don't explain why), and Ricimer replaced him as *magister militum per Gallias* with his friend, the Burgundian king Gundioc, in exchange for land around Lyon. Ricimer had in effect ceded southern Gaul to the Burgundians in exchange for their protection.

But while Ricimer was busily giving away what was left of Roman Gaul to the barbarians, Aegidius had other plans.

Priscus suggests he was considering invading Italy to avenge Majorian's death: 'Aegidius ... who had served with Majorian and who now possessed a sizeable force was incensed at the murder of the emperor.'[132] The Visigoths, now Ricimer's allies, lay in his path and in 463, although the month is unknown, he led the Roman forces into battle with them near Orléans. The result was a Roman victory, and king Theodoric's brother, Frederic, was killed in the battle. However, the Roman advance stopped there. We have no knowledge why Aegidius' advance suddenly petered out other than a brief comment from a Frankish source that Aegidius' Frankish allies, who were an important part of his army, fell to fighting each other.

This was a big let-off for Ricimer but he had plenty of other enemies to contend with. Gaiseric was increasingly frustrated that no one was taking his claims on the western throne seriously and so he stepped up his attacks on Sicily, Sardinia and the Italian mainland. Meanwhile, in 464, northern Italy was invaded by the Alans led by their king, Beorgor. This was a direct threat to Ricimer and he responded well, as he always did whenever he was directly threatened, defeating them in a pitched battle near Bergamo.

Meanwhile, the puppet emperor, Libius Severus, died in November 465. One source says that Ricimer poisoned him,[133] although why he would have wanted to do that remains unclear. Libius Severus' death passed as unnoticed as his life had been. Indeed, the only person who seems to have noticed it was Ricimer who now wondered whether there was any need for a western emperor at all. Having a puppet emperor hadn't really helped him. He was still surrounded by enemies. Marcellinus in Dalmatia was itching to depose him. Aegidius wanted to do the same until he died in 465, whereupon he was succeeded by his capable son, Syagrius, who maintained just as hostile a position to Ricimer as his father had done. Gaiseric and the Vandals were also upping the pressure on Ricimer by raiding the Italian coastline and occupying Sicily and Sardinia. Ricimer must have been wondering how long he could hold out against this rising tide of enemies. But just as his future was starting to look decidedly grim, suddenly everything changed. For the eastern empire woke up to the chaotic position in the west.

Let us pause to catch up with matters in the east. Despite the rebuilding of its army in the 440s in response to Attila's threat, the eastern empire had been too preoccupied with the break-up of Attila's empire along the Danube frontier to take much notice of the western empire's plight. Although, as discussed in Chapter 20, the number of eastern field armies had probably increased from two or three to five in the 450s and 460s, Leo had been using these to fend off the Goths and Huns who crossed the Danube frontier as Attila's empire imploded.

As mentioned in Chapter 28, a decisive victory over the Huns was achieved in 467 when Attila's son Dengizich was defeated and killed by an eastern Roman army led by Anagastes, the son of the general Arnegisclus, whom Attila had defeated and killed at the Battle of the Utus River back in 447. At exactly the same time, Gaiseric made a major political mistake. His frustration at the lack of recognition for his claims on the western throne had reached boiling point, and he launched an attack on Greece, which was, of course, part of the eastern empire. Gaiseric hoped to put pressure on Leo to support his preferred candidate, Olybrius, for the western throne and depose Ricimer. But it had the opposite effect. It provoked Leo into launching the greatest Roman military campaign of the entire fifth century – the reconquest of Carthage.

34

The Roman Armada

The harbours around Constantinople are filled with noise: men shouting, hammers banging, horses neighing. Row upon row of ships is being prepared for war. Through the Golden Gate comes the sound of hob-nailed boots marching. Long columns of infantry and horsemen are pouring into the city from the barracks at Hebdomon. An invasion force is assembling on a scale not seen since the emperor Julian the Apostate launched his invasion of Persia a hundred years before.

At some point in 466 or 467, Leo decided to use the eastern empire's new praesental armies to destroy the Vandal kingdom in North Africa. His first step, before his armada sailed for Africa, was to sort out the shambles in what remained of the western empire. After Libius Severus' death in 465, Ricimer had not appointed a successor. For two years, the western empire had no emperor. Taking no notice of Ricimer, Gaiseric or Olybrius, in the spring of 467 Leo made his own choice for the purple: Anthemius. He came from a distinguished family and had proved himself a capable general fighting for Marcian on the Danube front.

He had even been a candidate for the eastern throne when the emperor Marcian died. Indeed, Leo was almost certainly rewarding him for his support.

There was also of course the small matter of what to do with Ricimer. Leo had no time for him but chose not to depose him. Instead, to keep him in order he sent Marcellinus, the governor of Dalmatia and one of Ricimer's fiercest opponents, with Anthemius to Rome. He made Marcellinus joint *patricius* with Ricimer. Anthemius wanted to make friends with Ricimer and offered him his daughter, Alypia, in marriage. We have no record of who Ricimer was married to previously, if anyone. The poet and chronicler, Sidonius Apollinaris, wryly observed that Alypia's marriage was purely a marriage of convenience designed to keep Ricimer onside.[134] The marriage produced no children that have been recorded and Alypia is never mentioned again.

But this game of thrones in the west was of little interest to Leo. He had more important things to think about. In 467, he mustered one of the largest invasion forces in Roman history. We have various sources for this and they all agree on one point: the huge scale of the expedition. The sixth-century chronicler, Procopius, has left us with the most detailed account of the story based on the facts provided by Priscus in a lost section of his history.

Procopius describes a great armada of 1,100 ships. This was nearly four times the size of Majorian's fleet that Gaiseric destroyed in 461. The figure seems plausible since the eastern empire was certainly at least four times as wealthy as the dilapidated western empire. Procopius also says 100,000 soldiers were mustered. This is almost certainly an exaggeration. As discussed in Chapter 19, I estimate the eastern army had at most 100,000 elite soldiers in its five field armies.

Most historians think the army was probably about half Procopius' number so around 50,000, although even that would have been an immense force, and probably the size of the western coalition that Aetius formed to fight Attila at the Battle of the Catalaunian Plains in 451. It's worth noting that Procopius, whose writings are eulogistic about Belisarius, probably somewhat exaggerated the size of Leo's expedition in 468 to flatter Belisarius' smaller and far more successful expedition against the Vandals in 533.

I suspect the eastern expeditionary force was around 30,000 strong, and comprised two field armies, presumably the two *praesental* armies stationed around Constantinople, which were no longer needed for the city's defence since the threat from Attila's empire and the fallout from its demise were over. Not surprisingly, the cost to the eastern Roman treasury was said to be gigantic at 130,000 pounds of gold, equivalent, for example, to nearly 62 years of annual tribute to Attila.[135]

The success of the invasion was crucially important to Leo. He worked tirelessly on the plan of campaign. The main fleet would sail to Sicily and thence to Carthage. Marcellinus and his Dalmatian troops were to secure the island from the Vandals prior to the fleet's arrival, as well as ridding Sardinia of the Vandals. A third force, recruited from the army of Egypt, led by the eastern general, Heraclius, was to be transported to Tripolis in modern-day Libya, and would march along the Mediterranean coastline towards Carthage, taking the towns belonging to the Vandals along the way.

Despite Leo's wish to make the expedition a success, Procopius was keen to point out a fatal flaw in its organisation. Leo gave overall command of the entire operation to his brother-in-law, the general Basiliscus. Although Basiliscus had proved himself a reasonably competent general in the Hunnic wars along the Danube, Procopius claims he had designs on the throne himself and wanted to discredit Leo. He also says he was in league with the Gothic general, Aspar, who had fallen out with Leo. Indeed, he goes so far as to say Aspar wanted the expedition to fail.

Historians have never known quite how to interpret this view of Basiliscus. The obvious flaw in Procopius' argument is that, if the expedition failed, Basiliscus would look just as much of a dummy as Leo. Because of this, most historians dismiss it as a conspiracy theory. Instead, they favour the argument that Leo was controlled by his formidable wife, Verina, who simply wished to promote her brother, Basiliscus.

The truth, as is usual with most historical debates, probably lies somewhere in the middle. It's doubtful Basiliscus really wanted the expedition to fail since this would have reflected badly on him. But he may have been hoping to claim success for himself while playing down the participation of others which in turn made teamwork difficult. And for such a large venture, teamwork was essential.

Whatever the truth about the back-stabbing politics, the great expedition started well. Marcellinus seized Sicily and Sardinia from the Vandals. Heraclius' Egyptian army landed in Tripolis and began its march towards Carthage largely unopposed. Meanwhile, the main fleet set sail for Sicily. One minor chronicler, Theophanes, quoting Priscus, suggests there was a naval battle off Sicily in which the Roman fleet triumphed over the Vandals: 'he [Basiliscus] engaged in naval battles with Gaiseric's force and sank a great many of his ships.'[136]

So far so good for the Romans. Gaiseric must have been getting nervous. Probably in June 468, Basiliscus crossed with the fleet from Sicily to North Africa. With a favourable wind, it might have taken only a day for it to reach the African coast. The great armada anchored in the shelter of a bay called Cape Bon, about 40 miles from Carthage, between modern Ras el-Mar and Ras Addar in Tunisia. This place was no doubt chosen because the winds in summer were normally easterly and would help a quick descent on Carthage. Basiliscus was probably aiming to land his army at the bay of Utica, a short march from Carthage, since the harbour of Carthage was protected against enemy shipping by a chain.

Gaiseric must have been desperate by now. The Roman armada was far more powerful than his own forces. Procopius said that if Basiliscus '...had undertaken to go straight for Carthage, he would have taken it at the first onset, and ... reduced the Vandals to servitude without their even thinking of resistance...'.[137]

But it was not to be. Gaiseric was a cunning old fox. He wanted Basiliscus to believe that he had given up hope and was about to surrender. So, he sent a deputation asking for a five-day truce while in reality he prepared for war. Why did Basiliscus fall for this old trick? Contemporaries and historians have universally labelled him either an imbecile or a traitor. Procopius' anger with Basiliscus leaps out from the pages of his history. He even suspected Basiliscus had accepted a bribe from the Vandal king: 'They say that he [Gaiseric] also, without the knowledge of Basiliscus' army, sent quite a sum of gold and in fact purchased this truce.'[138] In exasperation, he says Basiliscus fell into Gaiseric's trap for any of three reasons: one, he simply wanted Gaiseric's money; two, as previously mentioned, he was in league with Aspar against the emperor Leo and wanted the expedition to fail; or three, he was just plain stupid.

My sense is that Basiliscus was naïve enough to think Gaiseric really was about to surrender. With an overwhelmingly large Roman fleet and army at his disposal, Basiliscus was complacent. But if there was only one lesson to be learned from fifth-century Roman history, it was never to underestimate Gaiseric. By offering the truce, Gaiseric was more cunning than Basiliscus had realised. He was waiting literally for the wind of fortune to change. No doubt advised by expert native African sailors, for it is doubtful the Vandals ever truly mastered seamanship, he was told that victory or defeat depended on using the sea winds to your advantage.

The wind in question was an easterly one that was blowing when the Romans arrived and would have propelled them forward to Carthage making it difficult for the Vandals to resist them. As Procopius said, if Basiliscus had attacked immediately, victory would almost certainly have been his. But he delayed. Gaiseric was hoping that the wind would change to a north-westerly that would pin the Romans to the coastline and allow him to launch his attack. And again, no doubt advised by his African sailors, he had a trick up his sleeve. He was going to use fire ships. Procopius wrote: 'Arming all his subjects in the best way he could, he filled his ships, but not all, for some he kept in readiness empty, and they were the ships which sailed most swiftly.'[139]

Fortune can be fickle. Rome had had its fair share of good luck during the centuries of its rise to greatness. But in the years of its decline, its luck ran out. And there is no better example of this than what followed next, as Procopius will now describe for us:

> *But the Vandals, as soon as the wind had arisen for them which they had been expecting during the time they lay at rest, raised their sails and taking in tow the boats which, as stated above, had been made ready with no men in them, they sailed against the enemy. And when they came near, they set fire to the boats which they were towing, when their sails were bellied by the wind, and let them go against the Roman fleet. And since there was a great number of ships there, these boats easily spread fire wherever they struck, and were themselves readily destroyed together with those with which they came into contact. And as the fire advanced in this way the Roman fleet was filled with dread, as was natural, and with a great shouting that rivalled the noise caused by the wind and the roaring of the flames, as the soldiers together with the sailors shouted orders to one another and pushed off with their poles the fire boats and their own ships as well, which were being destroyed by one another in complete chaos.*[140]

Fire ships could be deadly in ancient warfare. Fire was one of the gravest threats to ancient wooden ships, whose sun-dried decks and sails burned quickly. Ironically, it was the Carthaginians, Rome's greatest enemy in its early days, and the predecessors to the Vandal kingdom of Carthage, who had used fire ships to devastating effect against a Roman fleet six hundred years before in 149 BC. Centuries later, the Byzantines would learn how to use 'Greek Fire' to destroy several enemy fleets. And a more modern example was the English defeat of the Spanish Armada in 1588. Very similar to the Roman fleet in 468, the vast Spanish fleet outnumbered the small English navy. The situation looked as hopeless for the English as it did for the Vandals. Yet, only eight English fire ships sufficed to cause enough damage to disperse and defeat the Spanish.

The same happened to the Romans at the Battle of Cape Bon in 468. We don't know how many Vandal fire ships were released into the midst of the vast Roman fleet. We don't know how many Roman ships were burned and sank. All we know is that Procopius says the Vandals destroyed the Roman fleet in a fiery haze. He ends his description by praising the bravery of many of the Roman soldiers and sailors who fought to the death to prevent the fires from spreading while they also tried to fight the Vandal ships. He describes a Roman general, named John, who went down with his ship rather than surrender:

> *He [John] stood on the deck and, turning from side to side, kept killing very great numbers of the enemy, and when he realised there was no hope left, he jumped wearing his heavy armour, from the deck into the sea … uttering that he would never surrender to the barbarian dogs.*[141]

The Romans fought bravely but in just a few hours the wily Gaiseric had won by far his greatest victory. Back in Italy, Ricimer smiled. He had stopped what ships the western empire had from participating in the expedition. Fearful of Marcellinus, who was still in Sicily, he plotted his assassination. Shortly after the destruction of the Roman fleet, one of Marcellinus' officers stabbed him to death. Although Ricimer escaped prosecution for this treacherous act, historians universally regard him as the instigator.

Meanwhile Basiliscus, the architect of the disaster, survived the battle and sheepishly returned to Constantinople. Fearing for his life, he took sanctuary in the church of St Sophia. There, the formidable Verina, his sister and Leo's wife, intervened to save him. Although he had been responsible for one of the Roman Empire's worst defeats in its entire history, his life was spared and in future years he would even very briefly become emperor of the east. He had much to thank his sister for. But the western empire was not so lucky. Its last hope had been dashed. Within just eight years it would cease to exist.

35

Once Upon a Time in Noricum

So far, this book has focused almost entirely on political, military, economic and climate history. I have said little about what life was like for the 'ordinary' person. One reason for this is that we have almost no literary records of what life was actually like for the ordinary person in this tumultuous time. Although the letters of Sidonius Apollinaris provide a fascinating insight into life for aristocratic senators in Gaul and Italy, when it comes to ordinary people the historical record is almost completely silent. Except for one extraordinary document. Quite unlike Sidonius' pompous rhetoric designed to flatter the rich and powerful, this provides a glimpse of the struggle for existence in a small frontier region of the western empire as the empire collapsed.

This document is *The Life of Saint Severinus*. Severinus was a holy man, in the tradition of holy men that developed in the late Roman Empire – that is, an utterly devout Christian who wandered the roads, helping the poor and sick, assisted by an ability to work miracles courtesy of his devotion to God. *The Life* was not written by Severinus himself but by a monk called Eugippius in 511, who wanted to record the good deeds of the saint. The account begins at the time of Attila's death in 453 and lasts until Severinus died nearly thirty years later in 482. Thus we have a vivid vignette of the last days of the western empire in a small, fairly remote location. That location was Noricum, in what is now Lower Austria, a beautiful mountainous landscape nestling between the Alps and the upper Danube. Enter Severinus, a wandering holy man from the faraway east – we are not told exactly from where, but probably Egypt or Syria – who could perform miracles and spoke perfect Latin.

We get a vivid picture of the last days of the regular Roman army. When Severinus arrived in Noricum, he found the remnants of the Roman legions still at their posts guarding the frontier wall along the Danube. But something was very wrong. They had not been paid for a long time. So, a small unit of soldiers set out for Italy to find out what was going on. They met a sticky end as described:

> *So long as the Roman Empire lasted, soldiers were maintained in many towns at the public expense to guard the frontier wall. When this arrangement ceased, the regiments of soldiers disbanded and the wall fell into disrepair. However, the garrison stationed at Batavis in Noricum continued to hold out. When they stopped receiving their pay, a group of soldiers went to Italy but they were killed by the barbarians although no one in Noricum knew that. One day, when Saint Severinus was reading, he suddenly closed his book and began to sigh and to weep. He told those who were present to go at once to the inn beside the river which he said was now*

> *red with human blood. There they found the dead bodies of the soldiers who had gone to Italy, washed ashore by the current of the river.*[142]

The point of the story was to highlight the omniscient powers of Saint Severinus, who knew what had happened to the soldiers before anyone else. But for the historian it paints a vivid picture of the last Roman soldiers looking out from their watchtowers and hoping that somehow, they would hear the blare of horns announcing reinforcements. When all hope was gone, the legions simply disbanded. Exactly where they went is not clear. It seems likely that some of them stayed with the locals, especially if they had married local women, while others perhaps looked to find a new life elsewhere. The evidence for the former is the mention in *The Life* that the Noricans fortified their settlements and established a string of *castella*, or castles, to defend themselves. Presumably this meant some of the regular Roman army became a sort of local militia.

To return to Severinus' story, he finds the locals clinging on to the Roman order that had existed for centuries but was struggling to survive the growing pressure from a complete breakdown of law and order and frequent barbarian incursions. This is probably what had happened in Britain nearly fifty years before Noricum. The result was a time of chaos. There was almost constant raiding by barbarians. The Heruli, Alemanni, Ostrogoths and Rugi, all of whom had been part of Attila's empire and were now mainly fighting each other, came and went, raiding and pillaging the Roman towns in Noricum.

The key point from the historical perspective was that, with the Roman army gone, life for ordinary people was transformed. And very much for the worse. No longer did they live in a prosperous land connected to a vast empire and marketplace by well-made roads. Suddenly, they were cut off from all contact with the outside world and transported into a nightmarish existence of constant danger, where if you ventured out from your fortified settlement even at midday to pick fruit, you might be captured by marauding barbarians. *The Life* describes how whole settlements suddenly disappeared overnight, their inhabitants slaughtered or enslaved. In the midst of this twilight world, we read how Saint Severinus gained the respect of the Noricans for his good deeds and his magical powers. In particular, he helped to win over the local barbarians in the form of the Rugi, who were sometimes paid to protect the Noricans against the Ostrogoths and others.

The Life abounds with morality stories. For example, the king of the Rugi, Feletheus, is impressed with Severinus and accepts him as his spiritual leader but his feisty wife, Giso, is not so sure. She is more interested in making the Noricans her slaves and demanding their gold and silver. But when Severinus saves the life of her adventurous little son, Fredericus, she is deeply grateful and he uses the opportunity to confront her saying: 'Giso, which lovest thou the more, your husband or gold and silver?' And when she answered that of course she prized her husband above all riches, the man of God, in his wisdom continued, 'Therefore, cease to oppress the innocent, lest their affliction result in the destruction of your power.'[143] The proud queen humbly promised to mend her ways.

We read about Saint Severinus wandering through Noricum, reminding people of their moral duty, and of the divine favour they will receive if they do: 'While the towns of riverside Noricum yet stood, and hardly a castle escaped the attacks of the barbarians, the fame and reputation of Saint Severinus shone so brightly that the castles vied with each other in inviting his company and protection; believing that no misfortune would happen to them in his presence.'[144]

The Life of Saint Severinus was written to demonstrate the importance of a pious life, but for us it paints a unique picture of the collapse of Roman society. And that collapse was truly frightening. For we are witnesses to the end of civilisation, at least as the inhabitants of the Roman Empire knew it. A life of material prosperity was replaced by a life of fear and deprivation in which religion offered the only hope.

This view is supported by archaeology. The best way of measuring the effect of the fall of the western empire is to compare the archaeological records before and after it fell. And one distinguished archaeologist[145] has done just this by comparing the four main surviving artefacts of Roman civilisation: pottery, roof tiles, coinage and graffiti. His analysis is highly informative. In many archaeological digs from Britain to Africa, he sees a fundamental change in living conditions that took place in the west in the fifth century and in the east in the seventh century.

In the west, the Romans led a life of relative comfort and even of luxury until the early fifth century. The sheer volume of finds of Roman pottery, roof tiles and coins evidences this. But this archaeological treasure trove comes to an abrupt end in the fifth century in the west. It was not until the beginning of the modern era, in the fifteenth and sixteenth centuries, that a similar quantity of archaeological finds comparable with those from ancient Rome began again. We are not just talking about quantity, but also quality. For example, Roman pottery was consistently high quality. Light and smooth to the touch, and very tough, it was amazingly 'modern' and was mass-produced in centres across the empire, which exported their products to its remotest corners. Archaeological discoveries show humble villages and isolated farmsteads enjoyed the use of this superb pottery just as much as the great urban centres.

Remains of roof tiles are equally impressive. Almost all Roman buildings had sturdy and high-quality roof tiles, from agricultural sheds and barns, to temples and basilicas. They protected Roman livestock from the wind and rain just as much as their human owners. Yet starting in the fifth century in the west, roof tiles almost disappeared from more humble dwellings for over a thousand years. Thatched roofs replaced tiled ones, a regression only favoured as a fashion statement today, since a thatched roof is far inferior to a tiled one, requiring remaking every 30 years compared to hundreds of years for well-made tiled roofs, and even then, it is normally less successful at keeping out wind and rain.

Coinage was another victim of the fall of Rome in the fifth century. Until then, Roman coins were abundant and available in three metals: gold, silver and copper. But in the west, during the fifth and sixth centuries, coins disappeared. Some of the new Germanic kingdoms in the west minted them for a short time, more for prestige than for economic purposes, but by the seventh century coinage had all but disappeared.

Surviving remains of graffiti also provide us with an insight into the scale of change for ordinary people. Graffiti was written to be read and the abundance of graffiti found in Pompeii (destroyed by the fatal eruption of Vesuvius in AD 79) suggests ordinary Romans were highly literate. Pompeii's walls were covered in graffiti, some of it vulgar but much of it nuanced and amusing, such as with the following famous inscription found four times in Pompeii, each time in different handwriting:

> *Wall, I admire you for not collapsing in ruins*
> *When you have to support so much tedious writing on you!*[146]

Although Pompeii remains our only source of Roman graffiti, we can assume that it was widespread in Roman towns and cities until the fifth century, after which the Germanic invasions resulted in a staggering loss of literacy, so much so that during most of the Middle Ages, literacy was confined to a few monks.

We should also recognise that not all the empire's inhabitants lived a life of comfort before its fall. Roman society comprised haves and have-nots. There was a substantial slave population in both halves of the empire, whose lives are poorly documented and about whom we know little. Common sense would suggest that while some slaves led lives of unimaginable suffering, such as those labouring until they dropped dead in mines, quarries and on the vast agricultural estates of the wealthy, others lived in relative comfort, such as domestic servants, many of whom were cooks, hairdressers and even teachers. We also know that there was an underclass of peasants happy to rise in rebellion when the central authority of the empire collapsed. These are well documented in Gaul, and as mentioned in previous chapters, were called the *bagaudae* (meaning warriors in Gallic) and comprised lawless peasantry and slaves who turned to pillage and plunder just as violently and destructively as the barbarians. Nevertheless, the *bagaudae* were a minority and for the great majority of the empire's inhabitants in the west, the fall of Rome was a decidedly bad thing.

One conspicuous example of this was fifth-century Britain. As mentioned, Noricum in the 460s and 470s was probably similar to Britain 50 years earlier in the 410s. When Constantine III rebelled against the emperor Honorius in late 406, he crossed over to Gaul with the British legions never to return. Abandoned, Britain declared its independence from Rome in 409, and thereafter we have no idea what happened on the island for over 100 years. About the only thing mentioned in Roman sources is that some of the wealthier Britons fled across the channel to Amorica, which became known as Brittany, the land occupied by the Britons, the name it still keeps in modern France.

Apart from that, there is almost no surviving source material covering the period from 410 to the mid-sixth century, when Gildas, a British monk, recounted the story of the Anglo-Saxon conquest of most of the western half of the British Isles. What happened to the Romano-Britons remains a mystery. The absence of almost any archaeological records suggests Britain reverted to a prehistoric level of society, less advanced than before the Romans arrived, when there had been a flourishing pottery industry, trade with Gaul, and even the minting of native silver coins. What little has survived shows the art of making pottery on a wheel completely vanished in the early fifth century and was not reintroduced for almost 300 years. Building in mortared stone or brick also disappeared. No coinage was minted. There is no evidence of any trade.

This dystopian post-Roman future is the stuff of horror stories, and a grim reminder of what can happen when a sophisticated economy, reliant on specialisation, is suddenly cast adrift to survive on its own. We in the twenty-first century, with our hugely complex and specialised global economy, would do well to heed the warning of what happened in fifth-century Britain.

But the example of Britain was extreme, even by fifth-century Roman standards, and it is also important to emphasise that the experiences of the two halves of the Roman Empire were quite different – a subject to which we will return in the next book in this series. Although the western economy collapsed in the fifth century, its eastern cousin prospered until the Arab invasions of the seventh century reduced it to a state similar to that of the west. In short, when Britain was reverting to a prehistoric lifestyle, Roman civilisation in the eastern Mediterranean was booming.

In conclusion, archaeological records after the sack of Rome suggest that a life of relative luxury continued in the west only for a small minority such as wealthy landowners, clerics, aristocrats and the ruling elites. For most people, the fall of the western empire plunged them back into a primitive lifestyle not experienced for centuries, an uncertain life of insanitary dwellings, undernourishment and the absence of quality manufactured goods.

So, perhaps we can see Saint Severinus' spiritual guidance as a consolation for this collapse of civilisation. Religion, in the controversial words of Karl Marx, was 'the opium of the people',[147] designed to ease their material suffering. He would no doubt have viewed Saint Severinus in this light.

36

Not with a Bang but a Whimper

The eastern emperor Leo made many mistakes when he organised the great expedition to Carthage. For the western empire, or what little remained of it, one of the worst of these was to allow Ricimer to survive. Ricimer not only undermined Leo's expedition by preventing the western Roman fleet from joining the eastern armada but, as mentioned in Chapter 34, as soon as news of the Vandal victory reached Italy, he instigated the assassination of his rival and co-patrician, the capable general Marcellinus, who had driven the Vandals out of Sicily.

With Leo firmly on the back foot after the disastrous defeat at Cape Bon, Ricimer only had to get rid of Anthemius to reinstate himself as the virtual king of Italy. Anthemius was aware of this, and he seems to have thought Ricimer tried to kill him through sorcery when he became ill. According to John of Antioch, in 470: 'Anthemius, the emperor of the west, fell into a serious sickness by sorcery…'.[148] His response was to execute one of the suspected perpetrators, a man named Romanus: '[he] punished many men involved in this crime, especially one named Romanus, who held the post of

Master of the Office, and was enrolled among the patricians, being a very close friend of Ricimer.'

This was a mistake. Romanus was a friend of Ricimer and Ricimer did not take his execution lightly. He gathered his German mercenaries, said to be 6,000 strong, and advanced to meet Anthemius in battle near Milan.

Meanwhile, in Constantinople, the eastern emperor Leo watched Anthemius' plight with growing concern but there was little he could do since he was himself embroiled in his own power struggle with his own version of Ricimer, the German general Aspar. In 471, this reached boiling point, and with the help of his Isaurian general, Zeno, he had both Aspar and his son Ardabur executed. Although Leo had re-established his authority, he still could not spare troops to help Anthemius. So, he did the next best thing. He announced the marriage in 471 between Anthemius' son, Marcian, and his daughter Leontia. It worked. Ricimer was sufficiently worried about retribution from the east to come to terms with Anthemius. Using Epiphanius, the bishop of Pavia, as their go-between, both men met and, according to the Roman chronicler, Ennodius, traded insults, Anthemius telling Ricimer he was a 'skin-clad Goth' while Ricimer said Anthemius could not control his temper.[149]

But Ricimer's and Anthemius' bickering was a sideshow. The real story lay elsewhere. The many Germanic tribes in possession of the great majority of the western empire's territory – the Visigoths, Burgundians, Franks, Suevi and of course the Vandals – knew that the defeat of the eastern armada in 468 marked a point of no return for the western empire.

Perhaps surprisingly, it was not the Vandals who rushed to drive the last nail into Rome's coffin. Instead, it was Euric, king of the Visigoths. He was the younger brother of Theodoric II, and had turned against him and murdered him in 465. Ruthlessly ambitious, he saw that the civil war between Ricimer and Anthemius was an opportunity. As Jordanes recounted: 'Becoming aware of the frequent changes of Roman emperor, Euric, king of the Visigoths, took the initiative to seize the Gallic provinces on his own authority.'[150]

First he tried to seize the north of Gaul. In 469, he defeated the pro-Roman Bretons led by king Riothamus. He took control of Tours and Bourges, and Riothamus fled to find sanctuary with the Burgundians. But Euric's progress in the north was halted by the still-powerful Roman enclave around Soissons, that fragment of the old empire that historians call the kingdom of Soissons, ruled by Aegidius' son, Syagrius. So, he turned his army south and marched on Arles, the Roman capital of southern Gaul.

His approach coincided with the rapprochement between Anthemius and Ricimer. It prompted Anthemius to gather an army to meet the Visigoths in battle. Ricimer was still keen to placate the eastern emperor Leo and may even have contributed some of his own troops. The Roman army assembled in northern Italy in 471 under the command of Anthemius' son, Anthemiolus. It would be the last time that a western Roman army would go into battle to save the empire. Anthemiolus led it across the Alps. The Visigothic army crossed the River Rhone to meet it. At an unknown place north of the Alps, the two sides met. The result was a crushing Roman defeat. Anthemiolus and all his senior officers and most of his troops were killed. Euric was now the effective master of southern Gaul although the Roman enclave in the north would hold out for several years even after the official end of the western empire in 476 (see Map 8 – it was finally destroyed by the Franks in 486). But Euric did better in the south. In the next two years, he took Arles and Marseilles and officially ended Roman control of Provence.

The western empire was slipping beneath the waves. But Anthemius and Ricimer continued to play their game of fighting over deckchairs on the *Titanic*. Seeing Anthemius' position gravely weakened, Ricimer spotted his opportunity to finish him off. He gathered his German mercenaries and called on his nephew, Gundobad, the son of Gundioc, king of the Burgundians (whom he vaingloriously named *magister militum* in Gaul) to join him. With a formidable army, he marched from Milan to Rome where Anthemius manned the Aurelian walls surrounding the city with what few troops he had and sent messengers to Gaul begging one of the survivors of the disastrous defeat there, a man named Bilimer, to rush to Rome to save him.

In March 472, Ricimer laid siege to Rome but with no success. The Aurelian walls defied him. Then a truly bizarre train of events was triggered by the eastern emperor Leo who had been watching this spectacle of self-destruction in the west with growing distaste. Although he still had no spare troops to send to Anthemius after the catastrophe of 468, he tried a different tactic somewhat similar to his previous attempt to secure peace by marrying his daughter to Anthemius' son. This time, he sent an embassy from Constantinople to Rome to negotiate a settlement between Anthemius and Ricimer. It was led by Olybrius, Placidia's husband, and the favourite of the Vandal king Gaiseric.

What followed must be regarded as one of the most back-stabbing plans ever conceived. Our main source for this event, John Malalas, says that Leo wrote a letter to Anthemius in which he asked him to murder first the bearer of the letter, Olybrius, and then Ricimer. Why did Leo want Olybrius dead? Because he feared he would join Gaiseric. If true, it stands as one of the most bizarre deceptions in all of Roman history. I will quote Malalas in some detail since it is so strange:

> *The emperor Leo, however, suspected that Olybrius favoured Gaiseric and would secretly take his side. He therefore feared for his own sake, lest Olybrius, who had a tie of marriage with Gaiseric, would betray Constantinople to Gaiseric if Gaiseric declared war upon him. Therefore, Leo ... gave a message ... to Anthemius [saying] you must kill your son-in-law Ricimer, lest there be anyone who might betray you. Moreover, I also have sent the patrician Olybrius to you; I wish you to kill him, so that you might reign, ruling rather than serving others.*[151]

But the story gets even more outrageous. Leo entrusted this letter to the hands of a messenger who was intercepted on his way to Rome by Ricimer and the contents of the letter were thus revealed. This suited Ricimer perfectly. He showed the letter to Olybrius who was horrified, and more than willing to become Ricimer's man. In April or early May 472 – our records do not make the exact date clear – Ricimer proclaimed Olybrius emperor of the west.

What can we make of this bizarre incident? Some historians have suggested that Ricimer made the whole thing up. And they may well be right given that it suited him so well. But my sense is that the incident could be true for two reasons: the first is that Leo had recently had the Gothic general, Aspar, executed and might have been worried that his supporters would back Olybrius, who had a stronger claim on the purple than Leo because of his marriage to Placidia. Therefore, sending Olybrius to Italy, and even arranging for his execution, was not as stupid as it might seem. What about the unwise decision to send a letter that Ricimer could intercept? It's quite possible this was a genuine mistake since it was sent to Anthemius in Rome before Leo heard Ricimer was besieging the city.

Whatever Leo's true motives, his incompetent handling of the situation meant the die was cast for Anthemius. Without eastern support, and now facing a rival emperor, his troops started to desert to Ricimer. Ricimer seized his opportunity and launched an attack, pushing his way into the city. Despite Bilimer's arrival with the troops from Gaul, Anthemius was defeated and Bilimer killed. Anthemius fled to a church, either Saint Peter's or Santa Maria in Trastevere, where the Burgundian prince, Gundobad, found him disguised as a beggar. On 11 July 472, he beheaded him. Ricimer's dislike of him was so intense that he wouldn't give him a proper burial.

And it wasn't just Anthemius who was treated brutally. The city of Rome now paid the price for this civil war. Filled with Burgundians and Ricimer's German mercenaries, the city was sacked so thoroughly that Pope Gelasius (Pope 492–496) later called it the third sack of Rome. We can only imagine what was left of the once proud capital of the Roman Empire.

The western empire was now truly on its last legs. Abandoned by the eastern empire, it only had four years to go. But the story still has a few twists and turns. The first surprise was with Ricimer. About a month after Anthemius was executed, he keeled over dead. No, he was not killed in a bloodthirsty palace coup, such as he himself had perpetrated on so many others. Instead, he died rather tamely of natural causes on 18 August 472. The historical record says that he died after 'vomiting much blood'.[152] The most widely accepted verdict is that he suffered some sort of haemorrhage. At long last the scheming tyrant was dead, and the man in charge of Italy was now the emperor Olybrius.

This was of course cause for celebration in faraway Carthage where Gaiseric, king of the Vandals, had at last achieved his dream. His daughter-in-law's brother-in-law was now emperor of the west. The time must have seemed ripe for a second Vandal trip to Rome. Who knows, perhaps Gaiseric would even move into the crumbling imperial palace on the Palatine Hill in Rome?

But Gaiseric's smile quickly vanished when he learned that only a few months into his reign, in either October or November 472 – it is not clear which – Olybrius also dropped down dead. There was no sign of foul play. The cause of death stated in our sources was oedema, probably because of heart failure. The leaders of the western empire were dropping like flies. Into the breach strode Ricimer's nephew and right-hand man, who had helped him depose Anthemius – Gundobad, prince of the Burgundians. On 3 March 473, Gundobad assumed the role of virtual king of Italy and proclaimed Glycerius, a high-ranking officer and Count of the Domestics, the next emperor.

But by this time, did anyone really care who was western emperor?

Probably not. Except for one man. That was Julius Nepos, nephew and successor to Marcellinus, the ruler of Dalmatia, who had been murdered back in 468, no doubt on Ricimer's instructions. Nepos was backed by the eastern emperors Leo, and then Zeno. At the same time, Gundobad lost interest in the whole charade. When his father Gundioc died, he returned to Gaul to stake his claim to the Burgundian throne.

This opened the door for Julius Nepos, who landed at Ostia in July 474, marched on Rome and deposed Glycerius without a fight. Nepos was generous enough to give him a position as the bishop of Salona in Dalmatia, well known to Roman historians because of its close proximity to Diocletian's palace in Split, the remains of which are still spectacular.

We are nearly at the end of the history of the western empire, but Julius Nepos seemed for a moment to offer it one last hope. But if the eastern emperor Leo's great armada had failed, what could Nepos do to snatch victory from the jaws of defeat? The answer was very little. The situation rapidly turned against him. In Gaul, Nepos' general, Ecdicius, was defeated by the Visigoths. In Italy, Nepos could not control his German mercenaries who backed their own commander Orestes.

It is a curious coincidence that this was the same Orestes who, as recounted in Chapter 21, had been one of the Hunnic ambassadors accompanying Priscus' expedition to see Attila in 449. Born in Pannonia, when this region beside the Danube had been overrun by the Huns, he had learned the Hunnic language and become one of Attila's most trusted secretaries and ambassadors. After the break-up of Attila's empire, he had found his way back to the western court and resumed his remarkable career, this time as the chief general of the German mercenaries, and effective heir to Ricimer.

Orestes now seized what was left of the western empire. He turned against his master, Nepos, who fled Ravenna in August 475, and returned to Dalmatia. Orestes made his own son, Romulus, western emperor, on 31 October 475. Because he was only aged somewhere between 10 and 15 years old, he was nicknamed Augustulus, the little Augustus. Historians have never understood why Orestes made his son emperor rather than taking the title himself. Perhaps he felt his association with Attila was inappropriate.

But the truth was it did not matter whether it was Orestes or his son who claimed the throne. Neither of them would last long. The problem was that Orestes could not control the German mercenaries. Our sources are limited, but the Germans wanted a significant settlement of land, perhaps one-third of the land owned by the Roman senators. Orestes resisted for reasons that are not clear. Perhaps he wanted to keep the backing of the senate who were opposed to giving the Germans more power. Whatever the truth, he misjudged the situation badly. The Germans proclaimed his deputy,

Odoacer, himself a German mercenary, king of Italy, and marched to depose Orestes.

It is interesting to note that Odoacer was connected to Attila since he was the son of Edeco, the Hunnic ambassador who, as recounted in Chapter 20, was bribed by the Romans to assassinate Attila in 449. He had been one of Ricimer's barbarian mercenaries, described by the author of *The Life of Saint Severinus* as 'a young man, of tall figure, clad in poor clothes'.[153] Now, his sights were set on becoming the king of Italy.

Orestes responded by gathering a small force, what we can perhaps call the last Italian legion. But it did not replicate the heroic feats of the ancient Romans. At Piacenza on 28 August 476, Odoacer defeated Orestes and executed him. He advanced on Ravenna, where he executed Orestes' brother Paul, but spared the young Romulus, out of pity it seems. Our main source says he persuaded Romulus to abdicate with the senate's agreement and sent a letter to the eastern Roman emperor, Zeno, saying: 'they [the senate] had chosen Odoacer, a man of military and political experience, to safeguard their own affairs, and that Zeno should confer upon him the rank of Patrician and entrust him with the government of Italy.'[154]

Zeno had no wish to intervene in the affairs of the west. He had enough problems of his own. So, he reluctantly complied with the senate's request and recognised Odoacer as Patrician and governor of Italy, although in his reply he referred to Julius Nepos as the rightful western emperor.

But no one else cared about Julius Nepos. Although he would live until 480, in most historians' eyes it was Odoacer who brought the western empire to a close in 476 by sending the imperial vestments, including the diadem and purple cloak, to Constantinople explicitly stating he did not want them back.

The western empire was dead. And it died not with a bang but a whimper.

Conclusion

The Road to Justinian

Attila's legend has become a story in its own right.

Either towards the end of his life or soon thereafter, some Christian chroniclers named him 'the Scourge of God'. Although none of his exploits had any religious motivation that we are aware of, he was a pagan and the epithet caught on. In particular, it caught the imagination of the late Roman papacy which nurtured his image as the Antichrist principally so that it could celebrate his downfall at the hands of Christian heroes such as Pope Leo and St Genevieve of Paris. By the modern era, the Attila legend was firmly embedded in the popular psyche. Verdi wrote an opera about him. Wagner's Ring cycle of operas was partly inspired by him. In 1870, when Prussia invaded France, French newspapers termed the Prussians Huns and recalled how St Genevieve had saved Paris. First World War British soldiers referred to the Germans as Huns. 'To the right of Attila the Hun' is a cliché used today to denigrate extreme conservatives as if the man from the steppes had a modern political manifesto.

But this legend is, if anything, a hindrance to our understanding of the real Attila.

This has to be largely based on the observations of Priscus of Panium, the only man who met him to leave a written record, which I have appended since it is such a remarkable document. Priscus was a gifted writer and a biting critic of Roman society. He presents Attila, who he clearly admired, as the opposite of the complacent and dull Theodosian emperors. He describes him as a complex man, quick-witted, charismatic, witty, passionate, loyal to his family and friends, a practical soldier and an astute ruler.

How did Attila affect Rome?

This is arguably the most important question. And historians are deeply divided. He is mostly regarded as either a bungler or a genius. Gibbon saw him as a flawed genius who accelerated the decline of the western empire while the distinguished Irish historian JB Bury suggested he had some surprising benefits for Rome, first, because his subjugation of the eastern Germanic tribes prevented them from invading the empire and, second, because Hunnic mercenaries helped Aetius to prolong the Roman presence in Gaul.

Modern historians mostly view Attila as an under-achiever because he never subjugated the Romans, and the Hunnic state collapsed within a few years of his death. One has commented that he 'was no more than a sideshow in the drama of western imperial collapse.'[155] I think this is wrong. I regard Attila as the most determined and dangerous adversary the Romans had faced, in both east and west, since Hannibal threatened to conquer Italy some 650 years earlier. Just as with Hannibal, the sheer scale of the conflict between Attila and Rome was staggering. It was touch and go throughout the 440s, and right until 452, whether either Constantinople or Rome would survive.

For example, the Battle of the Catalaunian Plains in 451 was a close-run thing. Had Attila been victorious, I think he would have shattered the western empire very quickly. The Visigoths would have become his vassals, as the Ostrogoths already were. There would have been no military force capable of resisting him, except possibly for the eastern Romans. Attila could have marched on Rome without opposition and maybe taken Honoria as his wife. I suggest history would have taken a different course had Attila won in 451.

Second, Attila inadvertently gave the Vandals an enormous advantage by diverting Roman resources from defending North Africa. Not only was Carthage captured by them in 439, largely because Aspar had returned to the Danube front to protect it from the growing Hunnic threat but after that, when the eastern army was assembling in Sicily in 441 to recover Carthage, Attila's and Bleda's sack of Naissus sent them scurrying back to defend Constantinople. Without this Hunnic distraction, I doubt Gaiseric would have established one of the most successful German states, and one of the most damaging for Rome.

But there is a third, and for me the most significant part, of Attila's legacy. This was the remilitarisation of the eastern Roman army caused by the shock of Attila's invasions in the 440s. The evidence for this lies in a simple fact. In either 443 or 444, Theodosius II's government stopped paying the annual tribute to Attila agreed after the sack of Naissus in 442. This could only have happened had the eastern army been expanded to a size capable of resisting the Huns. Therefore, I suggest it was during the early 440s that the two praesental armies (as detailed in the Notitia Dignitatum) were recruited and trained to provide Constantinople and its Balkan provinces with the extra strength needed to resist Attila. The praesental armies were an addition to the existing field armies of Illyricum and Thrace, meaning that there were four field armies ready to resist the Huns – the fifth field army (for the Oriens) remained in situ to defend the eastern frontier against the Persians.

Constantinople's defiant stance succeeded better than anyone could have imagined. No tribute was paid for four years. Part of the reason for this was Attila's preoccupation with internal politics for much of this time, in particular the elimination of his brother Bleda. But I suggest he hesitated to take on the new eastern army until a suitable opportunity arose.

This happened on 26 January 447, when an earthquake devastated the walls of Constantinople. The Hunnic army was immediately unleashed. The field army of Thrace (probably with the addition of one of the praesental armies) met the Huns. A large battle was fought beside the Utus River, in which the Huns sustained heavy casualties but defeated the Romans and killed the magister militum, Arnegliscus. The size and significance of this battle has been underestimated by historians. It was significant because the sources are clear Attila had not trounced the Romans, as you will mistakenly read in most historians' narratives. Instead, just the opposite – he had been given a bloody nose. Because of this, he dared not attack Constantinople, especially when he discovered the walls had been repaired. After defeating another Roman army (probably a praesental unit) near the Chersonesus, again with heavy casualties, he retreated home, having failed to win a decisive victory but with just enough kudos to demand the reinstatement of the annual tribute (at an increased level) and the back payment of tribute not paid.

The point which most historians have overlooked is that the tribute was paid for only three years until the new soldier-emperor Marcian (who succeeded Theodosius II in 450) cancelled it. This is compelling evidence that the Roman field armies had been brought back up to strength and were ready to fight Attila again. This time, it was Attila who backed down. He gave into Constantinople and turned his attention to the west, hoping Aetius and the array of Germanic tribes would provide easier pickings.

To the best of my knowledge, no one has ever offered this view of Attila's wars before, although it is supported by the findings in Anthony Kaldellis' and Marion Kruse's recent work,[156] as described in Chapter 19. I find this theory of remilitarisation particularly plausible because not only does it make sense in explaining why Attila attacked the west, but it also helps to explain two unsolved mysteries central to both the history of the fifth century and the fall of the western Roman Empire.

First, where did the great Roman armada of 468 suddenly spring from? Not since the Battle of Adrianople have we heard about a Roman army being a major attacking force, such as it was throughout the period of the Republic and the classical empire. After Adrianople, as Themistius put it, 'our armies vanished like shadows.'[157] The answer I offer is that it was the new praesental armies, created to fight Attila, that sailed with the armada to Carthage, where they perished.

Second, why did Constantinople send a huge expedition

against the Vandals in 468, but stood by and did virtually nothing to help the west in the first half of the fifth century? Historians have normally ascribed this to the tension between the two halves of the empire, in particular the hostility between Stilicho and the court in Constantinople. While there is some truth in this, I suggest there was also a more basic reason – the eastern army was simply too weak to intervene in the west. This was because there were no praesental armies that could be despatched to save Rome in 410, such as those that existed in 468.

This remilitarisation was obscured by the catastrophic defeat at Cape Bon in 468. I estimate it took a full two decades for the army to recover, a process only completed in the emperor Anastasius' reign (491–518). Because of this long hiatus, historians have not made the link between Attila and Justinian.

But that link was a vital one. For, in 533, a second eastern Roman armada, led by Belisarius, sailed to reconquer North Africa from the Vandals. Said to be smaller than Leo's armada of 468, the risk was that it would meet the same fate. But it won a resounding victory. Belisarius would go on to reconquer Sicily and Italy from the Ostrogoths. On 10 December 536, he entered the city of Rome. His conquests were as extensive as those of Julius Caesar. For the first time in nearly two centuries, the Roman army was back on the offensive.

Most historians have ascribed this transformation to the genius of Justinian and Belisarius. But necessity is a more likely mother of invention. It was the white heat of war with Attila that engendered a new five field army system. And it was this which provided Justinian with the springboard for reconquest.

The road to Justinian began with Attila.

Extracts from Priscus' Account of his Journey to Attila's Court

Priscus of Panium's account of the Roman embassy to Attila's court in 449 is our only eyewitness description of Attila. It is such a remarkable document that I have presented below my own abridged translation of its highlights. I hope you enjoy it.

The Romans set out on their journey

We set out with the barbarians, and arrived at Serdica, which is thirteen days for a fast traveller from Constantinople. Stopping there, we decided it would be sensible to invite Edeco (Hun ambassador) and the barbarians with him to dinner. The inhabitants of the place sold us sheep and oxen, which we slaughtered, and we prepared a meal. In the course of the feast, as the barbarians praised Attila and we our own emperor, Vigilas (Roman translator) remarked it was not fair to compare a man and a god, meaning Attila by the man and Theodosius by the god. This made the Huns angry. So, we quickly turned the conversation in another direction and, after dinner, Maximinus (Roman officer leading the delegation) presented Edeco and Orestes (the Hun ambassadors) with silk garments and Indian gems to pacify them.

When we arrived at Naissus we found the city deserted (Attila had sacked it seven years before in 442); only a few sick people lay in the churches. We stopped a short distance from the river, in an open space, for all the ground next to the river bank was still covered with the bones of men slain in war. The next day, we arrived at the military headquarters of Agintheus, the commander-in-chief of the Illyrian field army, to bring him news of our mission and the emperor's command for five of the seventeen deserters who Attila wanted returned to him. We had an interview with him, and having treated the deserters with kindness, he handed them over to us. The next day, we continued on our journey from the district of Naissus towards the Danube. We traversed a valley with many winding paths. We got confused about the direction we were travelling in since we thought we were travelling west but when the day dawned the sun showed that we had travelled east in order to navigate the difficult roads. Having passed through this difficult terrain we reached a well-wooded plain. At the river, we were met by barbarian ferrymen, who rowed us across it in boats hollowed out of single trees. This transport had not been made for us but for a company of Huns. For Attila pretended he wanted to hunt in this country but he really wanted to spy on the Romans.

Having crossed the Danube, and travelled with the barbarians for about seventy miles, we were told to wait while Edeco and the Huns went to find Attila and inform him of our arrival. As we were dining in the evening we heard the sound of horses approaching, and two Huns arrived with directions for our journey to Attila. We asked them to share our meal, and they gladly dismounted and joined us. On the next day, under their guidance, we arrived at the tents of Attila, which were numerous, in the afternoon. When we wished to pitch our tent on a hill, the barbarians who met us prevented us from doing this because Attila's tent was on low ground.

A message is received from Attila, saying he would not receive them and they should leave. It later transpires this was because Edeco, the would-be assassin, had revealed the plot to Attila. It is surprising Attila did not have the entire embassy impaled for their impudence. Instead, when he found out Maximinus and Priscus knew nothing about the planned assassination attempt whatsoever, he decided not to punish them. I suspect this was because Edeco praised the young Romans as being courteous and brave. Attila always held brave men in high regard, no matter what their nationality – according to Jordanes he had a high opinion of Aetius in the western empire, as well as some of his own Germanic warrior-kings, Ardaric and Valamir (see Chapter 26).

The first meeting with Attila

When the baggage had been packed on the beasts of burden, and we were preparing to leave at night, messengers arrived from Attila telling us to wait on account of the late hour. Then men arrived with an ox and river fish, sent to us by Attila, and when we had dined on this feast, we retired to bed. At dawn the next day, we expected to receive a courteous message from Attila but again he told us to leave. We made no reply, and prepared to depart, although Vigilas insisted we should pretend we had some other information to convey. When I saw that Maximinus was very dejected, I went to Scottas (one of the Hun nobles and brother of Onegesius), taking with me Rusticius who understood the Hun language. He had come with us, not as a member of the embassy, but on business with Constantius, an Italian whom Aetius had sent to Attila to be his private secretary. I informed Scottas (with Rusticus acting as interpreter) that Maximinus would reward him with presents if he could secure us an interview with Attila.

Scottas successfully lobbies Attila to see the Romans, and Maximinus and Priscus gain their first audience with Attila.

As we were considering what to say to Attila, and how to present the emperor's gifts, Scottas came to fetch us, and we entered Attila's tent, which was surrounded by a multitude of barbarians. We found Attila waiting on a wooden chair. We stood at a little distance and Maximinus advanced and saluted the barbarian, to whom he gave the emperor's letter, saying that the emperor prayed for his and his family's safety. Attila replied: 'It shall be unto the Romans as they wish it to be unto me.' Then, having been polite to us, he turned to

Vigilas, calling him a shameless beast, and asking why he ventured to come when all the deserters had not been given up.

Attila's outburst against Vigilas was because Edeco had told him that Vigilas was part of the conspiracy to assassinate him. Edeco had also told him Maximinus and Priscus were innocent – hence Attila's gentler treatment of them. Indeed, Attila took such a liking to the two young Romans that he invited them to accompany him on a tour of his northern territories. As described by Priscus below, at one point they left Attila's entourage and found themselves lost in a storm. They are rescued by the Huns and given food and shelter, and offered female company for the night.

The Romans travel with Attila to his palace

Late in the evening, having travelled a long distance, we pitched our tents on the banks of a fresh-water lake, used for water by the inhabitants of the neighbouring village. But a wind and storm, accompanied by thunder and lightning and heavy rain, arose and almost destroyed our tents, with all our utensils rolling into the lake. Terrified by the mishap and the atmospherical disturbance, we left the place and lost one another in the dark and the rain, each following the road that seemed most easy. We all reached the village by different ways and cried out for help. The Huns in the village sprang out of their huts and, lighting the reeds they use to kindle fires, they asked us what we wanted. Our guides replied that the storm had alarmed us; so they invited us into their huts and provided warmth for us by lighting large fires of reeds.

The lady who governed the village—she had been one of Bleda's wives—sent us provisions and good-looking girls to console us (this is a Hun compliment). We shared our food with the young women but declined any physical contact with them. We remained in the huts until dawn and then went to look for our lost utensils, which we found partly in the place where we had pitched the tent, partly on the bank of the lake, and partly in the water. We spent that day in the village drying our things; for the storm had passed and the sun was bright. Having looked after our horses and cattle, we returned to the princess, to whom we paid our respects and presented gifts in return for her courtesy. The gifts consisted of things esteemed by the barbarians since they don't have them in their own country—three ornamental silver bowls, red skins, Indian pepper, palm fruit and other delicacies.

The Romans rejoin Attila's entourage, where they unexpectedly meet another Roman embassy from the western empire – it is interesting to note there was no co-ordination between the two halves of the empire in their dealings with Attila. They arrive at Attila's 'palace'.

Having waited for some time until Attila advanced in front of us, we proceeded, and having crossed some rivers we arrived at a large village, where Attila's house was said to be more splendid than his residences in other places. It was made of polished boards, and surrounded with a wooden enclosure designed not for protection but for appearance. The house of Onegesius was second to the king's in splendour, and was also encircled with a wooden enclosure, but it was not adorned with towers like that of the king. Not far from the enclosure was a large bath which Onegesius—who was the second in power among the Huns—built, having transported the stones from Pannonia; for the barbarians in this district had no stones or trees but used imported material. The builder of the bath was a captive from Sirmium, who hoped to win his freedom as payment for making the bath. But he was disappointed, and greater trouble befell him than mere captivity among the Huns, for Onegesius appointed him bathman, and he used to minister to him and his family when they bathed.

When Attila entered the village he was met by girls advancing in rows, under thin white canopies of linen, which were held up by the outside women who stood under them, and were so large that seven or more girls walked beneath each. There were many lines of young women thus canopied, and they sang Hunnic songs. When Attila came near the house of Onegesius, which lay on his way, the wife of Onegesius issued from the door, with a number of servants, bearing meat and wine, and saluted him and begged him to partake of her hospitality. This is the highest honour that can be shown among the Huns. To gratify the wife of his friend, he ate, just as he sat on his horse, his attendants raising the tray to his saddle. Having tasted the wine, he went on to the palace, which was higher than the other houses since it was built on an elevated site. But we remained in the house of Onegesius, at his invitation, for he had returned from his expedition with Attila's son. His wife and kinsfolk entertained us to a dinner, for he had no leisure for himself, as he had to relate to Attila the results of his expedition, and explain the accident which had happened to the young prince, who had slipped and broken his right arm. After dinner we left the house of Onegesius, and took up our quarters nearer the palace, so that Maximinus might be at a convenient distance for visiting Attila and his court.

Priscus writes a long passage in which he describes his meeting with a Roman working for Onegesius. The Roman was a merchant who had been captured by the Huns but had helped them in matters unspecified and been rewarded with marriage to a Hunnic woman. He explained to Priscus why he preferred living among the Huns to his previous life. He and Priscus compared the merits of the Hunnic and Roman lifestyles. The passage is interesting (but too long to include here) because it shows the cultural acclimatisation occurring between the Romans and Huns. Priscus then relates his meeting with Attila's wife, Kreka, who is portrayed as an independent and forceful personality. Her three sons born to Attila would inherit his empire on his death.

Priscus meets Attila's wife

The next day I entered the enclosure of Attila's palace, bearing gifts for this wife, whose name was Kreka. She had three sons, of whom the eldest governed the Acatiri and the other nations who dwell in Pontic Scythia. Within the enclosure were numerous buildings, some of carved boards beautifully fitted together, others of straight wood, fastened on round blocks which rose to a moderate height from the ground. Attila's wife lived here and, having been admitted by the barbarians at the door, I found her reclining on a soft couch. The floor of the room was covered with woollen mats for walking on. A number of servants stood round her, and maids sitting on the floor in front of her, were embroidering linen cloths with many colours.

Having approached, saluted and presented the gifts, I went out and walked to another house where Attila was, and waited for Onegesius who was with Attila. I stood in the middle of a great crowd—Attila's guards and his attendants knew me, so no one bothered me. The crowd was excitable and noisy because they were expecting Attila to appear at any moment. When he came out of the house, he walked with a dignified gait, looking around him from one side to the other. He was accompanied by Onegesius who stood in front of the house. Many people were pressing lawsuits and he listened to them and passed judgement. Then he returned into the house to meet ambassadors from various barbarian tribes.

Maximinus secures another audience with Attila who tells him to arrange for one of the emperor's senior generals to come and discuss the conditions of the treaty between the Huns and Romans. Later that day, Attila holds a great banquet and invites the two Romans to attend. By this time, Attila has clearly developed a liking for the two young Romans and gives them privileged access to his court. What follows provides our best insight into Attila's character and Hunnic court life.

Attila's banquet

When we returned to our tent the father of Orestes appeared with an invitation from Attila for both of us to attend a banquet that evening. When the hour arrived we went to the palace, along with the embassy from the western Romans, and stood on the threshold of the hall in the presence of Attila. The cup-bearers gave us a cup, according to the national custom, that we might pray before we sat down. Having tasted the cup, we proceeded to take our seats. All the chairs were ranged along the walls of the room on either side. Attila sat in the middle on a couch. A second couch was set behind him, and from it steps led up to his bed which was covered with linen sheets and wrought coverlets for ornament, such as Greeks and Romans use to deck bridal beds. The places on the right of Attila were held chief in honour, those on the left, where we sat, were only second. Berichus, a noble among the Huns, sat on our side but had precedence over us. Onegesius sat on a chair to the right of Attila's couch, and beside him sat two of Attila's sons; his eldest sat on a couch with his eyes fixed on the ground, as if in respect for his father. When all were arranged, a cup-bearer came and handed Attila a wooden cup of wine. He took it and saluted the first in precedence who, honoured by the salutation, stood up and did not sit until the king, having tasted or drained the cup, returned it to the attendant.

All the guests then honoured Attila in the same way, saluting him, and tasting or drinking from the cups, although Attila did not stand up. Each of us had a special cup-bearer who came forward to present the wine when Attila's own cup-bearer retired. When those second in precedence had been honoured in this manner, Attila turned to us and toasted us in the same way. When the whole ceremony was over, the cup-bearers retired, and tables, large enough for several people, were placed around Attila's table so that each of us could take food from the dishes without leaving their seat.

Attila's personal attendant entered with a dish full of meat, followed by many other servants carrying dishes with delicacies and bread, which they spread out on the tables. A luxurious meal, served on silver plates, was brought to us and all the barbarian guests. But Attila himself only ate meat from a wooden plate. Indeed, in everything he showed himself to be modest as if he despised ostentation. His cup was wooden in contrast to the golden and silver goblets given to the guests. His very clothes were simple. The only striking thing about his attire was that it was beautifully clean. Likewise, his sword, the straps of his shoes and his horse's bridle were all plain and undecorated with gold and precious gems like those of the other senior Huns.

When the meat and delicacies of the first course were all consumed, we all stood up and didn't resume our seats until each one of us, in the same order as before, drank Attila's health in the goblet provided. We then sat down and a second course of new delicacies was served. After this course, the same toasting ceremony was performed again. When evening fell, torches were lit, and two barbarians bowed before Attila and sang songs they had composed, celebrating his victories and deeds of valour in war. The guests responded to this performance in different ways: some looked proud as they heard the verses, others rose in excitement reminded of wars they had fought in, and many of the older guests shed tears in memory of past wars and mourning the fact their bodies were now too weak to fight in battle.

After the songs, a Hun, whose mind was deranged, made everyone laugh by uttering outlandish and senseless words. After him, Zerkon, the Moorish dwarf entered. He had been sent by Attila as a gift to Aetius but Edeco had persuaded him to return to recover his wife, whom he had left behind. She was a Hunnic lady who he had obtained in marriage through the influence of his patron Bleda (Bleda was Attila's brother and co-ruler until, according to the Roman sources, Attila murdered him). He did not succeed in recovering her since Attila was angry with him for returning. On this occasion, he gave a performance which caused everyone except Attila to laugh uproariously at his antics, which involved a ridiculous costume, voice and words which jumbled Latin, Hunnic and Gothic in a confused mess. However, Attila was not amused by this entertainment at all, and maintained a grim face. He only smiled when his youngest son, Ernak, joined the party. He hugged him and smiled at him joyfully.

I was surprised he made so much of his son and neglected his other children. But a barbarian who sat beside me and knew Latin, bidding me not to reveal what he told, gave me to understand that prophets had forewarned Attila that his race would fall but would be restored by this boy. As it became clear the drinking would continue long into the night, and not wishing ourselves to become drunk, we made our excuses to the barbarians and retired from the banquet.

Attila and his wife invite Maximinus and Priscus to attend further feasts. It is interesting to note Attila's wife invites the Romans separately to her own dinner party, suggesting aristocratic Hunnic women had considerable power and status. Finally, the Romans are released and allowed to return home.

At this time, Kreka, Attila's wife, invited us to dinner at the house of Adames, the man who oversaw her affairs. We joined him along with some of the nation's leading men, and had a cordial evening. He greeted us politely and offered us lavish food. Each of those present, with Hunnic generosity, arose and gave us a full cup and then, after embracing and kissing the one who was drinking, received it back. After dinner, we went back to our tent to sleep.

On the next day, Attila summoned us again to a banquet, and in the same way as before, we joined him and feasted. It happened that his older son was not sitting with him this time, but Ebarsios, Attila's brother, was there. He talked to us kindly and told us that we should ask the emperor to find a wealthy wife for Attila's private secretary, Constantius, who had been sent by Aetius to Attila as a gift (I have omitted a lengthy retelling of this story which seems to be a sort of Hunnic 'joke').

We left the banquet late at night, and three days later, having been given many gifts by the Huns, we were allowed to depart for home.

Priscus and Maximinus returned safely to Constantinople. Thereafter, they remained best friends. Maximinus continued his successful career and ended up as governor of Egypt, where he died of some illness. Before his death, Priscus travelled to Egypt to look after him. Priscus wrote a history of the fifth century, focusing on Attila. It became renowned and, although most of it has been lost, it was widely referred to in other surviving historical sources (especially Jordanes).

Find Out More About the Fall of the Roman Empire

The fall of the Roman Empire was one of the greatest events in world history.

Debate about why, when and how it happened has been as wide-ranging as the opinions on its significance. One historian has written that it was the greatest setback to humanity *in all of human history.*[158] Others have argued that it was a positive catalyst for Europe, releasing forces of creativity and mercantilism.[159] But whatever your view, no one can deny that we live today in the shadow of that great empire. For example, the letters I am now writing on this page are those of the Roman alphabet. Romance languages – such as French, Spanish and Italian – are derived from Latin and are still spoken, not only in former Roman territories but in much of the Americas as well. Roman law underpins many of the world's legal systems. Christianity was the religion of the late Roman Empire. Need I say more?

This book is the third in a projected six-volume series covering the full story of the fall of the Roman Empire from the 'crisis of the third century' to the rise of Islam in the seventh century. The first two books are described below.

The Roman Revolution – Crisis and Christianity in Ancient Rome

The first book in my series on the Fall of the Roman Empire, it describes the little-known 'crisis of the third century'. Although little has been written about this period due to a lack of surviving sources, in the years between AD 235–75, the Roman Empire was nearly destroyed by barbarian invasions, civil war and plague. The scale of destruction caused a radical realignment of classical society, resulting in the creation of a 'second' Roman Empire barely recognisable with the 'first' empire created by Augustus. The Roman state became highly militarised under Diocletian, and embraced both a new religion – Christianity – and a new capital – Constantinople – under the revolutionary emperor, Constantine.

The Fall of Rome – End of a Superpower

The second book in the series examines the period from Constantine to the sack of Rome by the Goths in AD 410. During this period, Rome lost its superpower status as it suffered a complete military collapse. This stemmed not only from the decline of the Roman army due to political incompetence, but also from climatic changes in the Asian steppes which caused the Huns to migrate westward, igniting a period of unprecedented barbarian pressure on the empire's borders, termed the *Volkswanderung*, or 'wandering of the peoples', by German historians. The empire became firmly divided into two halves – the eastern half remaining prosperous and powerful while its western half was overrun by Germanic barbarians.

Podcast
My podcast *The Fall of the Roman Empire* accompanies my books and is available on all the main podcast apps.

Website
If you want to find out more about the fall of the Roman Empire, visit my website www.nickholmesauthor.com where you will find a free ebook together with my other books, podcasts and special offers.

Please Leave a Review
I love to hear from my readers, and I'd be delighted if you would like to leave a review on the site where you purchased this book or contact me via my website.

Acknowledgements

I would like to thank all those people who have kindly helped me with this book, in particular my editor, Scott Pack, who has given me so much valuable input. Nick Castle, for his striking front cover. Bek Cruddace, for making the clear and elegant maps. Helen Peters, for making such a thorough and intelligent index. Jayne Lewis, for her thorough copy-editing. Sara Hall for her proof-read. I would like to thank the London Library and its staff for providing an excellent haven of study and creativity in the middle of central London. I have written most of this book in its elegant reading rooms and at the desks among its endless bookshelves.

Finally, I would like to thank my family. My now young adult children who are a constant source of admiration and pride for me as I see them establish themselves in their exciting lives. My wonderful wife, Sarah – all roads lead to Rome, and all my roads lead to you – you are my true love and companion in all I do. Thank you for your patience, support and understanding, and for putting up with me, the Romans and this time Attila as well. Yet again, this book is for you.

Roman Emperors

(Augustus to Romulus Augustulus)

Augustus	27 BC – AD 14
Tiberius	AD 14 – 37
Caligula	37 – 41
Claudius	41 – 54
Nero	54 – 68
Galba	68 – 69
Otho	69
Vitellius	69
Vespasian	69 – 79
Titus	79 – 81
Domitian	81 – 96
Nerva	96 – 98
Trajan	98 – 117
Hadrian	117 – 38
Antoninus Pius	138 – 61
Marcus Aurelius	161 – 80
Commodus	180 – 92
Pertinax	193

Didius Iulianus	193
Septimius Severus	193 – 211
Caracalla	211 – 17
Macrinus	217 – 18
Elagabalus	218 – 22
Severus Alexander	222 – 35
Maximinus Thrax	235 – 38
Gordian III	238 – 44
Philip the Arab	244 – 49
Decius	249 – 51
Trebonianus	251 – 53
Aemilianus	253
Valerian	253 – 60
Gallienus	260 – 68
Claudius Gothicus	268 – 70
Aurelian	270 – 75
Tacitus	275 – 76
Probus	276 – 82
Carus	282 – 83
Numerian	283 – 84
Diocletian (*Sole then Tetrarch*)	284 – 305
Maximian (*Tetrarch*)	286 – 305

Constantius (*Tetrarch*)	292 – 306
Galerius (*Tetrarch*)	293 – 311
Licinius (*Tetrarch*)	308 – 24
Constantine I (*Tetrarch then Sole*)	306 – 37
Constantine II (*West*)	337 – 40
Constans I (*Middle then West*)	337 – 50
Constantius II (*East then Sole*)	337 – 61
Magnentius (*Rebel in West*)	350 – 53
Nepotianus (*Rebel in West*)	350 – 50
Vetranio (*Rebel in West*)	350 – 50
Julian 'The Apostate' (*Sole*)	361 – 63
Jovian (*Sole*)	363 – 64
Valentinian I (*Sole then West*)	364 – 75
Valens (*East*)	364 – 78
Procopius (*Rebel in East*)	365 – 66
Gratian (*West*)	375 – 83
Magnus Maximus (*Rebel in West*)	383 – 88
Valentinian II (*West*)	388 – 92
Eugenius (*Rebel in West*)	392 – 94
Theodosius I (*East then Sole*)	379 – 95
Arcadius (*East*)	395 – 408
Honorius (*West*)	395 – 423

Constantine III (*Rebel in West*)	407 – 11
Theodosius II (*East*)	408 – 50
Johannes (*usurper in West*)	423 – 25
Valentinian III (*West*)	425 – 55
Marcian (*East*)	451 – 7
Leo I (*East*)	457 – 74
Petronius Maximus (*West*)	455
Avitus (*West*)	455 – 56
Majorian (*West*)	457 – 61
Libius Severus (*West*)	461 – 5
Anthemius (*West*)	467 – 72
Olybrius (*West*)	472
Zeno (*East*)	473 – 91
Basiliscus (*East – interregnum during Zeno's reign*)	474 – 76
Glycerius (*West*)	473 – 74
Julius Nepos (*West*)	474 – 75
Romulus Augustulus (*West*)	475 – 76
End of Western Empire	476

Chronology of the Later Roman Empire

(AD 211–486)

211	Death of Septimius Severus
	Accession of Caracalla
216–217	Caracalla campaigns successfully against Parthia
226	Sasanian Persian dynasty founded by Ardashir, who overthrows the Parthians
235	Murder of Alexander Severus by his own troops and succeeded by Maximinus Thrax
238	Revolts against Maximinus result in Gordian III becoming sole emperor
	Sasanians attack Roman east
241	Death of Ardashir
	Shapur I becomes Shah of Persia
243–244	Philip the Arab concludes humiliating treaty with Shapur in order to go to Rome to be proclaimed emperor
248	Philip celebrates Rome's millennium
249–250	Goths cross Danube and invade Balkans
251	Battle of Abrittus – Gothic victory and Emperor Decius killed
252–253	Shapur's second great invasion of Roman east
	Antioch sacked

253	Valerian becomes emperor and makes his son Gallienus co-ruler in the west
260	*Annus horribilis* for Roman Empire
	Valerian defeated and captured by Shapur at Battle of Edessa
	Franks invade Gaul
	Postumus creates breakaway Gallic Empire
	Alemmani invade Italy and are defeated by Gallienus at Mediolanum
261	Odenathus seizes power in Palmyra
262–267	Odenathus defeats Sasanians
	Goths invade Balkans
	Heruli sail into Aegean
267–268	Goths and Heruli sack Athens
	Odenathus murdered and succeeded by Zenobia
268	Murder of Gallienus
	Claudius II becomes the first of the Illyrian soldier-emperors
269	Claudius defeats Alemanni at Lake Garda and Goths at the Battle of Naissus
270	Claudius dies of plague
	Aurelian becomes emperor after brief reign of Quintillus
	Palmyra invades Arabia and Egypt
271	Aurelian defeats Juthungi invasion of Italy
	Riots at Rome
	Postumus killed by his own troops and succeeded by Tetricus
	Aurelian defeats Goths and initiates the evacuation of Dacia
272	Aurelian campaigns against Palmyra

	Egypt recaptured by Probus
	Aurelian defeats Palmyrene army at Immae and Emesa, and captures Palmyra
273	Revolt in Palmyra suppressed and city sacked
274	Aurelian defeats Tetricus and reintegrates west into empire
	Triumph held in Rome
275	Aurelian murdered at Caenophrurium
	Tacitus made emperor
276	Tacitus defeats Gothic invasion
	Tacitus murdered
	Probus made emperor after brief reign of Florian (June–July)
279	Probus defeats Vandals in Pannonia
282	Probus assassinated and succeeded by Carus
283	Carus defeats Quadi and Sarmatians on Danube and defeats Sasanians, possibly capturing Ctesiphon
	Carus dies in mysterious circumstances
284	Diocletian proclaimed emperor by army of east
286	Diocletian makes Maximian co-emperor in west
	Carausius sets up breakaway state in Britain and northern Gaul
293	Diocletian establishes tetrarchy, appointing Constantius and Galerius junior emperors (Caesars) while he and Maximian remain senior emperors (Augusti)
296	Constantius subjugates breakaway British state
297–298	War with Persia won by Rome
301	Diocletian issues the Edict on Maximum Prices
303–304	Great Persecution of Christians
305	Diocletian and Maximian abdicate

	Tetrarchy continues with Galerius and Constantius as senior emperors and Severus and Daia as junior emperors
305–310	Tetrarchy breaks down
306	Constantine proclaimed western emperor by Roman army in York following his father's death (Constantius)
311	Edict of Toleration by Galerius grants Christians freedom of worship in the eastern empire
312	Battle of Milvian Bridge – Constantine defeats Maxentius and secures western empire; Licinius rules the east with Daia
313	Licinius defeats Daia
324	Constantine defeats Licinius and becomes sole Roman emperor
	Constantinople founded
325	Council of Nicaea
330	Constantinople dedicated and becomes the imperial residence
337	Death of Constantine
	His sons, Constantine II, Constans and Constantius II become co-emperors
340	Civil war between Constantine II and Constans in the West. Constantine II dies
350	Magnentius rebels in West and kills Constans
351	Constantius II defeats Magnentius at Battle of Mursa and becomes sole ruler of the empire
355	Julian made Caesar
357	Battle of Strasbourg: Julian defeats Alemanni
c.360	Hunnic attacks on Alans and Goths begin
361	Civil war between Julian and Constantius II; Constantius dies and Julian becomes sole emperor

363	Julian invades Persia and is killed in battle
363–364	Jovian succeeds Julian and makes humiliating peace with Persia
364	Death of Jovian; Valentinian becomes emperor and takes the West while his brother, Valens takes the East
367–368	War with Persia, Germans and Britain invaded by Saxons, Picts and Irish
371–372	Peace with Persia and revolt by Firmus in North Africa
375	Death of Valentinian I in a rage with Quadi
376–377	Migration of Goths across the Danube, fleeing the Huns, results in war
378	Battle of Adrianople: catastrophic defeat of the eastern Roman army and death of eastern emperor, Valens
379	Theodosius made emperor of east by Gratian
382	Treaty with Goths after several years of warfare; they are given land south of the Danube in unprecedented Roman capitulation to barbarians
383	Rebellion of Magnus Maximus in Britain, Gaul and Spain
388	Theodosius defeats Maximus at battles of Siscia and Poetovio
392	Valentinian II found hanged; rebellion of Arbogast and Eugenius
394	Theodosius defeats Arbogast and Eugenius at the Battle of the Frigidus River
395	Death of Theodosius; succeeded by his sons Arcadius in the east and Honorius in the west; Stilicho guardian of the west; Huns raid Middle East from Caucasus
395–397	Rebellion of Goths led by Alaric; Alaric made *magister militum* for Illyria

401–402 Stilicho defeats Alaric's first invasion of Italy at the battles of Pollentia and Verona

405–406 Treaty between Stilicho and Alaric; Radagaisus invades Italy and is defeated by Stilicho

406–407 Germans cross Rhine and devastate Gaul; Constantine III leads rebellion in the West

408 Stilicho executed; Alaric invades Italy and lays siege to Rome; minor Hunnic leader Uldin invades eastern empire;

409 Alaric's second siege of Rome; Germans cross into Spain

410 Third siege and sack of Rome by Alaric

411 Alaric dies

412 Visigoths enter Gaul

415 Visigoths cross into Spain

418 Peace treaty with Goths who settle in Aquitaine

421 Constantius made co-emperor with Honorius and dies

423 Death of Honorius and usurpation of Johannes

425 East Roman army puts Valentinian III on western throne

427 Gaiseric secures leadership of Vandals

429 Vandals cross straits of Gibraltar to Africa

433 Aetius becomes generalissimo of western empire

433–439 Aetius expands Roman control of Gaul

439 Vandals seize Carthage

441–442 Huns led by Attila and Bleda cross Danube and sack Naissus; Constantinople agrees to pay annual tribute of 1,400 pounds of gold to Huns but reneges on this in 443 or 444

444 Treaty with Vandals recognises their control of Carthage

c. 445 Attila murders Bleda and assumes sole leadership of Huns

447	Attila invades Balkans to force reinstatement of tribute; defeats eastern Roman armies at battles beside the Utus River and the Chersonesus but suffers heavy casualties; Constantinople agrees to pay tribute of 2,100 pounds of gold
449	Priscus participates in embassy to assassinate Attila
450	Marcian succeeds Theodosius II and stops payment of tribute
451	Attila invades Gaul and is defeated at the Battle of the Catalaunian Plains
452	Attila invades Italy; sacks Aquileia and Milan but not Rome
453	Death of Attila
454	Hunnic Empire starts to fragment at Battle of Nedao River; Aetius murdered by Valentinian III
455	Valentinian III murdered by Petronius Maximus who is killed by mob; Vandals sack Rome
457	Majorian becomes western emperor
461	Majorian's fleet destroyed in Spain; he is murdered by Ricimer; Libius Severus made western emperor
465	Libius Severus dies; no western emperor for two years
467–469	Attila's son, Dengizich defeated and killed; head displayed in Constantinople; Leo prepares major expedition to recapture Carthage; in preparation for this, he makes Anthemius western emperor
468	Leo's expedition to recapture Carthage disastrously defeated
472	Olybrius made western emperor by Ricimer; Ricimer dies; Olybrius dies
473	Glycerius declared western emperor
474	Glycerius deposed by Julius Nepos

475	Julius Nepos flees Italy and return to Dalmatia; Orestes declares his son, Romulus Augustulus western emperor
476	Odoacer defeats and kills Orestes; deposes Romulus Augustulus; returns imperial vestments to Zeno in Constantinople; widely recognised formal end of western empire although Julius Nepos claims he is still the true emperor
480	Julius Nepos dies – death of last claimant on western throne
486	Last remnant of western empire extinguished when Franks eliminate kingdom of Soissons in Gaul

Further Reading

Secondary Sources

Given that probably over a thousand books have been written about the Roman Empire, this relatively concise selection of scholarly works might be more useful for the reader than a general bibliography. I have divided these into relevant sections. The main primary sources are listed separately at the end.

My Top Five on the Fall of the Roman Empire

These are all landmark academic works which are also very readable. The two best ones in my view are Peter Heather's *The Fall of the Roman Empire* (Oxford UP, 2006), and Bryan Ward-Perkins' *The Fall of Rome and the End of Civilisation* (Oxford UP, 2005). Peter Brown's classic, *The World of Late Antiquity* (Thames & Hudson, 1971), is also a must read which presents a deeper insight into the post-apocalyptic world after Rome was sacked in AD 410. Arther Ferrill's *The Fall of the Roman Empire: The Military Explanation* (Thames and Hudson, 1988) is a forgotten classic on Rome's military decline, in my view. More recently, a compelling work which provides new and thought-provoking research, especially about the effects of climate change and pandemics on the

Roman Empire, is Kyle Harper's *The Fate of Rome: Climate, Disease, and the End of an Empire* (Princeton UP, 2017).

Attila and the Huns

The two most influential scholarly works on Attila and the Huns are Otto Maenchen-Helfen's *The World of the Huns* (University of California Press, 1973) and EA Thompson's *The Huns* (Oxford UP, 1948, updated in 1999 with an afterword by Peter Heather, Blackwell Publishing, 1999). Maenchen-Helfen was a meticulous German scholar, who spent a lifetime compiling a huge amount of information and analysis on the Huns which was only published after his death in 1969. It remains the most extensive analysis of the Huns used by scholars worldwide. Peter Heather has also developed clear views of the impact of the Huns on the Roman Empire described in *The Fall of the Roman Empire* (Oxford UP, 2006) mentioned above. More recently, an interesting new scholarly perspective of the impact of the Huns on Rome and Europe is presented, somewhat controversially, by Hyun Jin Kim, in *The Huns* (Routledge, 2016). Also relevant are Christopher Kelly's *The End of Empire: Attila the Hun and the Fall of Rome* (Norton, 2009); Ian Hughes' *Attila the Hun: Arch-enemy of Rome* (Pen & Sword, 2019) and John Man's *Attila the Hun: A Barbarian King and the Fall of Rome* (Bantam, 2005).

General Overview of the Later Roman Empire

For many decades, the most famous scholarly work on the late Roman Empire was by AHM Jones, *The Later Roman Empire 284–602*, Volumes I and II (Blackwell, 1964), although archaeological discoveries since it was written have made much of Jones' economic analysis redundant. JB Bury's two volumes on the *History of the Later Roman Empire: From the Death of Theodosius I to the Death of Justinian* (Dover Publications, 1958) still make compelling if somewhat outdated reading. Essential reading for the Roman economy is Richard Duncan-Jones, *Money and Government in the Roman Empire* (Cambridge UP, 1994). Walter Scheidel provides an entertaining new view of Rome's legacy in his *Escape from Rome: The Failure of Empire and the Road to Prosperity* (Princeton UP, 2019). Going further back in time, the classic work remains Edward Gibbon's *The History of the Decline and Fall of the Roman Empire* (first published in 1776 and more recently by Penguin, 2005). Hugely influential are two older works published in French with English translations – Ferdinand Lot's *The End of the Ancient World* (first published in 1931 and more recently by Routledge, 1996) and Henri Pirenne's *Mohammed and Charlemagne* (first published in 1939 and more recently by Martino, 2017).

The Crisis of the Third Century

The crisis of the third century was of huge significance not just for Rome but also for world history, and yet remains sadly under-researched because of the lack of surviving source material. Probably the most insightful works are Alaric Watson's *Aurelian and the Third Century* (Routledge, 1999) and John F White's *The Roman Emperor Aurelian: Restorer of the World* (Pen and Sword, 2015). Edward Luttwak's *The Grand Strategy of the Roman Empire: From the First Century A.D. to the Third* (John Hopkins, 1976) is interesting. More recent and thought-provoking are Ilkka

Syvanne's *The Reign of Emperor Gallienus: The Apogee of Roman Cavalry* (Pen and Sword, 2019) and, by the same author, *Aurelian and Probus: The Soldier Emperors Who Saved Rome* (Pen and Sword, 2020).

Diocletian and Constantine

Diocletian and Constantine have received more attention than the crisis of the third century. Strongly recommended on Diocletian are Stephen Williams' *Diocletian and the Roman Recovery* (Routledge, 1985) and Roger Rees' *Diocletian and the Tetrarchy* (Edinburgh UP, 2004). On Constantine: AHM Jones' *Constantine and the Conversion of Europe* (first published in 1948 and more recently by Medieval Academy of America, 1994); Timothy Barnes' *Constantine: Dynasty, Religion and Power in the Later Roman Empire* (Wiley-Blackwell, 2014) and David Potter's *Constantine: The Emperor* (Oxford UP, 2013). Extremely valuable on Christianity is Rodney Stark's *The Rise of Christianity* (Princeton UP, 1996).

Julian the Apostate

Of the many books written about Julian, three stand out: GW Bowersock's *Julian the Apostate* (Harvard UP, 1978); Robert Browning's *The Emperor Julian* (Weidenfeld and Nicolson, 1975); and Adrian Murdoch's *The Last Pagan: Julian the Apostate and the Death of the Ancient World* (Inner Traditions, 2008).

From Valentinian to the Sack of Rome in AD 410

The Valentinian and Theodosian dynasties are relatively under-researched. A good overview is provided in David Potter's *The*

Roman Empire at Bay: AD 180–395 (Routledge, 2004). The reign of Theodosius is well covered by Stephen Williams and Gerard Friell in *Theodosius: The Empire at Bay* (Routledge, 1998). Books on other main fourth-century figures are Neil McLynn's *Ambrose of Milan: Church and Court in a Christian Capital* (University of California Press, 1994); Ian Hughes' *Stilicho: The Vandal Who Saved Rome* (Pen and Sword, 2010); and Douglas Boin's *Alaric the Goth: An Outsider's History of the Fall of Rome* (Norton, 2020).

The Fifth Century

Since most of the main scholarly works on the fifth century are already included in the section above on *Attila and the Huns*, and in the other sections both above and below, I highlight the useful works by Ian Hughes which I have not listed elsewhere, and which provide a reliable and detailed narrative on many of the key figures of the fifth century. His works include: Ian Hughes, *Constantius III: Rome's Lost Hope* (Pen and Sword, 2021); Ian Hughes, *Gaiseric: the Vandal who Destroyed Rome* (Pen and Sword, 2017); Ian Hughes, *Patricians and Emperors: The Last Rulers of the Western Empire* (Pen and Sword, 2015) and Ian Hughes, *Aetius: Attila's Nemesis* (Pen and Sword, 2012). I would also recommend another classic by Peter Brown, *Augustine of Hippo: A Biography* (University of California Press, 2000).

Roman Army

There are a number of good books on the Roman army including the outstanding recent work by Anthony Kaldellis and Marion Kruse, *The Field Armies of the East Roman Empire, 361–630* (Cambridge UP, 2023). Otherwise, the most interesting works on the late Roman army are Pat Southern and Karen Dixon's *The Late Roman Army* (Yale UP, 1996) and Hugh Elton's *Warfare in Roman Europe AD 350–425* (Oxford UP, 1996). For an understanding of the development of the Roman army, Lawrence Keppie's *The Making of the Roman Army: From Republic to Empire* (Routledge, 1998) and Adrian Goldsworthy's *The Roman Army at War 100 BC–AD 200* (Oxford UP, 1996) are recommended. For the Praetorian Guard, see Sandra Bingham's *The Praetorian Guard: A History of Rome's Elite Special Forces* (Baylor UP, 2013).

Persia

Sasanian Persia remains very under-researched. Three useful books are Beate Dignas and Engelbert Winter's *Rome and Persia in Late Antiquity* (Cambridge UP, 2007); Eberhard Sauer's *Sasanian Persia* (Edinburgh UP, 2017); and Touraj Daryaee's *Sasanian Persia: The Rise and Fall of an Empire* (I.B. Tauris, 2013).

Climate Change

Paleoclimatology is rapidly becoming a major focus for historians. Kyle Harper's *The Fate of Rome* (Princeton UP, 2017) is the most comprehensive scholarly analysis yet published of how the climate (and pandemics) affected Roman history. I also strongly recommend Brian Fagan's *The Great Warming: Climate Change and the Rise and Fall of Civilisations* (Bloomsbury, 2008) for a fascinating account of the medieval warm period. The view put forward in this book that it was probably a megadrought that prompted the Huns to migrate west is informed by the research paper called 'Megadroughts, ENSO, and the Invasion of Late Roman Europe by the Huns and Avars' presented by Edward R Cook to the Dumbarton Oaks Workshop for Climate Change Under the Late Roman Empire in April 2009. Another relevant research paper is 'Climate and the Decline and Fall of the Western Roman Empire: A Bibliometric View on an Interdisciplinary Approach to Answer a Most Classic Historical Question' by Werner Marx, Robin Haunschild and Lutz Bornmann, published on 15 November 2018 in the Multidisciplinary Digital Publishing Institute (MDPI).

Primary Sources

For ease of accessibility, the sources listed below are only those referenced in this book that can currently be purchased in paperback/hardback. Other versions and more material are accessible online and in academic libraries. It should be noted that the history of the republic and early empire is so rich in sources that my list is very concise. In contrast, the third, fourth and fifth centuries have relatively few sources, the most significant of which are listed.

Republic/Early Empire

Cicero, *Selected Works* (Penguin, 1971)
Livy, *The Rise of Rome* (Oxford UP, 1998)
Marcus Aurelius, *Meditations* (Oxford UP, 2011)
Polybius, *The Histories* (Digireads, 2019)
Suetonius, *The Twelve Caesars* (Penguin, 1957)
Tacitus, *Annals and Histories* (Everyman, 2009)

Virgil, *The Aeneid* (Oxford UP, 1986)

Later Empire (AD 180–476)

Ambrose (Saint), *On the Mysteries and on Repentance* (Veritatis Splendor Publications, 2014)

Ammianus Marcellinus, *The Later Roman Empire* (Penguin, 1986)

Augustan History (Historia Augusta) – first half published as *Lives of the Later Caesars*, translated by Antony Birley (Penguin, 1976); full work published by Loeb Classical Library in three volumes as *Scriptores Historiae Augustae*, translated by D Magie (Loeb, 1932)

Cassius Dio – the first and last sections of his incomplete *Roman History* have been published i) by Penguin (1987) covering Books 50–6 from 32 BC to AD 14, and ii) by Echo Library (2007) covering Books 77–80 from AD 211 to 229

Claudian, *Volumes I and II* (Loeb Classical Library, 1922)

Eusebius, *Life of Constantine* (Oxford UP, 1999)

Eusebius, *Ecclesiastical History* (Baker Book House, 1989)

Gregory of Tours, *The History of the Franks* (Penguin, 1974)

Jerome, *Chronicle* (Akademie Verlag, 1956)

Jerome, *Letters* (Aeterna Press, 2016)

Jordanes, *The Gothic History* (Sophron Editor, 2018) Jordanes, *Romana and Getica*, translated by Peter Van Nuffelen (Translated Texts for Historians Vol 75, Liverpool University Press, 2020)

Julian, *Volumes I to III* (Loeb Classical Library, 1923)

Lactantius, *On the Deaths of the Persecutors* (Oxford UP, 1984)

Notitia Dignitatum – the original version in Latin compiled by Otto Seeck in 1876 has been reproduced by Forgotten Books (2018); a summarised English translation compiled by William Fairley in 1899 has been reproduced by BiblioLife (undated)

Procopius, *History of the Wars, Book 3* (Loeb Classical Library, 1916)

Priscus, *The Fragmentary History of Priscus* (translated by John Given), Christian Roman Empire Series Vol 2, (Evolution Publishing, 2014)

'Res Gestae Divi Saporis' ('The Great Inscription of Shapur I') are rock carvings located in modern Iran containing essential information on the Roman/Sasanian wars in the third century (see online for best accessibility)

Saint Severinus, *The Life of Saint Severinus*, translated by George Robinson, published by Leopold Classic Library (reprint of 1914 original by Harvard Translations)

Sidonius Apollonaris, *Poems and Letters* (Loeb Classical Library, 1936)

Themistius, *The Private Orations of Themistius*, translated by Robert Penella (University of California Press, 1999)

Vegetius, *The Military Institutions of the Romans (De Re Militari)*, (Ancient World Books, 2018)

Victor (Aurelius), *De Caesaribus* (Liverpool UP, 1994)

Zosimus, *The New History* (Byzantina Australiensia, 1984)

Notes

Part I The Origin of Our Destruction

1 Ammianus Marcellinus, *The Later Roman Empire*, translated by Walter Hamilton (Penguin, 1986) p. 416.
2 Ibid, p. 411.
3 Ibid, p. 411.
4 Ibid, p. 412.
5 Peter Heather, *The Fall of the Roman Empire* (Oxford UP, 2006), p.155.
6 Hyun Jin Kim, *The Huns* (Routledge, 2016), p. 28.
7 Ammianus Marcellinus, *The Later Roman Empire*, translated by Walter Hamilton (Penguin, 1986) p. 411.
8 Otto Maenchen-Helfen, *The World of the Huns* (University of California Press, 1973), p. 20.
9 Ammianus Marcellinus, *The Later Roman Empire*, translated by Walter Hamilton (Penguin, 1986) p. 416.
10 Ibid., p. 417.
11 Ibid., p. 329.
12 Ibid., p. 419.
13 Ibid., p. 426.
14 Ibid., p. 426.
15 Ibid., p. 410.
16 Ibid., p. 434.
17 Ibid., p. 435.
18 Ibid., p. 435.
19 Ibid., p. 435.

20 Ibid., p. 435.
21 Ibid., p. 436.
22 Stilicho's full title was *'comes et magister utriusque militiae praesentalis'*.
23 Peter Heather, *The Fall of the Roman Empire* (Oxford UP, 2006), p. 207.
24 Ibid., p. 207.
25 While the western empire came to a formal end in 476, the Roman outpost in Soissons survived until 486 when it was finally overwhelmed by the Franks.
26 Peter Heather, *The Fall of the Roman Empire* (Oxford UP, 2006), p. 221.
27 Zosimus, *The New History* (Odin's Library Classics, 2018), p. 108
28 Ibid., p. 108.
29 Ibid., p. 109.
30 The Salarian Gate was demolished in 1871 after it was damaged in the battle for Rome of 1870. It was subsequently rebuilt and then demolished a final time in 1921 to make way for the modern Piazza Fiume.
31 Sozomen, *The Ecclesiastical History*, Book IX, Chapter 10. Hermias Sozomen, *The Ecclesiastical History* (Jazzybee Publishing, 2019), p. 273.
32 Peter Brown, *Augustine of Hippo: A Biography* (University of California Press, 2000), p. 288.
33 Peter Heather, *The Fall of the Roman Empire* (Oxford UP, 2006), p. 231.
34 Bertrand Lançon, *Rome in Late Antiquity*, Trans. Antonia Nevill (Routledge, 2001), p. 119.

Part II The False Dawn

35 Ian Hughes, *Constantius III: Rome's Lost Hope* (Pen and Sword 2021), p. xi.
36 Peter Heather, *The Fall of the Roman Empire* (Oxford UP, 2006), p. 239.
37 JB Bury, *History of the Later Roman Empire, Vol 1* (Dover Publications, 1958), p. 216.

38 Gregory of Tours, *The History of the Franks* (Penguin, 1974), p. 119.
39 Ibid., p. 117.
40 Ian Hughes, *Aetius: Attila's Nemesis* (Pen and Sword, 2012), p. 97.
41 Jordanes, *The Gothic History*, translated by Charles Mierow, (Sophron Editor, 2018), p 113.

Part III The Scourge of God

42 Hyun Jin Kim, *The Huns* (Routledge, 2016), p. 38.
43 Edward R Cook, *'Megadroughts, ENSO, and the Invasion of Late Roman Europe by the Huns and Avars'*, 2009, Dumbarton Oaks Workshop for Climate change Under the Late Roman Empire.
44 Kyle Harper, *The Fate of Rome* (Princeton UP, 2019), p. 47.
45 Brian Fagan, *The Great Warming* (Bloomsbury, 2008).
46 Edward Gibbon, *The History of the Decline and Fall of the Roman Empire*, Vol II, (Penguin, 1994, first published 1781), p. 294.
47 Jordanes, *The Gothic History*, translated by Charles Mierow, (Sophron Editor, 2018), p 122.
48 Peter Heather, *The Fall of the Roman Empire* (Oxford UP, 2006), p. 302.
49 Anthony Kaldellis and Marion Kruse, *The Field Armies of the East Roman Empire, 361-630* (Cambridge UP, 2023).
50 Jordanes, *The Gothic History*, translated by Charles Mierow, (Sophron Editor, 2018), p. 125.
51 Christopher Kelly, *The End of Empire: Attila the Hun and the Fall of Rome* (Norton, 2008), p. 134.
52 EA Thompson proposed this until it was rejected by Otto Maenchen-Helfen.
53 The battle is mentioned by Marcellinus Comes, Pascal and by Jordanes in his *Romana.*
54 Jordanes, *Romana and Getica*, translated by Peter Van Nuffelen (Translated Texts for Historians Vol 75, Liverpool University Press, 2020), p. 197.
55 EA Thompson, *The Huns* (Blackwell, 1996), p. 228.
56 Peter Heather, *The Fall of the Roman Empire* (Oxford UP, 2006), p. 312.

57 Christopher Kelly, *The End of Empire: Attila the Hun and the Fall of Rome* (Norton, 2008), p. 141.
58 *The Fragmentary History of Priscus* (translated by John Given), Christian Roman Empire Series Vol 2, (Evolution Publishing, 2014), p. 48.
59 Ibid., p. 73.
60 Ibid., p. 73.
61 Ibid., p. 73.
62 Ibid., p. 71.
63 Christopher Kelly, *The End of Empire: Attila the Hun and the Fall of Rome* (Norton, 2008), p. 260.
64 *The Fragmentary History of Priscus* (translated by John Given), Christian Roman Empire Series Vol 2, (Evolution Publishing, 2014), p. 75.
65 Ibid., p. 76.
66 Christopher Kelly, *The End of Empire: Attila the Hun and the Fall of Rome* (Norton, 2008), p. 232.
67 Ibid., p. 237.
68 *The Fragmentary History of Priscus* (translated by John Given), Christian Roman Empire Series Vol 2, (Evolution Publishing, 2014), p. 98.
69 Ian Hughes, *Attila the Hun: Arch-Enemy of Rome* (Pen and Sword, 2019), p. 138.
70 Jordanes, *The Gothic History*, translated by Charles Mierow, (Sophron Editor, 2018), p. 125.
71 Christopher Kelly, *The End of Empire: Attila the Hun and the Fall of Rome* (Norton, 2008), p. 242.
72 Jordanes, *The Gothic History*, translated by Charles Mierow, (Sophron Editor, 2018), p. 124.
73 Ibid., p. 126.
74 Christopher Kelly, *The End of Empire: Attila the Hun and the Fall of Rome* (Norton, 2008), p. 245.
75 Ibid., p. 245.
76 Jordanes, *The Gothic History*, translated by Charles Mierow, (Sophron Editor, 2018), p. 129.

77 Ibid., p. 129.
78 JB Bury, *History of the Later Roman Empire* (Dover Publications, 1958), p. 294.
79 Edward Gibbon, *The History of the Decline and Fall of the Roman Empire, Vol II,* (Penguin, 1994, first published 1781), p. 340.
80 Jordanes, *The Gothic History*, translated by Charles Mierow, (Sophron Editor, 2018), p. 129.
81 Ibid., p. 131.
82 Ibid., p. 131.
83 Ibid., p. 132/33
84 Ibid., p. 134.
85 Ibid., p. 134.
86 Ibid., p. 134.
87 Ibid., p. 134.
88 Ibid., p. 135.
89 Ibid., p. 135.
90 Ibid., p. 135.
91 Ibid., p. 136.
92 Ibid., p. 136.
93 Ibid., p. 136.
94 Ibid., p. 137.
95 Ibid., p. 138.
96 Ibid., p. 138.
97 *The Fragmentary History of Priscus* (translated by John Given), Christian Roman Empire Series Vol 2, (Evolution Publishing, 2014), p. 103.
98 Ibid., p. 104.
99 Jordanes, *The Gothic History*, translated by Charles Mierow, (Sophron Editor, 2018), p. 140.
100 Ibid., p. 141.
101 Alexander Murray, *From Roman to Merovingian Gaul*, (University of Toronto Press, 2008) p. 74.
102 Christopher Kelly, *The End of Empire: Attila the Hun and the Fall of Rome* (Norton, 2008), p. 260.
103 Alexander Murray, *From Roman to Merovingian Gaul* (University of Toronto Press, 2008), p. 74.

104 Ibid., p. 92.

105 Peter Heather, *The Fall of the Roman Empire* (Oxford UP, 2006), p. 341.

106 Jordanes, *The Gothic History*, translated by Charles Mierow, (Sophron Editor, 2018), p. 143.

107 Ibid., p. 143.

108 Ibid., p. 164.

109 John Man, *Attila the Hun: A Barbarian King and the Fall of Rome* (Bantam Press, 2005), p. 326.

110 Jordanes, *The Gothic History*, translated by Charles Mierow, (Sophron Editor, 2018), p. 167.

111 Ibid., p. 168.

112 Ibid., p. 174.

113 Otto Maenchen-Helfen, *The World of the Huns: Studies in Their History and Culture* (University of California Press, 1973), p. 168.

114 Hyun Jin Kim, *The Huns* (Routledge, 2016), p. 122.

Part IV The Last Days of an Empire

115 *The Fragmentary History of Priscus* (translated by John Given), Christian Roman Empire Series Vol 2, (Evolution Publishing, 2014), p. 126.

116 Edward Gibbon, *The History of the Decline and Fall of the Roman Empire*, Vol II, (Penguin, 1994, first published 1781), p. 353.

117 *The Fragmentary History of Priscus* (translated by John Given), Christian Roman Empire Series Vol 2, (Evolution Publishing, 2014), p. 127.

118 Ibid., p.128.

119 Ibid., p. 128.

120 Ian Hughes, *Gaiseric: the Vandal who Destroyed Rome* (Pen and Sword, 2017), p. 112.

121 Ibid., p. 117.

122 *The Fragmentary History of Priscus* (translated by John Given), Christian Roman Empire Series Vol 2, (Evolution Publishing, 2014), p. 129.

123 Ian Hughes, *Patricians and Emperors: The Last Rulers of the Western Empire* (Pen and Sword, 2015), p. 45.

124 *The Fragmentary History of Priscus* (translated by John Given), Christian Roman Empire Series Vol 2, (Evolution Publishing, 2014), p. 130.
125 Ian Hughes, *Gaiseric: the Vandal who Destroyed Rome* (Pen and Sword, 2017), p. 140.
126 Ibid., p. 141.
127 Stewart Oost, *Libius Severus*, Classical Philology 65 (1970), pp. 228–240.
128 Edward Gibbon, *The History of the Decline and Fall of the Roman Empire*, Vol II, (Penguin, 1994, first published 1781), p. 370.
129 Ibid., p. 372.
130 The Novella Maioriani are preserved in a Visigothic compendium of Roman laws called the Breviarium.
131 *The Fragmentary History of Priscus* (translated by John Given), Christian Roman Empire Series Vol 2, (Evolution Publishing, 2014), p. 135.
132 *The Fragmentary History of Priscus* (translated by John Given), Christian Roman Empire Series Vol 2, (Evolution Publishing, 2014), p. 138.
133 Ian Hughes, *Patricians and Emperors: The Last Rulers of the Western Empire* (Pen and Sword, 2015), p. 115.
134 Sidonius Apollonaris, *Poems and Letters* (Loeb Classical Library, 1936), p. 361.
135 Attila's tribute from the eastern empire rose to a high of 2,100 pounds of gold in 447.
136 *The Fragmentary History of Priscus* (translated by John Given), Christian Roman Empire Series Vol 2, (Evolution Publishing, 2014), p. 158.
137 Procopius, *History of the Wars, Book 3* (Loeb Classical Library, 1916) p. 59.
138 Ibid., p. 59.
139 Ibid., p. 59.
140 Ibid., p. 61.
141 Ibid., p. 63.
142 *The Life of Saint Severinus*, translated by George Robinson, published by Leopold Classic Library (reprint of 1914 original by Harvard Translations).
143 Ibid., p. 48.

144 Ibid., p. 52.
145 Bryan Ward-Perkins, *The Fall of Rome and the End of Civilisation* (Oxford UP, 2005), p. 87.
146 Ibid., p. 154.
147 The full quotation contained in the introduction to Marx's *"A Contribution to the Critique of Hegel's Philosophy of Right"* (published posthumously) is "Religion is the sigh of the oppressed creature, the heart of a heartless world, and the soul of soulless conditions. It is the opium of the people.»
148 Ian Hughes, *Patricians and Emperors: The Last Rulers of the Western Empire* (Pen and Sword, 2015), p. 146.
149 Ibid., p. 150.
150 Jordanes, *The Gothic History*, translated by Charles Mierow, (Sophron Editor, 2018), p. 151.
151 Ian Hughes, *Patricians and Emperors: The Last Rulers of the Western Empire* (Pen and Sword, 2015), p. 154.
152 Ibid., p. 160.
153 *The Life of Saint Severinus*, translated by George Robinson, published by Leopold Classic Library (reprint of 1914 original by Harvard Translations), p. 45.
154 Peter Heather, *The Fall of the Roman Empire* (Oxford UP, 2006), p. 429.
155 Peter Heather, *The Fall of the Roman Empire* (Oxford UP, 2006), p. 435.
156 Anthony Kaldellis and Marion Kruse, *The Field Armies of the East Roman Empire*, 361-630 (Cambridge UP, 2023).
157 *The Private Orations of Themistius*, translated by Robert Penella (University of California Press, 1999), p. 216.

Find Out More About the Fall of the Roman Empire

158 Ian Morris, *Why the West Rules – For Now* (Profile Books, 2010)
159 Walter Scheidel, *Escape from Rome* (Princeton UP, 2019)

Index

NICK HOLMES is a British author, podcaster and historian. His passion is Roman history. He is currently writing a multi-volume series on the Fall of the Roman Empire. His podcast *The Fall of the Roman Empire* accompanies his books. In 2021, he gave up a career in investment banking to write full time.

Visit his website at nickholmesauthor.com for more on his books, podcasts, newsletter and special offers.

Milton Keynes UK
Ingram Content Group UK Ltd.
UKHW011522150624
444129UK00004B/152